THE

CATALAN COUNTRY KITCHEN

BY MARIMAR TORRES
With a Foreword by Gerald Asher

Aris Books

Addison-Wesley Publishing Company, Inc.

Reading, Massachusetts   Menlo Park, California   New York

Don Mills, Ontario   Wokingham, England   Amsterdam   Bonn

Sydney   Singapore   Tokyo   Madrid   San Juan

Paris   Seoul   Milan   Mexico City   Taipei

THE

CATALAN COUNTRY KITCHEN

▼ ▼ ▼

FOOD AND WINE FROM THE PYRENEES TO THE MEDITERRANEAN SEACOAST OF BARCELONA

Library of Congress Cataloging-in-Publication Data
Torres, Marimar.
     The Catalan country kitchen : food and wine from the Pyrenees to
the Mediterranean seacoast of Barcelona / by Marimar Torres : with a
foreword by Gerald Asher.
          p.   cm.
     "Aris books."
     Includes index.
     ISBN 0-201-57721-6
     1. Cookery, Spanish—Catalon style.   2. Cookery—Spain—
Catalonia.   3. Wine and wine making—Spain—Catalonia.   I. Title.
TX723.5.S7T658 1992
641.5946'7—dc20   91-19807
                                                                                                            CIP

Jacket and interior photographs by Oriol Maspons

Front jacket photo: a still life of Catalan ingredients at Cal Estevet restaurant in Barcelona.

Jacket and text design by Janis Owens
Set in 11-point Sabon by Shepard Poorman Communications Corporation

1 2 3 4 5 6 7 8 9-VB-95949392
First printing, January 1992

To my mother, Margarita,
who eventually became an enthusiastic supporter
of my cooking

and

to my daughter, Cristina,
who didn't exactly help in the kitchen
but provided so much joy while I cooked.

CONTENTS

RECIPE LIST

ACKNOWLEDGMENTS

▼　　▼　　▼

any people in the United States and Spain helped make this book possible. First of all, Sherry Virbila provided invaluable help in putting the manuscript together; she and I worked closely on it almost from its inception. My agent, Regula Noetzli, also collaborated with me from the beginning, as did my editor at Aris Books, John Harris. Joann Shirley and Judy Miller, at my Sausalito office, typed and proofread all the recipes.

In Spain, my assistants Montse Painous, Montse Rovirosa, and Fèlix Mascaró—who have been with me at my family's winery ever since I started to work there twenty-five years ago—coordinated my contacts, visits, and trips within Catalunya, and patiently answered my myriad of questions from here. My good Catalan friend Mauricio Wiesenthal, a living encyclopedia of gastronomy and wine, researched and wrote the Spanish draft of the section on Catalan wines. And Monica Brun, at the New York office of Wines of Spain, checked many of the facts with expedience and efficiency.

This book would not have been the same without the collaboration of Oriol Maspons, an outstanding Catalan photographer who went beyond the call of duty in obtaining the marvelous photographs. And, of course, all the members of my family need to be acknowledged, especially my brother Miguel for sharing not only his many contacts in the wine world but also the invaluable information in the many wine books he has written.

Finally, I have to thank all my friends who acted as "guinea pigs" and gave me their opinions about the numerous dishes I insisted they try at every single dinner—even though that often meant dieting the entire following week. And very specially, my housekeeper and nanny, Patricia Riquelme, who assisted me with everything connected with the recipe-testing dinners, from cooking and cleaning up, to looking after my two-year-old daughter and whatever else was necessary—very often all at once.

O

ur sense of food and of self are inseparable. It is not just for its restriction of bodily nourishment that a prolonged diet of bread and water is such fearful punishment. The greater ordeal is its inherent denial of identity. More than the way we dress, and even more than the language we speak, we are defined by what we eat. That is why, as adults, we all find comfort in the foods remembered from our childhood, even in those we ate, at the time, unwillingly. When we eat such dishes, sauced with recollection, we feel reassured and reconfirmed. We know that to be true of others, too. As we travel we expect to learn at least as much from restaurants and cafes and street markets as we do from cathedrals and museums.

What, then, was more natural than that Marimar Torres, far from her native Catalunya, should find contentment in the preparation of a *paella*, satisfaction in the pervasive aroma of the Catalan *sofregit*, and pleasure in offering her friends the fruit and nut tarts and the anise-scented fritters of her childhood?

Marimar tells us, in a book that condenses that contentment, satisfaction, and pleasure onto black and white pages, how she was introduced to the more exuberantly rustic tradition of Catalan cooking—particularly its garlic and snails and the tripe and rabbit her mother disapproved of—in spite of parental determination that she should eat with the reserved delicacy appropriate to her station in life. She uncovered the full vigor of her own culinary birthright at the farmhouse homes of family help, and in the household kitchen and larder where she was supposed to have no place. Disapproval can only have further enhanced what she learned, giving it, in the pagan or medieval sense, the qualities of a mystery, of a great wisdom made plain, of life's secrets unraveled and self-knowledge revealed. In sharing with us this precious patrimony, Marimar Torres makes the most generous gesture possible from one to another.

Gerald Asher
San Francisco, April 5, 1991

ne of my most vivid childhood memories is my mother's expression when someone asked me what I wanted to be when I grew up. I invariably answered, to her chagrin, "a cook or a ballerina"—and I remember her elegant eyebrows rising in horror. In Spanish society of those days, the kitchen was the cook's domain, not the place for a properly raised "aristocratic" young lady. Yet it was a fascinating world to me, and I was always trying to sneak into the kitchen to help the cook.

I grew up in Barcelona, the capital of Catalunya, in the days when kids were to be seen and not heard. When my mother gave one of her elaborate dinner parties, I watched all the preparations in the hope I'd be given a menial chore; if I was lucky I would be allowed to peel pears or potatoes, a task I would carry out with the concentration of a heart surgeon, relishing it as if it were the most important job in the world. And very often, whenever my brothers had teased me too much, I would retreat to the kitchen, where the cook would comfort me with a piece of freshly baked bread or a little pie. Sometimes she even let me put my hands in the soft sticky dough or help clean the squid.

My family has been growing grapes and making wine in Catalunya since the seventeenth century; Jaime Torres established the Torres winery in 1870, and from then on the business has been handed down from father to son for four generations. After my father took over the business at age thirty-two, he traveled with my mother all over the world to promote Torres wines. Whenever they went away, because I was too little—and a girl—I stayed home with the nanny and the cook. I actually looked forward to those occasions, for then we could eat whatever we wanted. Things like watermelon, which my mother never liked—or tripe or snails, which she considered too rustic. On rainy days, just after the rain stopped we would go out secretly and collect snails, hiding the box in the basement; on more than one occasion, a snail would escape and almost give us away.

My mother didn't like rabbit either, so it was always a great treat for me when my nanny, Mercedes, took me to her family's farm in the countryside. I remember the wonderful old-style kitchen, the long table covered with oilcloth, and the great loaves of crusty bread her uncle cut with a knife. We would feast on *pa amb tomàquet,* toasted bread rubbed with a ripe tomato and doused in olive oil, and I literally stuffed myself with grilled rabbit—accompanied with *allioli,* of course, another forbidden pleasure I never had at home, for my mother despised garlic. Sometimes we ate cabbage and potatoes drizzled with exquisite, greenish olive oil; thick wedges of potato and onion omelet; and rustic *botifarra* sausage served with *fasolets,* crunchy sautéed white beans. The men would pass the *porró,* a wine-drinking vessel with two spouts: a larger one for filling it with wine, and a smaller one for pouring the wine straight into your mouth while holding the *porró* high with one hand. This down-to-earth way of eating, reflecting the Catalans' true love for food, is still closest to my heart, and I always try to bring the same warm spirit to my own table.

As I grew up, my studies kept me busy and I rarely ventured into the kitchen anymore. Once I began working for my family, being groomed as export director, I traveled a great deal with my father; and on our business trips, he always took me to the best restaurants. I always enjoyed trying new dishes and began to acquire an appreciation of fine food and wine. However, all the fun I had in the kitchen as a child was put out of my mind—until I married an American and moved to California. My husband was a restaurant and wine critic, and his entire circle of friends in the San Francisco Bay Area were passionate about food.

It was 1975 and California cuisine was just taking off. Here, I discovered an entirely different attitude toward food. Alice Waters, a friend of my husband, had recently opened her celebrated restaurant Chez Panisse in Berkeley, cooks and chefs were becoming hometown heroes, and all sorts of wonderful new produce was available in the markets. Every one of our friends cooked—including the men—and could easily spend a whole day in the kitchen preparing festive meals. I began to see that cooking was really an art, and the memories of my childhood forays into the kitchen started to come back to me. Nostalgic for Catalan food, I began to try a few long-forgotten dishes as my contribution to these dinner parties.

To be honest, my first efforts were not a great success. I particularly remember an elaborate three-tiered omelet I attempted to cook in the mountains. The eggs would not set, and my husband's pork roast burned while we were all waiting for my first course. I soon realized my memories weren't detailed enough to cook from, so to bone up on basic techniques, I took cooking lessons both here and abroad. I was now working as the export director for my family's wines in North America, and each time I went back to Spain, I gathered recipes for the Catalan dishes I loved so much as a child. My family's cook and childhood mentor Rosalia was at a nursing home; I sat by her side for hours with a pad and paper, while she talked me through her best recipes. And as I traveled around Catalunya and Spain I also met inspiring cooks who were generous enough to share their recipes.

Most of the dishes, I found, could easily be adapted to ingredients available here; after all, California has a Mediterranean climate, and tomatoes, peppers, eggplants, fresh herbs, and so on—all the staples of Catalan cuisine—could be found at the local supermarket. Whenever I entertained I prepared traditional Spanish specialties, particularly country-style dishes from home. My friends thoroughly enjoyed Catalan cuisine; flavors that seemed so commonplace to me, like the combination of pine nuts and raisins, the medley of ingredients in a *paella,* or a typical fisherman-style seafood stew, to them seemed very exotic.

At the time, some Americans barely knew where Spain was, let alone my home region of Catalunya. I found myself explaining again and again that Catalunya was a semi-autonomous region in northeast Spain, that we have our own unique culture and an entirely separate language—not a dialect—and that our cuisine is one of the most distinct in Europe.

Since Barcelona was chosen as the site for the 1992 Summer Olympics, my hometown and its region have been very much in the news. Barcelona has been rediscovered as one of the most exciting and cosmopolitan cities in Europe, celebrated for its great art and architecture, its music and literature, its gastronomy and earthy lifestyle. After the long Franco years, when the Catalan language and culture were suppressed, the region is enjoying an exuberant new flowering of its unique spirit. And Catalan cuisine is very much a part of all this: with over ten thousand eating establishments, Barcelona boasts one of the hottest restaurant scenes in Europe today. It is very much an urban, sophisticated city—yet the food everybody loves to eat is unabashedly country.

What is Catalan Cuisine?

Catalan cuisine is cooking from the heart. It encompasses flavors we all love—tomatoes, olive oil, garlic, onions, nuts, dried fruits, lots of fresh herbs—many of the same ingredients that appear in French, Italian, and other Mediterranean cuisines, but put together in a different way. After all, parts of Provence and Roussillon were annexed to the Kingdom of Aragon and Catalunya for several centuries, as were Naples and Sicily from the late thirteenth through the fifteenth centuries. And

Lombardy with its capital, Milan, was a Spanish possession from the mid-sixteenth until the early eighteenth century. But whether it is rustic farmhouse or sophisticated restaurant fare, Catalan cuisine is based on thousands of years of country cooking.

L'Empordà, the area at the far northeast corner of Catalunya, was the site of the ancient Greek city of Empùries, and today is renowned for its fine gastronomy. When the Romans came to the Iberian Peninsula, they established Tarraco—today Tarragona—on the coast south of Barcelona as the capital of Hispania, as they called their Spanish empire. Remnants of other old cuisines, such as the Arabic and Jewish custom of using lemon, honey, and cinnamon in certain dishes, can still be found in Catalan cooking. And the first Spanish cookbook, one of the earliest surviving in Europe, was the *Llibre de Sent Soví,* written in Catalan in the first half of the fourteenth century.

Catalan Cuisine Today

Catalunya boasts two well-defined styles of cooking: one built around the fisherman-style dishes of the Mediterranean coast, the other on the more solid, sturdy preparations of the mountains. Seafood stews, dishes such as black rice with squid cooked in its own ink, grilled fish, and *suquet* (a fish and potato stew) are typical of the first style, while hearty stews of rabbit and game in red wine come from the mountain tradition.

The wealth of Catalan cuisine relies on the wide range of ingredients available from this varied region, which encompasses the Pyrenees Mountains, the rugged Costa Brava, and the gentler Costa Dorada in its twelve thousand square miles. A visit to La Boqueria, Barcelona's premier marketplace in the historic Gothic quarter, demonstrates the quality of materials cooks have to work with: scarlet peppers that seem to glow in the dark; pyramids of perfect peaches, plums, and melons; baskets filled with a dozen types of wild mushrooms from the hills; lobsters, tiny cuttlefish, and giant shrimp from the Costa Brava; partridge, quail, and wild hare from the Pyrenees.

Classic Catalan dishes range from the brilliantly simple *pa amb tomàquet* (toasted bread rubbed with tomato and drizzled with olive oil) and *esqueixada* (a salad of shredded raw salt cod) to *arrossejat* (pasta sautéed in olive oil and cooked in a fish broth) and the baroque, sumptuous flavors of *mar i muntanya* ("sea and mountain," a stew of lobster or prawns and chicken cooked in a rich sauce flavored with herbs, spices, hazelnuts, and a touch of chocolate).

Techniques and Essentials

A few techniques, such as *sofregit* (p. 12) and *picada* (p. 12), are essential to Catalan cuisine. The word *sofregit* (*sofrito* in Castilian) means "long sautéing"; in this technique, onions and sometimes tomato, garlic, peppers, or other ingredients are slowly sautéed in olive oil until the onions soften and start to caramelize. It is used as the base for many dishes and sauces. *Picada,* which literally means "pounded" in Catalan, is usually a mixture of garlic, parsley, and nuts, along with toasted or fried bread, and perhaps a pinch of saffron or other spices, pounded to a paste in a mortar and pestle. Added to a dish toward the end of the cooking, *picada* thickens a sauce and adds a final burst of flavor.

Other essentials include *samfaina* (p. 74), a mélange of vegetables (usually tomato, pepper, eggplant, and zucchini) cooked together rather like the Provençal rattatouille (which is, of course, a relation of *samfaina*), and the two beloved and ubiquitous sauces *allioli* and *romesco* (p. 113). *Allioli* is a heady garlic mayonnaise that accompanies grilled fish and meats, and is sometimes stirred into a dish toward the end of the cooking. In Provence, it goes by the more familiar name *aïoli,* but its origin is definitely Catalan. *Romesco* evolved from a fish stew of the Tarragona area on the coast south of Barcelona. A ruddy sauce that is the perfect accompaniment for all sorts of grilled vegetables, fish, and meats, *romesco* is made primarily with tomatoes, fresh or dried red peppers, garlic, and toasted almonds.

How This Book Was Conceived

In my first cookbook, *The Spanish Table* (Doubleday, 1986), I covered all the regions of Spain, and in its Catalan section I included some of my best recipes. Naturally, when I began to collect and test recipes for this book, I had to include many of these traditional favorites. They've all been retested, and many have been revised to new or simplified versions that I now prefer to the originals. The truth is that cooked the traditional way, many of these dishes are just too laborious for today's lifestyle.

The Spanish Table showcased the new Spanish cooking from restaurants all over Spain. In this more personal book, I have emphasized family recipes and the rustic country dishes I've enjoyed all my life. Of course, not everything in this book is traditional; the recipes reflect the way I cook Catalan dishes here in California. In fact, a few of my favorite dishes have been omitted, simply because the ingredients are not available here.

California has obviously had a big influence on me. For one thing, the concept of a dinner is much less complicated here. When my mother gave a dinner party, it became a marathon three-day project for everyone involved; as a consequence, she attempted it just two or three times a year. Admittedly, her dinners were quite lavish ones, but even so, it is normal in Spain to serve hors d'oeuvres followed by a first course, a fish course, a meat course, and *two* desserts. I was astonished to find how easy it can be to entertain in California, where buffet dinners often consist of a single entrée with pasta or rice, a salad, and a dessert.

I have also become much more health conscious here. Even today menus are not well balanced in Spain—they are too heavy on protein, fat, and starch, with very little emphasis on vegetables or greens. In California, we are much more aware of the need to balance a meal.

With its unique Mediterranean flavors, Catalan cuisine is ideal for our American palate and lifestyle. My love of good food has grown here, and ironically, my appreciation for Catalan cooking has also blossomed in California. In Spain, as in all of Europe, the tradition of food and wine is so old and so deep that we take it for granted, and it often takes an outsider to fully appreciate it. By living in California, I've had the opportunity to look at Catalan tradition with a different eye and have come to love it all the more. It is my hope that this book will bring Catalan country cooking into the hearts and homes of American food and wine lovers.

Mar Cantábrico

Océano Atlántico

La Coruña
Santiago de Compostela
GALICIA
Pontevedra
ALVARIÑO
RIBEIRO
Orense
Valdeorras

Lugo

ASTURIAS
Oviedo
CORDILLERA CANTÁBRICA
PICOS DE EUROPA
CANTABRIA
Santander
Laredo

León

Zamora

Burgos

Palencia

Valladolid

CASTILLA - LEÓN

Ribera del Duero

Río Duero

Rueda

Salamanca

Ávila

Segovia

Guadalajara

MADRID

Madrid

Toledo

Río Tajo

Cáceres

Río Guadiana

Badajoz

EXTREMADURA

Jabugo

Huelva

Sevilla

Sanlúcar de Barrameda
Jerez de la Frontera
Puerto de Santa María
Cádiz

ANDALUCÍA

Córdoba

Río Guadalquivir

Jaén

Málaga

Granada

SIERRA NEVADA

Almería

CASTILLA - LA MANCHA

Ciudad Real

Valdepeñas

SIERRA MORENA

Albacete

Murcia

MURCIA

MAR MENOR

San Sebastián
Bilbao
Vitoria
PAÍS VASCO
Río Ebro
Logroño
Haro
LA RIOJA
Tudela

Soria

Pamplona

NAVARRA

ARAGÓN

Huesca

Zaragoza

Cariñena

Alcañiz

Teruel

Cuenca

PAÍS VALENCIANO

Castellón de la Plana

Valencia

Río Júcar

LAKE ALBUFERA

Alicante

FRANCIA

CORDILLERA PIRENAICA

Lleida

CATALUNYA

Girona

Barcelona

Sant Sadurní d'Anoia
Vilafranca del Penedès
Tarragona

ISLAS BALEARES

MALLORCA
Palma

IBIZA

Mar Mediterráneo

N

ESPAÑA

0   MILES   100
KM   100

FRANCIA

ANDORRA

Martinet

LA CERDANYA

LLEIDA

L'EMPORDÀ

Pals

GIRONA

L'Escala

ARAGÓN

Vic

Girona

BRAVA

Palamós

Sant Felíu de Guixols

Lleida
(Lérida)

BARCELONA

COSTA

Les Borges
Blanques

Argentona

Sant Sadurní
d'Anoia

Siurana

Valls

Vilafranca del Penedès

Barcelona

TARRAGONA

Sitges

Vilanova i Geltrú

Tarragona

Ebro River

N

CATALUNYA

Mar Mediterráneo

PAIS VALENCIANO

ISLAS BALEARES

Castellón de le Plana

MALLORCA

THE BASICS OF

CATALAN

CUISINE

▼ ▼ ▼

INGREDIENTS

T his section covers some exotic ingredients such as saffron and salt cod, but I have also included tips on more basic items like salt and olive oil. While none of these ingredients are exclusive to Catalan cuisine, they are important elements in many of my recipes.

Anchovies
Anxoves

The Costa Brava anchovy is so plump, sweet, and subtle in taste that it bears almost no resemblance to the skinny fillets tasting of salt that garnish pizza in this country. Palamós, L'Escala, and Sant Felíu de Guixols, all fishing villages along the rugged Costa Brava north of Barcelona, are famous for the quality of their salt-cured anchovies. During the season that runs from May until September, the shimmering silver fish are still prepared the old-fashioned way, first brine-cured for weeks in big wooden barrels, then layered with coarse sea salt to mature for several months more. They are sold either whole, layered with salt in large glass jars, or filleted and packed in olive oil.

Needless to say, the real thing is difficult to find here, so I generally substitute salt-cured anchovies from Spain, which are often available in fine food markets. Before using, rinse the anchovy fillets and pat dry. For whole salt-cured anchovies, separate the two fillets from the spine under running water, then pat dry.

Brandy
Brandy

In those recipes that use brandy, I have specified either full-bodied brandy or finest-quality brandy. The former refers to a style of brandy that is more robust and intense, aged in American oak; it is generally used in flambéed dishes. The latter is made by the classic *charentais* process used in Cognac, of double distillation in copper pot stills, and aged in French Limousin oak; it is more delicate, smooth, and complex, so I reserve it for desserts and other recipes in which it is used strictly as a flavoring.

Of course, I recommend using Catalan brandies, which warrant a special mention here. They are less sweet than most Spanish brandies, and the finest are distilled from the area's white wines following the *charentais* method just discussed. Naturally, in my recipes I use our own Miguel Torres brand as the finest-quality and Tres Torres as the full-bodied brandy; other good Catalan brandies include those from Mascaró.

Ham
Pernil

Spain's incomparable raw-cured ham, *jamón de Jabugo*, hails from a miniscule village nestled in the high peaks of the western end of the Sierra Morena mountain range, in the region of Andalucía. (*Jabugo* is a special Appellation of Origin of *jamónserrano*, which is the name given to Spain's excellent cured mountain hams.) The village of Jabugo is surrounded by leafy oak forests, which provide the acorns that the placid black Iberian pig, *cerdo ibérico*, loves to eat. The cool mountain climate is also ideal for curing the hams.

Jamón serrano is expensive; that from *Jabugo* even more so. That's because the Iberian pig is rare, and the process of curing the mountain hams takes from fifteen months up to three years. First, they are stored in salt for fifteen to twenty days, then rinsed and hung from the rafters in special drying rooms, and finally transferred to dark, humid cellars for maturing.

A favorite Catalan snack is *pa amb tomàquet i pernil,* literally Bread with Tomato (p. 41) and ham, topped with fine hand-cut slices of ruddy *jamón serrano* or *jamón de Jabugo*. Unfortunately, neither of these hams is imported into this country, but you can substitute a top-quality prosciutto, Black Forest ham, or *jambon de Bayonne*.

Honey
Mel

At country markets in Catalunya I always enjoy searching out fragrant wildflower honey, thick and opaque. It is especially delicious poured over the fresh white cheese we call *mató*. In the simple and very popular dessert *mel i mató*, honey is mashed into the snowy cheese with a fork, and pine nuts or walnuts are served alongside. In this country, I look for unfiltered honey sold in natural foods shops, fine food stores, and local farmers' markets.

Olive Oil
Oli d'Oliva

Olive oil is indispensable for cooking in Catalunya and all over the Mediterranean. A heritage of the ancient Greeks and Romans, the olive and its prized oil arrived in Catalunya—and Spain—via Eastern Mediterranean traders some three thousand years ago. Today, together with Italy, Spain heads the list of the world's olive oil producers. While most of the Spanish olive oils are produced in the provinces of Jaén, Córdoba, and Sevilla, in Andalucía, some of the finest oil comes from Catalunya. The village of Les Borges Blanques and its surroundings, east of Lérida, and the area of Siurana, west of Tarragona, are renowned for the quality of their oil and are two of the four olive oil–producing areas in Spain with their own Appellation of Origin. Both oils are made from the *arbequina* olive, a small round variety noted for its low acidity and delicate, fruity flavor.

Fortunately, several Catalan olive oils are available in this country. Among them are Verge de Borges, Siurana, and Lérida. The best-quality olive oil is called extra virgin and comes from the first (cold) pressing of the olives. It has the lowest acidity—under 1 percent—as well as an intensely green color and fruity taste. It is excellent for seasoning salads or used as a condiment, but I find it too strong for cooking. The second and third pressings yield what is called refined olive oil, with a higher acidity and limpid yellow color. The so-called "pure" olive oil is actually a blend of refined oil with 5 to 10 percent of first-press olive oil. I find this is the best choice for cooking and frying.

Unlike wine, olive oil does not improve with age. Check to see if the tin or bottle is dated, and try to purchase oil from the current year or, at most, the year before; store it in a cool, dark place, away from direct sunlight, at a temperature between 50° and 60° F.

Olives
Olivas

Olives, along with almonds, Manchego cheese, sausages—and potato chips—are the most common *tapa* in Spain. Special stands in Barcelona's turn-of-the-century covered markets proffer olives from all over Spain. Some of the most flavorful are the tiny grayish-green *arbequinas*, which also produce Catalunya's exquisite olive oils.

Many of my recipes call for pimiento-stuffed green Spanish olives; these are easy to find, since they're the most popular of the Spanish table olives. California also produces olives in a similar style.

Orange Liqueur
Licor de Taronja

Whenever a recipe calls for orange liqueur, I naturally use Gran Torres, my family's product. It is made from brandies steeped in an extract of herbs, honey, and Valencia oranges, carefully aged in American oak casks. Grand Marnier works equally well in any of the recipes that require orange liqueur; others, however, such as Triple Sec, are not recommended because they have a different flavor and consistency.

Rice
Arròs

In Catalunya and the rest of Spain we normally use short-grain rice from Valencia. It has a very particular texture and is more flavorful than long-grain rice. Short-grain rice is essential to prepare any of my rice recipes; long-grain rice should not be substituted.

Valencian rice is sometimes available in Latino markets and at some locations of the San Francisco–based chain of cookware shops, Williams-Sonoma. Italian Arborio rice is the best substitute; you can also use California short-grain rice.

Saffron
Safrà

The finest saffron in the world is produced in the plains of La Mancha in central Spain. Every October, the landscape there is a checkerboard of newly harvested vineyards and broad fields carpeted in purple saffron flowers. The plant is native to Asia, and arrived in Spain with the Arabs (*azafrán*, Castilian for saffron, derives from the Arabic word *za'faran,* or "yellow," for the color its dried pistils give to rice or other food).

Today, because of the enormous amount of labor required to produce "the gold of La Mancha," the saffron's red pistils are the costliest spice in the world. During the harvest, the men collect the flowers very early in the morning, their backs bent over for hours, while the women carefully separate the flower from its three precious pistils, accompanying their work with singing around the table. An experienced "peeler" will do at most two to three ounces a day, or about ten thousand flowers. The pistils must be dried the same evening, a process that will reduce the crop to one quarter of its size.

Yes, saffron is expensive, but it takes very little to give a stunning effect. I prefer to use saffron "threads" (the term for the whole, dried pistils), rather than the powdered form, which often disguises lower quality or adulterated saffron. The best quality is Mancha Superior. Before using, mash the saffron slightly in a mortar with a pestle, or between the palms of your hands. And always soak or simmer the threads in warm liquid for at least 5 minutes, to further release the flavor. Remember, a small amount of saffron goes a long way; too much of it will impart a medicinal flavor.

Stored in airtight containers, away from direct sunlight, humidity, and extreme heat and cold, saffron will keep for several years. In La Mancha, the farmers treat it just like gold, storing it and selling it in time of need.

Salt
Sal

We hear so much these days about how we should cut down on salt for our health. In my recipes, I have kept the salt to a minimum; however, the dishes are so well flavored that few will find it necessary to add salt at the table.

I prefer to use sea salt, rather than processed commercial salts; because it has a more intense flavor, you will need to use less. Though it is sold in both coarse and fine crystals, I prefer the coarse type, which has no magnesium carbonate added, and I use a salt grinder whenever I need a finer salt.

Salt Cod
Bacallà

Catalans have a special love for salt cod, which is known as *bacallà;* and we prepare it many different ways. Made from fresh cod, preserved by salting and drying, it is a staple all over the Mediterranean. Most of it comes from northern climes: from Norway (where it can be traced as far back as the ninth century), Scotland, and Newfoundland. Salt cod has been used in Catalunya since at least the fifteenth century, and is a particular favorite in Provence, which was once linked to Catalunya and Aragón. In fact, the famous *brandade de morue* (shredded salt cod with olive oil, garlic, and milk) is original to Nîmes, only we call it *brandada de bacallà* (p. 64)

When buying salt cod, ask for the thick pieces called "middles," or buy the boxed fillets. The flesh should be white; if it is yellowish, the salt cod is old and may be stringy when cooked. Stored in your refrigerator, it will keep at its best for 2 or 3 months.

Before it can be used, however, salt cod has to be soaked in cold water to remove excess salt. Two days' soaking, changing the water 5 or 6 times during the process, will be sufficient. The only way to check is by tasting; it should be no saltier than fresh fish. One shortcut: If the recipe requires shredded cod, you can cut the soaking time by shredding it beforehand.

Sausages
Salsichas

Stands festooned with garlands of sausages are among my favorite haunts in Catalan markets. Along with rustic mountain hams, they feature dozens of sausages: everything from the famous *botifarra de Vic* (a white sausage sliced and eaten raw) and the creamy white *botifarra* (served grilled or as an accompaniment to bean dishes) to the dried salami-type sausages, rich blood sausages, and mild or spicy pimiento-stained *xoriço* (*chorizo* in Castilian).

Unfortunately, not even the cured or dried types of sausages can be imported into this country. But although the selection here is more limited than in Spain, I find it is not worth all that's involved to make my own sausages. Instead, I have adapted the recipes to suit the sausages available here. For *botifarra,* I substitute a mild Italian pork sausage (without fennel); for *botifarra negra,* or blood pudding, I use an Italian blood sausage, French *boudin noir,* or Spanish-style *morcilla.* The fatty, loosely textured Mexican-style *chorizo* little resembles the Spanish version; choose a firm, lean style of *chorizo* or *linguiça* sausage instead.

Sherry
Xerès
(*Jerez* in Castilian)

True sherry is produced in a relatively small region in southwest Spain, in the triangle formed by the towns of Jerez de la Frontera, Sanlúcar de Barrameda, and Puerto de Santa María. By international agreement, Spain is the only country that can use the word "sherry" alone on the label. California and Australian sherries, for example, must be labeled "California sherry" or "Australian sherry," respectively. For my recipes, it is best to use Spanish sherries; those from other areas may have an entirely different taste.

The key factor in *jerez* wines is the *flor*, a film of *Saccharomyces* yeast that protects the wine from oxidation and transforms the alcohol into acetaldehyde, giving sherry much of its flavor, aroma, and character. The *Saccharomyces* yeast thrives on oxygen and develops perfectly around 60° F—the fall and spring temperature in Jerez—in wines of an alcohol content around 15.5 percent. As soon as the fermentation is finished, the new wine is transferred to 130-gallon *botas,* or butts, made of American oak. To encourage development of the *flor*, they are not filled to the top. For reasons not fully understood, the *flor* will not develop in every cask, and its presence determines a sherry's classification.

Sherries are classified as *finos, amontillados,* and *olorosos. Finos,* with at least a year's contact with the *flor,* are light, very dry wines of pale straw color, with clean, pungent aroma and a special, almost green-olive taste; they should be served cold. Aged longer on the *flor, amontillados* have an elegant amber color, more body, and a marked dry palate reminiscent of hazelnuts. The butts with no good growth of *flor* are classified as *olorosos,* and fortified to 18 percent alcohol to eliminate further growth.

Most of the *olorosos* on the market are semisweet; the dry versions are much rarer. At its best, a dry *oloroso* will have an old-gold amber color, acquired after long aging in wood. The bouquet will be intense and clean, with a luscious first impression on the palate evolving into a complex aftertaste with hints of walnuts.

Snails
Cargols

Snails are very popular in Catalunya, where they have typically been considered more an earthy peasant dish than elegant or refined. They are part of a classic *paella* and appear as an ingredient in many country-style stews. Snails were customarily eaten in the past on vigil days—traditionally on Holy Thursday, Good Friday, and Christmas

Eve—when Catholics were not allowed to eat meat (and snails did not qualify as such). It is interesting that the tastiest snails are said to come from the vineyards.

In most cases, unless you can buy them fresh or prepare them yourself, I find snails add little flavor to a dish in the readily available canned form. However, they do provide an interesting texture, and their meat is an excellent "boat" for sauces.

Wine Vinegar
Vinagre de Vi

Like wines, wine vinegars can vary in quality and taste. Before buying one, it is wise to do some comparative shopping and purchase the best quality you can find. A red wine vinegar that has been aged in oak is preferable. The best is the one that you make yourself.

To make your own vinegar: You'll need a small oak barrel fitted with a spigot, or a 1-gallon or larger earthenware crock, plus a bottle of vinegar mother (available from beer- or wine-making suppliers). Rinse and dry the container and add 1 part vinegar mother to 3 parts wine, enough to fill the container about two-thirds full; cover the opening with cheesecloth. The vinegar mold that transforms wine into vinegar needs exposure to the air in order to do its work. Place the container in a corner of your kitchen or pantry where it will be undisturbed.

After about 6 weeks, taste the contents of the barrel or crock; if it tastes like vinegar, you can begin to draw off a small quantity of it. Replenish the container from time to time with odds and ends of wines left over from a dinner party. (Save them in a large covered container and then add all at once.) You can mix red and white wines, though some people prefer to keep them separate. Use only dry wines of good quality; never add sweet or fortified wines. And always keep the barrel or crock two-thirds to three-fourths full.

Sherry vinegar is another staple in my kitchen. It is less sharp and more mellow in flavor than red wine vinegar. There are several imported sherry vinegars on the market, most from sherry producers; Sandeman is the one I like best.

Making Orange and Lemon Zest

Orange or lemon rind—without any of the bitter white pith—is referred to as *zest*. Whenever a recipe calls for grated lemon or orange peel or zest, I recommend using a handy "zester" (available in kitchenware shops) to cut fine strips of rind, and then mincing the peel very finely by hand. Grating the peel releases the bitter oils. If you don't have a zester, use a vegetable peeler or sharp paring knife to make very thin strips of peel; trim away any pith before chopping the peel.

Making Fresh Bread Crumbs

In Catalan cooking, soft white bread crumbs are often used to bind a stuffing. An all-meat filling tends to be too heavy; bread crumbs lighten the texture. And I find that the stuffing is also tastier, because the bread crumbs soak up the seasoning.

Bread crumbs can be made from either white or whole-wheat bread, but, being somewhat of a traditionalist, I always use white bread simply because that is what we use in Catalunya. In a few recipes I have called for commercial (dried) bread crumbs. These finely textured crumbs are more suitable for coating foods or lining a mold. Fresh homemade bread crumbs are always the best choice for any stuffing or filling.

To make your own bread crumbs: Use day-old bread, if possible. Cut away the crusts and, with the metal blade fitted in a food processor, whirl to mince the bread. A 1-pound loaf should yield about 5-1/3 cups or 1/2 pound of crustless bread crumbs. Three ounces of bread (weighed before removing crusts) will make 1 cup of bread crumbs. Quantities for bread crumbs in my recipes are always loose measurements; avoid packing the bread crumbs into the measuring cup.

Roasting and Peeling Peppers

Sweet red and green bell peppers appear in many recipes in this book, very often roasted and peeled. Here are a few tips on how to do it easily.

Preheat the oven to 400° F. Roast the whole peppers on an ungreased baking sheet for 30 minutes, turning them occasionally, until the skin blisters and starts to blacken. Remove from the oven and immediately place them in a paper bag. Twist it shut and leave the peppers for 15 to 30 minutes. While they are still warm, remove the skin by scraping with a small, sharp knife; don't worry about getting every bit of skin. And never peel the skins under running water; much of the peppers' flavor will wash off with the blackened skins.

This procedure will only precook the peppers; if they are to be baked later, they will not be overcooked. In fact, I prefer peppers on the well-done side, not only because they are easier to digest but also because their flavors are intensified.

To peel just a few peppers, you may find it faster to spear each pepper on a fork and hold it over a gas burner until the skin starts to blacken, turning so it scorches evenly all over. After each pepper has blistered, place it in a paper bag as directed above.

Peeling Garlic

Slice off the root end of each garlic clove, lay the flat of a large knife on top of the clove and give it a light tap with the heel of your hand; the papery skin should easily slip off.

Peeling and Seeding Tomatoes

Bring a pot of water to a boil, plunge the tomatoes into the boiling water, and count to 10. Immediately drain and run cold water over the tomatoes; the skin should slip off easily. With a sharp paring knife, cut out the hard core.

To seed the tomatoes, cut them in half *crosswise* and gently squeeze out the seeds.

Toasting Almonds, Hazelnuts, and Pine Nuts

Almonds, hazelnuts, and pine nuts are typical ingredients in Catalan recipes, and are almost always toasted to accentuate their flavor. To toast the nuts, preheat the oven to 350° F. Spread the nuts on an ungreased baking sheet and bake 15 minutes for whole almonds (10 if they are blanched, 4 or 5 if sliced) and 12 minutes for hazelnuts.

Unless it really makes a difference in the recipe, I don't bother to blanch the almonds. However, since some of the hazelnut skins blister and loosen when they're toasted, they are easily removed by rubbing the nuts gently in a damp cloth, while still warm.

To toast pine nuts, stir them in a dry skillet over medium heat until golden.

Whole roasted nuts can be stored in an airtight container in the refrigerator or freezer.

Making a *Sofregit*

The secret to making a good *sofregit*, the flavorful base for so many Catalan dishes, is to slowly sauté the onions in a little olive oil over low heat for a long time, stirring often, especially at the end. Old-fashioned Catalan cooks insist that in certain dishes the onions should be cooked for as long as an hour, until they darken and caramelize—and actually, I do sometimes cook them for 45 minutes or even an hour.

Tomatoes are frequently part of a *sofregit,* too, and sometimes garlic; shallots are occasionally substituted for onions, and chopped red peppers may replace tomatoes. In many of my recipes, onions and garlic are cooked together for only 10 or 15 minutes before adding tomatoes, then the sauce is cooked briskly until dry.

Making a *Picada*

Picada, a paste of various ingredients such as garlic, nuts, herbs, spices, and often fried bread, adds a special twist to Catalan dishes. It is used as a thickening and flavoring agent and is generally stirred in toward the end of the cooking to contribute a burst of flavor and complexity.

To make a *picada*, you can pound the ingredients in a mortar with a pestle or, as I generally do, grind them to a paste in a food processor.

Cooking with Wine and Spirits

Using quality ingredients is very important in cooking, and I cannot emphasize it enough. If the raw material that goes into a dish is inferior, the most skilled cook will not be able to produce a truly wonderful dish.

However, even those who understand this principle often make the mistake of using poor-quality, old or rancid wines and spirits in their kitchens. When wine or liquor is used in cooking, the alcohol burns off, leaving the flavor or essence of the product; the better its quality, the better the dish. Of course, it is not necessary to use an expensive bottle; a decently priced wine with good flavor is all that's required.

Flambéing

Catalan chefs are very fond of flambéing, and they use this technique more as part of the preparation, to add flavor and a bit of color to a dish, than as a dramatic presentation. The harsh alcohol flavors burn off quickly, leaving only the essence of the brandy or spirit used.

It is important to use a liquor with a high alcohol content; you cannot flambé with wine, for example. It is also essential to use a shallow pan. Both the alcohol and the ingredients should be hot; pour in the alcohol, shake the pan and, as soon as the liquor is heated, ignite it with a match. Avert your face and stand somewhat away from the pan, as the alcohol will burst into flames right away.

Deglazing

This technique is used to cook off the alcohol in a wine or spirit, leaving only the essence of its flavor in the pan. To deglaze, cook the wine or liquor over medium-high heat, stirring and scraping the bottom of the pan with a wooden spatula to loosen any browned bits of food attached to the pan, until the liquid is reduced to a glaze.

Caramelizing

Caramelizing is used in Catalan recipes to add color and flavor to savory dishes or to line a flan mold. The method is simple: dissolve sugar with a little water (about 1 tablespoon water to 1/4 cup sugar is a good rule of thumb) in a heavy saucepan and cook over brisk heat. (You can actually caramelize sugar all by itself, without dissolving it in water, but I find this method easier.) Don't stir, just shake the pan gently; after about 4 or 5 minutes, the water will evaporate and the sugar will begin to melt and turn to a thick golden liquid. At this point, you must decide how dark a caramel you want—and quickly, since the color goes from light golden to amber to burnt brown very fast.

In savory dishes, the caramel is usually added to a hot liquid; it will hiss and smoke at first, but the caramel will soon dissolve, contributing a rich color and extra depth of flavor. When used to line a mold, caramel will not only add richness and flavor to your dessert but will also make it easier to unmold.

A final bit of advice: Never touch the caramel with your fingers, as it gets extremely hot and can cause a bad burn. It is also very sticky, but easy to remove from pans and utensils: Soak them in hot water, and the caramel will dissolve by itself.

I love the look and feel of my handsome Catalan implements in the kitchen. They can be used not only for Catalan cuisine, but for all sorts of cooking. In fact, you don't need any special equipment to prepare the recipes in this book. You can easily substitute an oven-proof glass, iron, or ceramic casserole for the rustic terra-cotta *cassola*, a large skillet for the *paella* pan, and a food processor for the mortar and pestle.

Cassola (Cazuela)

The *cassola* (*cazuela* in Castilian) is a shallow clay casserole, an old classic of Catalan folk pottery. Simple in its design, it is a wonderful cooking implement because it can be used in the oven or on top of a gas stove (not on an electric stove, though), and can go straight from the kitchen to the table. Glazed only on the inside, these versatile, inexpensive casseroles are the original nonstick pans and are extremely easy to clean. (The glaze doesn't hold up in the dishwasher, however.) In Catalunya they are used for everything from bread soups and rice dishes or country-style stews to *crema catalana*, the classic Catalan custard. I also use it to serve cold salads, appetizers, and sauces.

Over the years, I've carried back dozens of *cassoles* from Spain, for myself and as presents for friends. I have them in all sizes, from the 5- or 6-inch individual versions all the way up to 18 inches across for a big party. Before they are used for the first time, they require a very simple seasoning: Fill with water, add a dash of vinegar, and bring slowly to a boil on top of the stove. Simmer for 30 to 45 minutes, turn off the heat and let sit overnight. And that's it.

To ensure a long life, it is important to avoid abrupt temperature changes, or the *cassola* can crack. Don't ever put it straight from the refrigerator into the oven, for example, or add cold water when it is hot. On top of the stove, always start with a low flame and gradually increase the heat (and never set the casserole directly on an electric heating element).

Check international groceries and Latino markets for imported *cassoles*, which will probably go by their Castilian name *cazuelas*. Also, the San Francisco–based chain of cookware shops, Williams-Sonoma, sells both individual and larger clay casseroles. (See "Mail Order Sources," p. 167.)

Paella Pan

The name for Spain's renowned rice dish *paella* comes from the Catalan word for the iron skillet in which it's cooked. Round, with two handles and shallow slanted sides, a good-sized *paella* pan is about 15 inches across. This is a dish to cook for a crowd! In some parts of Catalunya, village festivals are often celebrated with the making of a gigantic *paella* many feet across, requiring hundreds of pounds of rice and other ingredients—that is, large enough to feed all the celebrants!

In Spain, *paella* is traditionally cooked outdoors over a wood fire. The best pans feature a thin bottom, which ensures plenty of *socarrat*: the tasty crust of burnt rice on the bottom. For me, this was always the best part of *paella* at home. On today's stoves, however, a heavier pan distributes the heat from the burners more evenly. You will still have to shift the pan on the burner as the *paella* cooks; otherwise, the rice cooks only in the middle. And after 10 minutes or so on top of the stove, it is easier to finish cooking the rice in the oven.

Check specialized kitchenware shops, international groceries, and Latino markets for *paella* pans in iron or speckled enamel; also see Mail Order Sources, p. 167.

Mortar and Pestle

Despite the availability of modern conveniences such as the blender and food processor (which I use for the most part), a mortar and pestle are still frequently used in Catalunya to pound nuts and spices for a *picada* and to prepare sauces such as *allioli* and *romesco* by hand.

The typical Catalan mortar is not marble or wood, but ceramic with a lovely glaze of canary yellow splashed with green. These basic utensils are very inexpensive and make a great gift to bring back from a trip to Catalunya—buy the largest size you can carry.

Food Processor

The food processor has dramatically reduced the time necessary to make some of these recipes. It is invaluable for chopping and mincing vegetables, grinding nuts, and making bread crumbs. I also love the food processor for making pastry and bread doughs. I use it for just about everything except chopping meat and mashing potatoes, both of which are better done by hand.

ESSENTIAL STOCKS
FOR GOOD COOKING

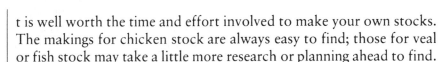

I t is well worth the time and effort involved to make your own stocks. The makings for chicken stock are always easy to find; those for veal or fish stock may take a little more research or planning ahead to find.

Fortunately, you needn't make a batch of stock each time it appears as an ingredient in a recipe. Stocks will keep for 3 or 4 days in the refrigerator, or for 6 months if frozen. Before freezing, divide stock into small containers (1- or 2-cup sizes are best) and label with the date and the quantity. Another idea is to freeze stock in ice cube trays and store the frozen cubes in a plastic freezer bag. Then, whenever you need a small quantity of stock, you can quickly defrost a few of the cubes.

You might want to keep separate bags of chicken and veal parts in your freezer, adding to them whenever you have spare pieces. Chicken backs, necks, wing tips, and gizzards all go into my poultry bag, as well as leftover veal bones in another bag for the veal stock. When you have accumulated several pounds, it's time to make a batch of stock.

Let the strained stock cool to room temperature, then chill for several hours or overnight in the refrigerator. The fat will form a solid layer at the top and can be easily removed. Then—and only then— you may want to cook the stock over medium-high heat and reduce it by half. This will produce a very rich stock, which will add great flavor to sauces. Never boil a stock before you have removed the fat, or the fat will bond with the stock and become impossible to remove.

It is a good idea not to season a basic stock; since it is just one element of the final dish, it is usually better to season the dish once it is assembled—unless you are using any of the following recipes as a soup on its own.

Chicken Stock

Yields about 12 cups.

Keep this basic stock on hand in your freezer to add rich flavor to your dishes without extra calories.

5 or 6 pounds chicken backs, necks, and/or wing tips
1 pound onions, coarsely chopped
1 pound unpeeled carrots, trimmed and coarsely chopped
2 or 3 leeks, coarsely chopped, with two thirds of green part

1 cup dry white wine
1 large bay leaf
3 parsley sprigs
8 black peppercorns
1 fresh thyme sprig (optional)

Preheat oven to 450° F. In a large roasting pan, brown chicken pieces, onions, carrots, and leeks in preheated oven for 1 hour or more, turning chicken and vegetables occasionally, until they are browned.

Transfer contents of roasting pan to a stockpot. Add wine to roasting pan; over medium heat, stir and scrape bottom and sides to get all browned bits of vegetables and chicken left in the pan. As you scrape, let wine boil for a few minutes to evaporate the alcohol. Transfer this liquid to stockpot; add remaining ingredients and 3 quarts water, or to cover. Bring to a boil and immediately reduce heat to low.

Remove the scum that forms on top. Simmer stock, partially covered, for about 3 hours. During this time, remove scum occasionally as it rises to the top; don't worry about fat on the surface, as it is easily removed after the stock is chilled.

Strain stock through a colander and then through a fine sieve. Let cool at room temperature and refrigerate overnight. The next day, carefully remove the hardened layer of fat from the surface. The stock is now ready to use as is, or to be reduced for a richer, more concentrated stock.

Veal Stock

Yields about 6 cups.

This dark stock provides a deep background of flavor for meat dishes and sauces. You might want to double the recipe and store the extra stock in your freezer.

4 or 5 pounds veal bones and/or veal breast (see *Note* below)
3/4 pound unpeeled carrots, trimmed and coarsely chopped
1 large onion, coarsely chopped
2 leeks, coarsely chopped, with two thirds of green part

1/2 celery stalk, with leaves, chopped
1/4 cup chopped shallots
1 cup dry white wine
1 bay leaf
4 parsley sprigs
1 teaspoon whole black peppercorns

Note: The best bones for making a veal stock are knuckle and marrow bones. Veal breast is also excellent, although more expensive, but it is often available on special. It is usually sold by the piece (about 2 or 3 pounds). If you do use it, ask your butcher to cut the breast and an additional 2 pounds of veal bones in small pieces.

Preheat oven to 450° F. In a large baking pan, roast bones and vegetables in preheated oven for 1-1/4 hours, or until bones and vegetables are browned. Turn them from time to time, especially toward the end of the cooking, so as not to burn the vegetables in the corners of the pan.

Transfer contents of roasting pan to a stockpot. Add wine to roasting pan; over medium heat, stir and scrape bottom and sides to get all browned bits of vegetables and veal left in the pan. As you scrape, let wine boil for a few minutes to evaporate the alcohol.

Add this liquid to stock pot. Add remaining ingredients and 2 quarts water, or to cover. Bring to a boil and immediately reduce heat to low. Continue as directed in Chicken Stock recipe, p. 18.

Fish Stock (Fumet)

Yields about 8 cups.

A good homemade fish stock, or fumet, is essential for many fine seafood dishes. Do not be tempted to substitute bottled clam juice; it is too salty and has none of the delicacy or complexity of a good homemade fish stock. Unlike chicken or veal stocks, this recipe is quick and very easy to make. All you need are fish heads and bones, available often at fine food markets or by special order from your grocer or fishmonger. It is important to use only white fish—any sole or flounder type, halibut, red snapper, lake trout, pike, whiting, ocean perch, rockfish, etc. (I also use salmon.) Avoid oily fish, such as bluefish or mackerel. When preparing the fish bones, discard the oily skins and fins. Unlike other stocks, this one does not benefit from long cooking; once it is finished, be sure to strain it immediately.

3 pounds fish heads, collars, and/or bones
1/4 cup olive oil
2 large or 3 small leeks, coarsely chopped, with two thirds of green part
1 large onion, coarsely chopped
1 medium unpeeled carrot, trimmed and coarsely chopped
2 cups dry white wine
2 parsley sprigs and plenty of stems
1 bay leaf
2 or 3 fresh thyme sprigs, or 1 teaspoon dried thyme

Rinse fish bones and heads thoroughly; unless they are absolutely fresh, soak them in cold water for 10 to 15 minutes. Drain.

Heat oil in a large stock pot. Add leeks, onion, and carrot; sauté for about 5 minutes, stirring, until they start to color. Add wine and boil for 5 minutes to evaporate the alcohol. Add fish heads/bones, herbs, and 6 cups cold water; bring to a boil, immediately reduce heat to very low, and remove scum on surface. Simmer slowly, partially covered, for 30 minutes. During this time, skim off several times any scum that rises to the surface.

Immediately strain fish stock through a colander, gently pressing down bones and vegetables with a spoon, and then through a fine-mesh strainer into a storage container. Let cool before refrigerating or freezing.

MENU
PLANNING

▼ ▼ ▼

A NOTE ON SERVING
WINE WITH FOOD

▼ ▼ ▼

In Catalunya and Spain, as in all of Mediterranean Europe, wine is considered as much a part of the meal as the food on the table. And in fact, most people don't pay that much attention to either one. They drink the wine of the region and usually serve just one wine throughout the meal. Very few really worry about choosing the right wine for each dish. And certainly the wine and the cooking are rarely topics of lengthy conversation.

Of course, it is very different with food lovers (like us), especially those in a winemaking family. I pay a lot of attention to the choice of wines, and carefully consider both the guests and the food when planning a menu. Different foods can dramatically change one's appreciation of the wine and vice versa. However, I don't believe in insisting on a specific wine with a specific dish. Just as in planning a garden, you have to bear in mind the entire context and imagine how each element will fit into the whole. Whether it is a simple menu or a more elaborate one affects the choice and number of wines. Not only that but the season, the purpose of the meal (business or pleasure), and whether your guests are wine knowledgeable or even wine lovers, are all factors that come into play. I confess, I keep some of my most precious wines to enjoy with good friends, because we appreciate them all the more in good company.

There are no hard and fast rules on serving wine with food, only general guidelines. As my friend, wine writer Larry Walker maintains, "the integrity of neither the food nor the wine should be violated." Although there may be one traditional "perfect" match, the fact is that many wines will work with the same recipe. Also, it is not necessary to choose a different wine for each dish on a menu. A single wine may do for several courses, or I may serve more than one wine with a single dish. Often, I serve more than one wine at the start, then let the guests decide which wine they prefer with each dish. But then, wine has always flowed quite freely in my family!

Keeping all of this in mind, I have given general wine recommendations for all the main-course dishes and occasionally, where the match was particularly good, also for recipes in other chapters. Of course, since regional wines tend to go with regional cuisine, Catalan wines will always be good matches. But, although I can always think of one, I'm not going to cite a specific Torres wine, nor indeed any other brand. Rather, I've tried to give more general guidelines, such as "a complex oak-aged white," or "a barrel-fermented, oak-aged Chardonnay". I feel it is just as confusing to make a blanket recommendation for Chardonnay—which includes a tremendous range of characteristics and styles—as it is to recommend a specific wine and producer from a specific vintage.

CATALAN MENUS FOR ALL OCCASIONS

▼ ▼ ▼

ollowing are several menus I have gleaned from the notebooks I've kept on all my dinner parties back to 1975. These menus should give you an idea of how my recipes can work together for many styles of entertaining and different seasons.

I must point out that I do tend to entertain lavishly—it seems to run in the family. When I set aside time to cook for a dinner party, I find myself adding dishes to the menu, rather than subtracting; but you can easily simplify things by taking out one or more dishes. And I often serve some *tapas*, or appetizers, in the living room before sitting down at the table.

If at all possible, I try to prepare the desserts or whatever other dishes are appropriate the day before. Some, in fact, often benefit from cooking them ahead, such as stews and terrines.

As for wines, of course those I serve most often are my family's— and we do have one for every occasion! But just as I have not recommended any wines from specific producers to accompany the recipes, here too I have suggested one or more types or styles of wine for each menu, rather than listing specific wines and producers.

A Festive Catalan Picnic

Flatbread with Tomato and Peppers, Topped with Anchovies and Pine Nuts

Orange and Celery Salad with Mint

Chicken Galantine with a Classic Spanish Stuffing

Grilled Leg of Lamb and Mediterranean Vegetables with Romesco Sauce

Peasant Bread

Wine — **A medium-bodied, young red, such as a Merlot, Zinfandel, or a fresh Gamay, slightly chilled to 55° or 60° F**

Crunchy Twice-Baked Almond Cookies

▼ ▼ ▼

An Elegant Catalan Repast

Eggs Stuffed with Anchovies, Garlic, and Cheese
Terrine of Rabbit and Pork with Prunes, Carrots, and Herbs
Apple Garlic Mayonnaise

Wine **A delicate, young, fresh white, such as a Parellada from Catalunya
or a light Chardonnay; or a Catalan brut cava**

Mushroom Flan in Port Cream Sauce

Wine **A flavorful, aromatic white wine, such as an Alvarinho from Galicia, or a
Riesling from Alsace, or a Muscat-Gewürztraminer blend from Catalunya**

Prawns and Chicken in a Sauce with Nuts, Herbs, and Chocolate
Rice with Saffron Threads

Bread Rings Basted with Olive Oil

Wine **An elegant, well-aged Cabernet, Cabernet-Tempranillo blend, or a
mature Zinfandel**

Orange and Celery Salad with Mint

Fresh Blackberry Flan with a Blackberry Cassis Sauce
Almond Meringue Cookies

Wine **A late-harvest Sauvignon Blanc or Riesling**

A Hearty Autumn Supper

Snails in a Piquant Sauce of Tomatoes, Herbs, and Almonds

Thyme and Garlic Soup

Red Cabbage Salad with Anchovies

Catalan-style Lima Bean Stew with Sausages and Fresh Mint

Peasant Bread

Wine **A hearty Mediterranean wine, such as a Garnacha-Cariñena blend from
Catalunya or the southern Rhône**

Aunt Oriola's Pears in Red Wine with a Fresh Cheese Filling and Strawberry
Sauce

A Rustic Winter Meal

Kitchen Garden Soup

Cabbage Dumplings Stuffed with Pork, Chorizo, Pine Nuts, and Raisins

Rabbit Stewed in Red Wine with Tomatoes, Chocolate, and Herbs

Wine **An older, oak-aged red wine, such as a fine Merlot or Cabernet, or a
reserva Tempranillo from Rioja or Ribera del Duero**

Red Wine Sherbet with Orange Lemon and Mint
Dried Fruit Tart with a Topping of Mixed Nuts

Fisherman-style Flamed Coffee and Brandy with Lemon and Orange Peel

An Informal Kitchen Supper

Bacon-wrapped Dates Stuffed with Almonds

Zucchini Cake Cristina

Rosalia's Chicken Stew with Mushrooms, Onions, and Carrots in an Almond
Saffron Sauce

Wine **A fresh red, such as a young Pinot Noir, Beaujolais, or Zinfandel, or a
Cabernet from Chile**

Caramelized Apple Flan Scented with Cinnamon and Brandy

A Warm-Weather Brunch

Charcoal-grilled Mediterranean Vegetables

Tuna Salad with Anchovies, Olives, and Romesco Sauce

Braised Peaches with a Pork and Almond Filling in a Brandy and Muscat Sauce
Glazed Onion Relish
Potato and Onion Cake with Fresh Rosemary Leaves

Wine **A fruity, 2- or 3-year-old Pinot Noir or Merlot from California or
Catalunya, slightly chilled to 55° or 60° F**

Three Kings' Sweet Bread with an Orange Almond Filling
Meringue Sherbet with Cinnamon and Brandy

Tapas Dinner I

Bread with Tomato
Potato and Onion Omelet
Prawns in Garlic Sauce with Sweet Red Peppers
Glazed Leek and Cheese Tart

"Russian" Vegetable Salad with Endive in a Fresh Tarragon Dressing

Bread Rings Basted in Olive Oil

Salt Cod in a Classic Catalan Sauce with Pine Nuts and Raisins
Rabbit in an Herb and Garlic Sauce
Flank Steak Roll with Green Bean Omelet and Sausage Filling
Potato and Onion Cake with Fresh Rosemary Leaves

Wine   **Any wine goes well with tapas.**

Prune Ice Cream with Coffee and Brandy
Variations on Yam and Almond Cookies

Tapas Dinner II

Mushroom Caps Stuffed with Chorizo Sausage
Mediterranean Seafood Terrine
Snails in a Piquant Sauce of Tomatoes, Herbs, and Almonds
Peppers and Zucchini Sautéed with Garlic

Shredded Monkfish and Tomato Salad with a Creamy Sherry Dressing

Wreath Bread with Rosemary, Raisins, and Pine Nuts

Braised Peas with Clams and Fresh Mint
Braised Veal with Small Caramelized Pears in a Pear Brandy Sauce

Braised Potatoes, Onions, and Artichokes with a Pork and Herb Stuffing
Sautéed Spinach with Pine Nuts and Raisins

Wine   **Any wine goes well with tapas.**

Rice Pudding Ice Cream
Almond Meringue Cookies

A Summer Seafood Dinner

Steamed Mussels in a Wine, Tomato, and Almond Sauce
Shredded Salt Cod Salad with Tomatoes, Peppers, and Onions

Barcelona-style Shellfish Stew with Tomatoes, White Wine, and Saffron

Wreath Bread with Rosemary, Raisins, and Pine Nuts

Wine **A dry, crisp white wine, such as a Parellada from Catalunya, a Viura from Rioja, or a fresh Chardonnay from California or Chile**

Frozen Orange Soufflé

A Paella Dinner

Creamy Eggplant Mousse

Ham Terrine with Herbs in a Fresh Tomato and Parsley Sauce

Paella with Chicken and Shellfish, Rosemary and Saffron

Wine **A full-bodied white wine, a dry rosé, or a fresh young red wine**

Honey Ice Cream with Caramelized Nuts and Brandy
Grandma Pepeta's Apple Fritters Scented with Anise

A Classic Catalan Meal

Salt Cod Fritters
Charcoal-grilled Catalan-style leeks with Romesco Sauce for Grilled Seafood, Meats, and Vegetables
Fava or Lima Bean Salad with Cured Ham and Mint

Fish in a Burned Garlic Sauce

Wine **A medium-bodied Chardonnay or a Chardonnay-Parellada blend from Catalunya**

Braised Partridge or Game Hen with Cabbage Croquettes, Empordà Style

Brown Rice with Pine Nuts and Raisins

Wine **A mature red wine, such as a Pinot Noir or Pinot Noir–Tempranillo blend**

Catalan Caramel Custard
Crunchy Twice-Baked Almond Cookies

A Traditional Christmas Feast

Ham and Olive Croquettes

Wine **A top-of-the-line Catalan *brut* cava**

Grandmother's Pot of Meats, Sausages, and Vegetables with the Broth Served as a Pasta Soup

Wine **A medium-bodied red, such as a Tempranillo from Catalunya or Rioja, a fresh Zinfandel, or a Gamay**

Roast Turkey Stuffed with Dried Fruits, Nuts, and Sausage

Wine **A mature fine oak-aged red wine, such as Cabernet, Zinfandel, or Merlot**

Meringue Sherbet with Cinnamon and Brandy
Bread Pudding with Dried Fruits and Orange Liqueur

Wine **A glass of Orange Brandy Liqueur, such as Grand Marnier or Gran Torres**

THE COUNTRY FOOD OF

CATALUNYA

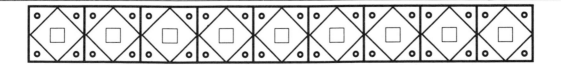

TAPAS AND FINGER FOODS
TAPES I PLATS PER A PICAR

n Spain—and Catalunya—*tapas* are a way of life, a delightful excuse to meet with friends over a glass of wine and an array of colorful dishes. Before lunch and dinner (which are both very late in Spain) neighborhood bars and taverns fill up with regulars of all ages who engage in animated conversations as they nibble on morsels of Manchego cheese or *serrano* ham, potato chips, olives, or almonds. Some bars set out a tantalizing display of little dishes, anything from thick wedges of potato omelet, tiny fried fish, or prawns in sizzling hot olive oil, to stuffed mushroom caps, salt cod fritters, and small casseroles of stew. *Tapas* can turn into a movable feast as you hop from bar to bar, sampling a dish or two here and a few specialties there—or you may adjourn to a sit-down restaurant for a regular meal after visiting just one or two bars.

The origin of the word *tapa*, which literally means "cover," can be traced back to the middle of the last century and the south of Spain. In Andalucía, roadside innkeepers used to cover the glass of wine they served to tired and thirsty horsemen with a slice of ham, cheese, or bread. This *tapa*, or cover, was meant to protect the glass of wine from dust or rain. In fact, the *tapa* was always free—the patron paid only for the wine.

Tapas are served only in bars or restaurants, never at home. In most restaurants, as soon as you sit down the waiter will offer you a *tapita*, or "little *tapa*." Usually, it's a small oval plate with a few slices of sausage, olives, or some almonds; at an elegant restaurant, it may be a crouton with a delightful dab of Salt Cod with Potato and Garlic (p. 64), a miniature version of Bread with Tomato (p. 41) topped with a plump Costa Brava anchovy, or an *Escalivada* (p. 92) of red peppers and eggplant.

But at home in California, I call all my buffet meals *tapas* dinners; I've included two examples in the section on menu planning (p. 25). Calling it a *tapas* dinner adds color and spirit to a convivial evening. The wine should be something simple and fresh that will go with all the dishes; never serve a great wine with *tapas*. A dry white, a fruity rosé, or a young red is best; I have always found that at stand-up parties, no one ever pays much attention to the wine anyway.

Creamy Eggplant Mousse

Mousse d'Albergínia

Makes 1-1/2 to 2 cups.

This eggplant mousse makes a light, creamy, and zesty dip spread on warm toast or crackers. It's easy to whip up, too.

1 pound eggplant, preferably the narrow Japanese variety (see *Note*, below)
6 garlic cloves, unpeeled
2 egg yolks
1-1/2 tablespoons fresh lemon juice, or to taste

1 teaspoon salt
1/4 teaspoon freshly ground black pepper, or to taste
1/4 cup olive oil, preferably extra virgin
2 tablespoons heavy cream, whipped
2 tablespoons snipped fresh chives

Note: The narrow Japanese eggplants found in this country are very similar to the Spanish variety; they are less strong but more flavorful and delicate than the common oval eggplant.

Preheat oven to 350° F. Bake whole unpeeled eggplants and garlic cloves on an ungreased baking sheet for 45 minutes or until very soft. Halve eggplants and scoop out flesh. Peel garlic cloves and scoop out the pulp.

In a blender or food processor, purée eggplant and garlic with egg yolks, lemon juice, salt, and pepper. With the motor running, slowly add oil. Transfer to a medium bowl. Fold in whipped cream and 1-1/2 tablespoons snipped chives. Taste for seasoning. Sprinkle remaining 1/2 tablespoon chives over the dip. Let sit for 2 hours at room temperature before serving. Serve spread on warm toast or crackers.

Bacon-wrapped Dates Stuffed with Almonds

Escolanets

Serves eight.

Another little tapa *from my mother's repertoire, these are easy to prepare and delicious. I never really thought about why they were called* escolanets, *or "altar boys," but one day while making this recipe, it dawned on me. In Spain altar boys wear black robes with a white transparent garment on top—rather like the bacon wrapped around the dark dates.*

24 blanched whole almonds, toasted (see p. 11)

24 medium dates, pitted
8 thin slices bacon, cut in thirds

Preheat oven to 350° F. Stuff an almond inside each date, wrapping date around almond.

Wrap each date with bacon and secure with a toothpick crosswise. Bake in the 350° F oven on a baking sheet for 20 to 30 minutes, or until bacon is crisp. Drain on paper towels and serve while still warm.

Eggs Stuffed with Anchovies, Garlic, and Cheese

Ous Farcits amb Anxova

Serves six.

Stuffed eggs are just as popular in Catalunya as they are in this country; my mother often made this recipe for her lovely buffet dinners. The filling is especially appealing because of the rustic flavors of the anchovies and garlic. These eggs are delightful as a tapa, *or appetizer, but can also be used to garnish a salad or a plate of sliced sausages, raw-cured ham, and tomatoes.*

6 small eggs, or 12 quail eggs

For the filling:
One 2-ounce can flat anchovy fillets, drained, well rinsed, and patted dry
1 medium garlic clove, coarsely chopped
Pinch of hot red pepper flakes
1/4 cup extra virgin olive oil

1 ounce freshly grated Parmesan cheese (about 1/2 cup, loosely packed)
2 tablespoons fresh lemon juice

As a garnish:
6 (or 12 if making with quail eggs) Niçoise olives, or other small black flavorful olives with pits

To cook the eggs: Place eggs in a saucepan, cover with cold water, and bring to a boil. Immediately reduce heat to very low and simmer, covered, for 15 minutes (less for quail eggs). Run cold water over eggs to stop the cooking. Peel eggs, cut them in half lengthwise, and carefully remove yolks. Set aside.

To prepare the filling: In a food processor, purée anchovies with garlic and pepper flakes; add olive oil and Parmesan, and whirl until a thick paste is formed. Add egg yolks and lemon juice, and mix thoroughly. Taste for seasoning.

To assemble the stuffed eggs: Using a pastry bag, pipe filling into the egg white halves. Cut olives in half and remove pits; garnish each egg with half an olive. Refrigerate for at least 1 hour before serving.

Ham and Olive Croquettes

Croquetes de Pernil i Olives

Makes 30 to 40 croquettes.

These croquettes—a specialty of my parents' cook, Rosalia—make a perfect appetizer to pass around at parties. Rosalia used leftover ham, turkey, sausage, or anything she had around to make them; but whenever I had a party at home, I asked her to make this particular version. Because they can be prepared ahead of time and deep fried at the last minute, this recipe has become one of my standbys.

For the croquettes:
1-1/2 tablespoons butter
2-1/2 tablespoons flour
1/2 cup milk
1/2 cup (3 ounces) pimiento-stuffed green Spanish olives, chopped
3 ounces lean prosciutto, sliced thin, and finely chopped by hand
3 hard-boiled eggs (see p. 35), coarsely chopped
1/2 teaspoon freshly ground white pepper, or to taste

To fry the croquettes:
Abundant olive or vegetable oil for frying
About 1/4 cup flour
2 whole eggs, beaten with 2 tablespoons water
About 1/2 cup fine commercial dry bread crumbs

To make the croquettes: In a medium saucepan, melt butter and add flour. Cook over low heat, stirring, for about 1 minute. Slowly add milk and continue to stir with a whisk or wooden spoon for 3 minutes. Off heat, stir in remaining ingredients. Mix well and taste for seasoning; salt should not be necessary (depending on saltiness of ham and olives). Spread mixture on a pie plate, cover, and refrigerate for at least 30 minutes.

To form and fry the croquettes: In a deep fryer or a pan with high sides, heat oil, at least 1 inch deep, to 340° F. Place flour, eggs, and bread crumbs in separate dishes. Using a small spoon and the palms of your hands, form croquettes about 1 inch in diameter. Dip them first in flour, then in egg, then in bread crumbs. Fry croquettes quickly in small batches until golden. Remove with a slotted spoon and drain on paper towels. Serve immediately.

Salt Cod Fritters

Bunyols de Bacallà

Makes 50 to 60 puffs.

These salt cod fritters are often served as tapitas *in restaurants or* tapas *bars. They are light and airy, with the distinctive taste of salt cod. The secret is in the frying: Use abundant oil and make sure it's hot enough.*

Start preparation 2 days in advance, by soaking cod in water.

1 pound boneless dried salt cod
1 pound potatoes
1 bay leaf
2 large garlic cloves, minced (2 teaspoons)
4 tablespoons butter
1/4 teaspoon salt or more to taste, depending on saltiness of cod

1/2 cup all-purpose flour
4 eggs
2 tablespoons chopped fresh parsley leaves
1/2 teaspoon freshly ground black pepper
Pinch of cayenne
Abundant olive oil for frying

Soak salt cod in water to cover for 48 hours, changing water 5 or 6 times.

Drain and press cod with your hands to remove excess water. Discard any bones or skin and shred it finely with your fingers. In a medium saucepan, boil potatoes with bay leaf until tender; peel and mash potatoes (with a fork or potato ricer, not a food processor) in a bowl. Mix in potatoes with salt cod and garlic, mashing finely with a fork.

In a small saucepan, bring 1/2 cup water to a boil with butter and salt. When butter melts, add flour all at once and cook, beating, until mixture forms a ball and pulls away from the sides of the pan. Immediately transfer to a food processor and whirl. With motor running, add eggs, parsley, pepper, and cayenne; whirl until paste is smooth. Stir into the salt cod/potato mixture. Taste for seasoning and correct for salt if necessary.

In a deep fryer or a deep pan, heat oil, at least 1 inch deep, to 340° F. Cook a few puffs at a time, dropping them in by the teaspoonful, until golden. Drain on paper towels and serve immediately.

Mushroom Caps Stuffed with Chorizo Sausage

Xampinyons Farcits amb Xoriço

Serves six.

Whenever a friend presented my mother with a particularly good chorizo sausage, she would have Rosalia make these stuffed mushrooms. I often serve them as a tapa, but they also make a good first course. And be sure to provide plenty of crusty bread to soak up the delicious sauce.

18 large mushrooms (1 to 1-1/2 pounds)
1 tablespoon olive oil
1 medium onion, chopped
1/2 cup fresh bread crumbs (see p. 10)
2 tablespoons chopped fresh parsley
1 teaspoon chopped fresh oregano or marjoram, or 1/3 teaspoon dried

6 ounces firm, lean *chorizo* or *linguiça* sausage (or other spicy pork sausage with paprika), casing removed, crumbled (1 cup)
2 tablespoons dark raisins
About 1/4 teaspoon salt, or to taste
About 1/2 teaspoon freshly ground black pepper, or to taste
1 cup Chicken Stock (p. 18)

Wipe mushrooms clean; remove stems and chop them. Heat oil in a small skillet and sauté onion over low heat until soft; add mushroom stems and cook until dry, about 5 minutes. Transfer to a medium bowl and mix well with bread crumbs, herbs, *chorizo*, and raisins. Taste for seasoning; amount of salt and pepper needed will depend on sausage used.

Preheat broiler. Stuff mushroom caps with this mixture. Arrange them on a baking sheet, stuffing side up, and cook under the broiler for 4 to 5 minutes, or until tops turn golden. Transfer mushrooms to a large skillet and pour stock around them. Bring stock to a boil, and immediately reduce heat to very low, cover, and cook 20 minutes. With a slotted spoon, transfer mushrooms to a serving plate. Bring stock in skillet to a boil and reduce by about half. Pour over mushrooms and serve warm.

Steamed Mussels in a Wine, Tomato, and Almond Sauce

Musclos amb Salsa d'Ametlles

Serves six.

Tapas bars usually serve an array of mussel dishes: in white wine, in a fisherman-style tomato sauce, with mayonnaise, etc. This is my favorite version, an appetizer my mother served at her buffet dinners. It also makes a suitable first course or a luncheon entrée, accompanied with fresh Peasant Bread (p. 118). The thick ground-almond sauce is spiked with a little tomato to tint it a lovely pink.

1 cup dry white wine
2 pounds live mussels (about 40), scrubbed
2 tablespoons olive oil
6 large garlic cloves, minced (2 tablespoons)
1 pound ripe tomatoes (2 large), peeled, seeded, and chopped
1/2 teaspoon salt, or to taste
1/8 teaspoon cayenne, or to taste
1/4 pound (3/4 cup) whole almonds, toasted (p. 11) and finely ground
2 hard-boiled eggs (see p. 35), halved and yolks removed

In a large pot, bring wine to boil; place mussels on a rack, cover, and steam over medium-high heat for 4 to 5 minutes. Set them aside. (Discard all mussels that have not opened.) Strain liquid and reserve.

In a medium skillet, heat oil and sauté garlic over low heat until soft. Add tomatoes and reserved liquid from steaming mussels; increase heat to medium and cook for 15 minutes (it should not be too dry). Off heat, add salt, cayenne, and ground almonds. Mash egg yolks finely and reserve whites; add yolks to tomato sauce. Mix well and taste for seasoning. (If sauce is too thick, add some water to dilute it.)

Open each mussel and discard the half shell to which it is not attached. Arrange mussels on a serving platter, and coat each mussel with sauce. Finely chop egg whites by hand and sprinkle on top as a garnish. Serve at room temperature.

Prawns in Garlic Sauce with Sweet Red Peppers

Gambes a l'All amb Pebrots

Serves six to eight.

Tapas bars often serve garlic prawns in individual clay casseroles, sizzling hot. I find that red bell peppers add a lot to this dish, and have included them in my recipe. Be sure to serve this dish with plenty of crusty bread to dip in the flavorful garlicky sauce.

3 tablespoons olive oil
18 large garlic cloves, coarsely chopped (6 tablespoons)
1/2 teaspoon hot red pepper flakes
3 large red bell peppers (about 1-1/2 pounds total), seeded and cut into thin strips lengthwise
2 pounds medium prawns, peeled but with tails attached
1 teaspoon salt
1/4 cup fresh lemon juice
1/4 cup dry white wine
2 tablespoons finely chopped fresh parsley leaves

Heat oil in a large skillet. Add garlic, pepper flakes, and red peppers; cook over low heat until peppers are soft, 10 to 15 minutes, stirring occasionally. Season with salt. Increase heat to high and toss prawns in; stir and turn them over for 1 minute. Pour lemon juice and wine over and sauté quickly 1 or 2 more minutes, just until prawns are cooked through. Serve immediately, sprinkled with parsley.

Terrine of Rabbit and Pork with Prunes, Carrots, and Herbs

Terrina de Conill amb Prunes

Makes one 7-cup terrine.

This chunky country-style terrine, inspired by the restaurant Ampurdán in Figueras—a landmark of fine Catalan cooking—has the surprise contrast of rabbit, fresh herbs, and sweet prunes, with carrots adding a note of color. I always serve it with toasted baguette slices and Apple Garlic Mayonnaise (p. 117). If you can't find rabbit, try making the terrine with chicken or duck.

Start preparation 1 day or at least 10 hours ahead.

1/3 pound carrots, peeled and cut into 1/4-inch dice
1/2 pound boneless rabbit meat
1/2 pound lean pork, such as boneless pork loin
1/2 pound pork fat, including fat trimmed from the pork loin or other cut used
1/2 pound boneless boiled ham, cut into 1/2-inch dice
1 large onion, finely chopped
3 large garlic cloves, finely chopped
3/4 cup (6 ounces) coarsely chopped pitted prunes
1/2 cup full-bodied Spanish brandy
2 teaspoons finely chopped fresh rosemary leaves
2 teaspoons finely chopped fresh thyme, marjoram, or oregano leaves
1 teaspoon salt
1 teaspoon freshly ground black pepper
1/2 cup *fino* sherry, or another dry Spanish sherry

Blanch carrots for 2 minutes in abundant boiling salted water; drain and set aside.

Cut rabbit meat, pork, and pork fat in pieces, and coarsely grind them together in a meat grinder or food processor. (If using a food processor, do it in small batches and pulse only enough to chop the meat; don't grind it to a paste.)

In a non-reactive bowl, mix ground meats with ham, onion, garlic, prunes, carrots, and brandy. Let mixture marinate at room temperature for 2 hours or longer.

Preheat oven to 325° F. Add rosemary, thyme, salt, and pepper to meat mixture; mix well. Oil a lidded 7- or 8-cup terrine mold and pack mixture into it. Pour sherry over. Cover terrine with aluminum foil and put lid on top. Set mold inside a larger pan filled with boiling water halfway up the mold. Bake in 325° F oven for 2 hours. Let cool, covered, at room temperature, then refrigerate overnight or for at least 4 hours. Serve at room temperature.

Potato and Onion Omelet

Truita de Patata

Serves six.

This classic omelet, known as tortilla española *in Castilian, translates as "Spanish omelet"—although it's very different from the so-called "Spanish" omelet we see on breakfast menus in this country. That version inevitably includes peppers and tomatoes, while the true Spanish version is made with potatoes and onions. The word* tortilla *may be misleading, too: Mexican tortillas are practically unknown in Spain, where* tortilla *(or* truita *in Catalan) always means "omelet." And unless you order a* tortilla francesa *(French omelet) you are bound to get a high, round omelet that most resembles an Italian* frittata, *as in this recipe. Practically every bar in Spain serves* tortilla española *as a* tapa, *cut into small squares or wedges. (You can even order an omelet sandwich.) At home we often had it for supper accompanied by Bread with Tomato (p. 41)—a great combination for an impromptu meal. It also makes a perfect lunch or picnic dish, served at room temperature. Although it can be made ahead, I prefer to eat it warm, shortly after making it.*

2 pounds potatoes, peeled
3/4 teaspoon salt
1/2 teaspoon freshly ground black pepper
1/2 cup olive oil
2 large onions, thinly sliced
6 eggs

Slice potatoes by hand into thin flakes about the size of a nickel, or precut potatoes in strips and slice them very fine in a food processor. Season them with 1/2 teaspoon salt and 1/4 teaspoon pepper. Heat 1/4 cup oil in a medium nonstick skillet, add potatoes, and cook over medium heat until golden brown and crispy. Toss potatoes around with a spatula to avoid clumping, but if they stick a bit, don't worry. Meanwhile, heat 2 tablespoons oil in another medium skillet and sauté onions until soft and golden, about 20 to 30 minutes.

In a large bowl, beat eggs; stir in remaining 1/4 teaspoon *each* salt and pepper, and onions. Drain potatoes with a slotted spoon, wipe skillet clean, and heat remaining 2 tablespoons oil. Stir potatoes into egg mixture and pour into skillet. Reduce heat to low and cook until lightly golden on the bottom, about 8 to 10 minutes.

Place on top of the skillet an inverted plate slightly larger than the skillet and turn out omelet onto it; slide omelet back into skillet. Cook until eggs are set, 3 or 4 more minutes. Serve warm, preferably.

Bread with Tomato

Pa amb Tomàquet

Serves four.

Lluis Cruanyas, owner of one of Barcelona's best restaurants, Eldorado Petit, says that "in Catalunya the first thing you taste after the baby bottle is pa amb tomàquet." And Catalans carry a love for this simple country dish from childhood on. It is eaten as a tapa, as an after-school snack, as part of a lunch, a light supper, or a sandwich—we even love it in the morning as part of a hearty breakfast before skiing. What could be better than good bread, lightly toasted, rubbed with a ripe, flavorful tomato, and doused with fruity olive oil? Often it is topped with plump salt-cured anchovies, local sausages, or cured ham.

To make it right, the bread has to be cut thin, soaked in tomato, drizzled with lots of fruity Catalan olive oil, and sprinkled with salt. The authentic version of pa amb tomàquet is most often found in casual or country restaurants, but even elegant restaurants may serve it on tiny croutons, as Lluis Cruanyas does at his Eldorado Petit restaurants in Barcelona, Sant Felíu, and New York.

8 large 1/3-inch-thick slices Peasant Bread (p. 118), sourdough, or French-style white bread
2 large garlic cloves, peeled and cut in half lengthwise (optional)
2 very ripe large tomatoes, halved crosswise
2 tablespoons olive oil
Salt and freshly ground black pepper to taste

Toast bread on both sides. For garlic lovers, vigorously rub garlic, cut side down, on the warm, toasted bread. Cupping a tomato half in your palm, rub 2 pieces of bread with it; squeeze tomato so that not only the juice and seeds ooze into the bread but also some pulp. Only the skin should be left.

Drizzle the olive oil over and sprinkle with salt and pepper to taste. This bread is best served warm, right after making it.

Flatbread with Tomato and Peppers, Topped with Anchovies and Pine Nuts

Coca d'Anxoves i Pinyons

Serves eight.

The name coca *is given to a number of different breads or pastries in Catalunya. There are two basic kinds: savory and sweet. The savory versions have a bread-dough base and are particularly traditional in the northeastern regions of Catalunya, such as L'Empordà and Maresme. They are usually shaped like elongated ovals, and often toasted, rubbed with half a fresh tomato—or with garlic—and sprinkled with olive oil and salt in the style of Bread with Tomato (p. 41).*

Savory cocas *are sometimes topped with herring or anchovies, roasted peppers, pitted olives, cooked eggs, or cold cuts. The following version makes a great appetizer cut in small squares. It is best served warm (reheated at the last minute). For greater effect, serve it on a large wooden board and cut it at the table.*

For the dough:
1/2 cup yellow or white cornmeal
1 teaspoon salt
1 tablespoon olive oil
2 packages (4 teaspoons or 1/2 ounce) active dry yeast
2 teaspoons sugar
1-1/2 cups unbleached all-purpose flour

For the topping:
3 tablespoons olive oil
10 garlic cloves, coarsely chopped
2 large onions, thinly sliced
1 small red bell pepper, seeded and cut in strips
4 pounds tomatoes, peeled, seeded, and chopped
1/2 teaspoon salt
1/2 teaspoon freshly ground black pepper
1/4 cup (1.5 ounces) pine nuts, lightly toasted (see p. 11)
Two 2-ounce cans flat anchovy fillets, drained, rinsed, and patted dry

To prepare the dough: Bring 1/2 cup water to a boil and pour over cornmeal. Stir in salt and oil. Let cool.

In a food processor bowl, dissolve yeast and sugar in 1/4 cup warm water (105 to 115° F). Don't stir; just let it sit for 5 to 10 minutes to activate the yeast (when yeast starts popping to the top, that means it is ready to work). As soon as yeast is ready and cornmeal has cooled to at least 115° F, add cornmeal and flour to yeast. Whirl to combine well, until dough pulls away from the sides of the bowl or forms a ball. Oil a large bowl and put dough in it, turning to coat all sides with oil. Cover and put in a warm place until doubled in size, about 1 hour.

To prepare the topping: Meanwhile, heat oil in a large skillet and cook garlic and onions over low heat for 25 to 30 minutes, stirring occasionally, until very soft and golden. Add red pepper, tomatoes, salt, and pepper; cook briskly until dry. Taste for seasoning; it should be slightly undersalted because anchovies will add saltiness.

Preheat oven to 400° F. Punch down dough to release air. Oil a 10-by-15-inch jelly-roll pan or baking sheet. Press dough into pan, pushing edges up to make a border. Spread topping evenly over dough. Arrange anchovies on top of the *coca*, and sprinkle pine nuts over.

Bake in the 400° F oven for 30 minutes, or until edges of the dough are golden brown. Remove to a rack and let cool briefly before serving. (It is best served warm.)

n Spain a first course, especially at home, can be quite substantial. Usually it's a starch to fill you up, and is followed by some kind of protein served as the main course.

But in recent years, the trend has been toward serving lighter dishes such as Mushroom Flan in Port Cream Sauce (p. 44), or some kind of seafood such as Mediterranean Seafood Terrine (p. 15), as a first course. Even so, when I entertain here, I tend to serve smaller portions than I would in Spain. Some of these first courses also make ideal light luncheon entrées.

Zucchini Cake Cristina

Pastís de Carbaçó Cristina

Serves six to eight.

My daughter Cristina's nanny, Patricia, developed this recipe and named it after my daughter because it has all the good things a mother would want: vegetables, eggs, and lean cheese. We all love it, too!

Using a food processor, it only takes 1 hour to prepare from start to finish. But when Patricia made it at my parents' home on a visit to Spain, it took her 3 hours to do everything by hand. The next day I went out and bought my mother a food processor!

3/4 teaspoon salt, or to taste
3 pounds (about 10 medium) zucchini, grated
3 tablespoons butter
1 large onion, minced
1 cup (8 ounces) ricotta cheese
3 cups (12 ounces) grated Monterey Jack cheese
3 eggs, beaten
1/4 teaspoon freshly ground black pepper, or to taste

Sprinkle 1/2 teaspoon salt over grated zucchini and let sit for 15 to 20 minutes, to release liquid. Squeeze inside a cloth and discard liquid.

Preheat oven to 375° F. Heat 1 tablespoon butter in a medium skillet and sauté onion slowly for 10 minutes. Transfer to a bowl. Add remaining 2 tablespoons butter to skillet and sauté zucchini for 10 minutes. Transfer to bowl and let cool. Add ricotta cheese, 2-1/2 cups grated cheese, eggs, remaining 1/4 teaspoon salt, and pepper. Mix well and taste for seasoning.

Oil or butter a 9-by-5-inch rectangular mold and pour in the mixture. Sprinkle remaining 1/2 cup grated cheese on top. Bake in the 375° F oven for 1 hour, or until cheese on top is golden brown. Let cool.

Unmold and serve at room temperature or reheated (if served straight from the oven, it's more difficult to slice).

Mushroom Flan in Port Cream Sauce

Flam de Bolets

Serves six to eight.

I have fond memories of mild fall afternoons spent picking baskets full of fragrant rovellons, *the unique mushrooms that grow wild in Catalunya. I can still smell their earthiness mingled with the clean, fresh air after the rain. We would then simply grill them and serve them sprinkled with minced fresh garlic and parsley. But they can also be turned into a more elaborate dish such as this flan.*

During the season in Barcelona, stands at the lively La Boqueria market display a dazzling array of rovellons *and other wild mushrooms neatly arranged with their tops up on the counter or in handwoven baskets. Few local markets in this country carry such specialized produce; but when you do see fresh* chanterelles *or any wild mushrooms you like, you might try this flan with them.*

For the flan:
4 tablespoons butter
1/2 cup minced shallots
2 pounds mushrooms, trimmed and finely chopped
1/4 cup finely chopped fresh parsley leaves
1/2 cup packed (2 ounces) grated Gruyère cheese
5 eggs, beaten
3/4 teaspoon salt
1/2 teaspoon freshly ground black pepper

For the sauce:
2 cups Veal Stock (p. 18)
1/3 cup port wine
1/3 cup heavy cream

To prepare the flan: In a large skillet, heat butter and sauté shallots over low heat for 5 minutes. Add mushrooms and cook over low heat until moisture evaporates, about 20 minutes. Reserve 1/2 cup of the mixture.

Preheat oven to 350° F. Butter a 4- or 5-cup round, rectangular, or ring mold. In a medium bowl, combine mushroom mixture with parsley, cheese, eggs, salt, and pepper. Pour into mold, cover with aluminum foil, and place in 350° F oven inside a larger pan filled with boiling water at least 1/2 inch up the sides of the mold. Bake for 45 minutes to 1 hour, until a needle stuck into the flan comes out clean.

To prepare the sauce: In a medium saucepan, cook reserved 1/2 cup mushroom mixture with veal stock over medium-high heat for 10 minutes, or until reduced to about 1 cup. Add port and cook for 2 minutes. Strain through a fine sieve into a small saucepan; add cream and cook over medium-low heat until reduced to about 1 cup.

When cool enough to handle, unmold flan onto a serving plate and pour sauce over. Serve warm.

Mediterranean Seafood Terrine

Pastís de Peix Mediterrani

Serves eight.

When I married and moved to California, this was one of the first family recipes I used, with great success. It comes from my sister-in-law Mahle, who often serves it at buffet dinners or as a first course. A chunky country-style terrine, it is quite easy to make, and it also works well as an appetizer spread on toast.

4 tablespoons olive oil
1-1/2 pounds flavorful fresh fish, such as rock cod, red snapper, monkfish, halibut, or sea bass
1-1/2 teaspoons salt
1 teaspoon freshly ground black pepper
1/4 cup full-bodied Spanish brandy
1 large onion, minced
3 garlic cloves, minced
2 pounds tomatoes, peeled but unseeded, chopped
1 tablespoon chopped mixed fresh herb leaves, such as thyme, oregano, marjoram, and rosemary
1/4 cup dry white wine
1/2 pound raw prawns, peeled and coarsely chopped
1/4 pound fresh cooked crab meat, shredded
6 eggs, beaten
About 2 tablespoons commercial dry bread crumbs

As a garnish:
1/4 cup large capers, drained
8 prawns, cooked and peeled, tail left intact

Heat 2 tablespoons oil in a large skillet and, over medium heat, sauté fish for 3 minutes. Sprinkle with some salt and pepper. Add brandy and, when hot, flambé (see p. 12). When the flames subside, remove fish and let cool.

Add remaining 2 tablespoons oil to the same skillet and, over low heat, sauté onion and garlic for 10 minutes. Add tomatoes, herbs, wine, and remaining salt and pepper; increase heat to medium-high and cook until thick. Purée half of the sauce in a food processor and reserve. Transfer remaining sauce to a large bowl.

Preheat oven to 350° F. Peel, bone, and crumble fish. Add to sauce in the bowl, together with raw prawns and crab meat. Taste for seasoning. Stir in beaten eggs and mix well.

Oil a 6- or 7-cup loaf pan (an 8-by-5-inch bread pan works well) or a round mold. Toss in bread crumbs and shake pan to coat bottom and sides; discard excess. Cover the bottom with buttered parchment or waxed paper cut to size. Pour in fish mixture. Place mold inside a larger pan filled with boiling water at least 1/2 inch up the sides of the mold. Bake in the 350° F oven for 30 minutes. Remove from the larger pan and bake for another 60 minutes, or until a cake tester comes out clean.

Unmold as soon as it's cool enough to handle. Serve either hot or at room temperature, covered with tomato sauce. Garnish upper edges of the terrine with capers and arrange prawns around the base.

Ham Terrine with Herbs in a Fresh Tomato and Parsley Sauce

Pastís de Pernil

Serves eight.

When my mother served this dish at her elaborate buffet parties, she always included a few precious fresh truffles. But those are much more affordable in Spain than in this country, so I've found that substituting fresh herbs such as sage or oregano gives the terrine a lift of flavor and doesn't bankrupt me in the process.

This dish has the consistency of a meaty country-style terrine, and it is best to make it ahead of time: The flavors will improve and it will be easier to slice. Only the fresh tomato sauce should be made shortly before serving.

For the terrine:
2 tablespoons butter
2 tablespoons flour
1 cup milk
4 eggs, beaten
1 pound baked ham, trimmed of fat and chopped
2 teaspoons finely chopped fresh herb leaves, such as sage, marjoram, and thyme
3 tablespoons *amontillado* or another flavorful Spanish sherry
1/2 teaspoon freshly ground white pepper, or to taste
1/4 teaspoon salt, or to taste

For the tomato sauce:
1/3 cup fresh parsley leaves
1-1/2 pounds ripe tomatoes, peeled and seeded
1-1/2 tablespoons tomato paste
1-1/2 tablespoons sherry vinegar or red wine vinegar, or to taste
3 tablespoons extra virgin olive oil
1/2 teaspoon salt, or to taste
1 teaspoon freshly ground black pepper, or to taste

As a garnish:
1 small bundle fresh chives (about 24)
16 cherry tomatoes, stemmed

To prepare the terrine: Preheat oven to 350° F. In a small saucepan, melt butter; add flour and cook over medium heat for about 1 minute. Add milk and continue cooking, whisking constantly, until sauce thickens or comes to a boil. Cook for 1 minute and remove from heat. Set aside.

In a large bowl, mix eggs with ham, herbs, sherry, and pepper. Add white sauce and blend well. Taste for seasoning; salt may not be necessary.

Butter a 5-cup rectangular mold and a piece of parchment or waxed paper cut to fit the bottom. Pour mixture into mold, cover, and place it inside a larger pan filled with boiling water at least 1/2 inch up the sides of the mold. Bake in the 350° F oven for 30 minutes; remove from water, uncover, and bake for another 25 to 30 minutes, or until a cake tester comes out clean. Let cool.

To prepare the tomato sauce: Finely mince parsley in a blender or food processor. Add remaining ingredients and purée. Taste for seasoning; the sauce should have a sharp flavor.

To assemble the dish: Unmold terrine onto a board and cut it into 8 slices. Spoon some tomato sauce on each of 8 dishes, and place a slice of terrine on top. Arrange 3 chives on one side of each slice of terrine and 2 tomatoes on the other. Serve at room temperature.

Glazed Leek and Cheese Tart

Pastís de Porros

Serves eight to ten.

Lola Pijóan was a great chef and a great lady. She died in 1990, leaving behind a legacy of old Catalan recipes that I have enjoyed at Can Borrell, the enchanting restaurant and inn she ran with her husband, Jaume Guillén, in the village of Meranges, high in the Pyrenees mountains. Reached by narrow winding roads running through bucolic valleys and mountain landscapes, this area—called La Cerdanya—is one of the most beautiful in Catalunya.
I chose this recipe from her extensive repertoire because not only is it one of my favorites, it was one of hers, too. And it can be served either as a first course, as a tapa *cut into small wedges, or as a light luncheon entrée with a salad.*

For the pastry:
1-1/2 cups unbleached all-purpose flour
1/2 cup (1 stick) frozen unsalted butter, cut into 1/2-inch pieces
1 egg yolk
1/2 teaspoon salt
5 tablespoons ice water

For the filling:
4 tablespoons butter
3 bunches leeks, thinly sliced, with one third of the green part (about 3 pounds after cleaning)
3/4 teaspoon salt, or to taste
1/2 teaspoon freshly ground black pepper, or to taste
1/8 teaspoon cayenne, or to taste
1/2 teaspoon freshly grated nutmeg, or to taste
4 eggs (plus 1 egg white, optional)
1 cup half and half
1 cup grated Gruyère or Emmenthaler cheese (1/4 pound)

To make the pastry dough: In a food processor, pulse flour and butter together until mixture has the consistency of cornmeal. In a small bowl, mix together egg yolk, salt, and ice water; add to flour and butter mixture. Whirl until a ball of dough forms. (If a ball doesn't quite form, remove dough and knead with your hands on a lightly floured surface for about 30 seconds.)

Wrap the ball of dough in plastic and refrigerate for at least 30 minutes before using.

To prepare the filling: In a large pot, melt butter and, over very low heat, sauté leeks until they are dry and almost caramelized; this will take 45 minutes to 1 hour. Season with salt, pepper, cayenne, and nutmeg. Let cool. In a large bowl, lightly beat eggs. Add cream and leeks; mix well and taste for seasoning.

To prepare the tart: Preheat oven to 425° F. On a lightly floured board, roll out pastry thinly to fit a 9- or 10-inch tart pan about 1-1/2 inches deep. Trim away any excess dough. Line pastry shell with aluminum foil and weight it with pie weights or beans. Bake in the 425° F oven for 15 minutes. Pick up foil by its edges and carefully lift it out of the pastry shell. Bake shell another 5 to 10 minutes, or until lightly golden. Remove from oven. Reduce oven temperature to 375° F.

To assemble the dish: Pour leek mixture into pastry shell. Sprinkle cheese on top. Bake in the 375° F oven for 45 minutes, or until cheese turns golden. Serve warm, cut into wedges.

Cabbage Dumplings Stuffed with Pork, Chorizo, Pine Nuts, and Raisins

Farcellets de Col

Serves six to eight; yields 16 to 18 dumplings. For a first course, use only half the recipe.

Cabbage is eaten a lot in Catalunya, and farcellets *("little bundles") are a classic Catalan recipe. They can be either stuffed, as they are here with a savory filling of pork and* chorizo *studded with pine nuts and raisins, or unstuffed, as in the Braised Partridge or Game Hen with Cabbage Croquettes, Empordà Style (p. 79). This dish makes a delicious first course as well as an entrée, and is a very special addition to a buffet or* tapas *dinner.*

The cabbage actually has to be overcooked for the flavors of the stuffing and the sauce to marry with the cabbage. That's why the curly Savoy cabbage is ideal; it holds up better than the firmer regular green cabbage.

1 large whole head green cabbage (about 2 pounds), cored

For the filling:
1 cup homemade bread crumbs (see p. 10)
1/2 cup milk
1 tablespoon olive oil
1/4 pound pancetta, sliced medium thick and cut into strips
3/4 pound medium-ground pork
One 3- or 4-ounce firm, lean *chorizo* or *linguiça* sausage (or other spicy pork sausage with paprika), casing removed, crumbled
1 small onion, finely chopped
1/4 cup (1.5 ounces) pine nuts
1/4 cup dark raisins
1 egg, beaten
1/4 teaspoon freshly ground black pepper, or to taste
Salt to taste, if necessary

For the sauce:
1 tablespoon olive oil
1 onion, chopped
2 pounds tomatoes, unpeeled, chopped
1 cup dry white wine
1/2 teaspoon salt, or to taste
1/2 teaspoon freshly ground black pepper, or to taste

As a garnish:
1 tablespoon finely chopped fresh parsley leaves
1/4 cup (1.5 ounces) pine nuts, toasted (see p. 11)

Bring a large pot of salted water to a boil and cook cabbage for 20 minutes, covered; it should be very tender, not crisp. Turn cabbage upside down to drain. Separate leaves and spread them on a cloth.

To prepare the filling: In a large bowl, soak bread in milk. Heat oil in a large skillet and sauté pancetta for 5 minutes over low heat. Add pork, *chorizo,* and onion; cook for 15 minutes. With a slotted spoon, add to bowl with bread; discard fat in the pan. Stir in pine nuts, raisins, egg, and pepper. Taste for seasoning.

Cup a cabbage leaf in your hand and scoop about 1/4 cup filling into it. Fold cabbage around filling, squeezing and shaping it into a ball. Divide filling among cabbage leaves (patch smaller leaves together). Place completed dumplings, seam side down, in one layer in a large clay casserole or baking dish.

To prepare the sauce: Preheat oven to 350° F. Heat oil in a large skillet and sauté onion over low heat for 5 minutes. Add tomatoes; cook over medium heat for 10 minutes. Add 1/2 cup wine, increase heat, and cook until dry. Add salt and pepper, and taste for seasoning. Purée in a blender or food processor.

Pour sauce and remaining 1/2 cup wine over dumplings; sprinkle with parsley and pine nuts. Bake in 350° F oven for 40 minutes. Serve warm.

Angel-Hair Pasta Sautéed and Cooked in Fish Stock with Lobster

Arrossejat de Fideus amb Llagosta

Serves six.

Best described as a pasta cooked in the manner of a rice dish, arrossejat employs the unusual technique of sautéing noodles (fideus) until golden brown before simmering them in a flavorful fish stock. Cooking noodles this way is an old tradition with fishermen along the Valencian and Catalan coast.

The trick here is to sauté the dry noodles in olive oil before cooking them in the stock, until they acquire a rossejat *(Catalan for "golden") color. It is important to use a rich, homemade fish stock, or fumet; commercial broth or clam juice won't be nearly as good.*

This was the sound advice that Blas Moreno, chef at the restaurant Eugenia in Cambrils, near Tarragona, gave me as I watched him in the kitchen while he sautéed the noodles, stirring all the time until they turned golden brown. Then he beamed—"See, now it is rossejat"—and went on adding ladles of his fragrant fish stock, until it was totally absorbed by the noodles. In Catalunya this dish is traditionally served with Garlic Mayonnaise (p. 116) on the side, although I find it really does not need it.

8 cups Fish Stock (p. 19)
Two 1-1/2- to 2- pound live lobsters
3 tablespoons olive oil
4 large garlic cloves, chopped
1-1/2 pounds unpeeled tomatoes, puréed
1/2 teaspoon (.2 gram) saffron threads
1/2 teaspoon salt, or to taste

1/2 pound dried angel hair pasta, or coiled *fedelini* or *capellini* (very thin dried pasta noodles rolled into coils)

As a garnish:
1 lemon, cut into 6 wedges
1/2 recipe Garlic Mayonnaise (p. 116) (make whole recipe and use half)

In a narrow flameproof casserole or a stock pot, bring fish stock to a boil with 4 cups water. Drop in 1 lobster; it will turn pink. As soon as it stops moving, after a minute or two, remove lobster from pot and set it aside. Bring water back to a rapid boil before dropping in the next lobster. Reserve cooking water.

Separate lobster bodies from tails: grasp body in one hand and tail in the other, twist tail, and pull; it will come free easily. Reserve any juices that ooze out. Pull out claws.

Bring lobster water to a boil again and add lobster bodies; simmer for 30 minutes, covered. Meanwhile, cut each tail, with its shell, crosswise into 3 pieces. Break claws (or remove meat from claws and discard shells, if preferred). Set aside.

Meanwhile, in a wide 2-quart saucepan, heat 1 tablespoon olive oil and add garlic. Cook until soft and add tomatoes; cook over medium-high heat for 3 minutes. Strain lobster water and juices into saucepan, bring to a boil, and reduce sauce to exactly 4 cups. Add saffron threads and salt; cover and set aside.

Heat remaining 2 tablespoons oil in a wide flameproof clay casserole or skillet. Add pasta, breaking it up with your hands in about 3-inch pieces as you add it. Over medium heat, stir pasta with a wooden spatula for 10 to 15 minutes, until it is golden brown (the more color the pasta acquires, the more flavor it will give to this dish; but be careful not to burn it).

Bring tomato sauce mixture to a boil and pour into casserole with noodles. Stir in lobster claws (or meat), together with tail sections. Cook over medium heat, stirring all the time, until the liquid is absorbed by the pasta. Cooking time will vary according to the size and material of casserole—it will probably be 10 to 15 minutes. Taste for seasoning.

If you have used a clay casserole, surround *arrossejat* with lemon wedges, arrange lobster bodies on top, and serve directly from the casserole, passing the Garlic Mayonnaise (*allioli*) in a sauce boat. Have guests squeeze a little lemon juice over their servings.

Wine Recommendation: Serve with an elegant oak-aged Chardonnay, a Catalan Chardonnay-Parellada blend, or an Alvarinho from Galicia.

Snails in a Piquant Sauce of Tomatoes, Herbs, and Almonds

Cargols Picants

Serves six to eight.

Equally at home as a tapa, *first course, or as part of a buffet dinner, this is a rustic, very Catalan snail dish, with its classic* sofrito *and* picada. *I treasure this particular version from El Celler del Penedès, a hospitable restaurant in the Penedès region that specializes in earthy Catalan country dishes. To welcome thirsty clients, chef/owner Pere Valls always keeps a giant* porró *full of wine outside. This is a glass drinking vessel with two spouts: a larger one for filling the* porró *with wine, a smaller one for pouring the wine straight into your mouth, raising the* porró *overhead with your hand. If you are able to lift it with one hand only, at El Celler you can drink as much as you like for free!*

For the *sofregit*:
1 tablespoon olive oil
1/4 pound pancetta, cut up small
3 large garlic cloves, minced
1 medium onion, chopped
1 pound tomatoes, peeled, seeded, and chopped
1/2 teaspoon hot red pepper flakes
1 cup Veal Stock (p. 18)
1 cup full-bodied dry red wine

For the *picada*:
1 tablespoon olive oil
1 medium slice bread (about 1/2 ounce)
2 tablespoons (about 12) whole almonds, ground
1/2 red bell pepper, or 1/2 cup packed canned pimiento, chopped
1 tablespoon chopped fresh parsley leaves
1 teaspoon chopped fresh thyme, oregano, or marjoram leaves (or 1/3 teaspoon dried)

40 to 50 large snails, frozen or canned (8 or 9 ounces, drained weight)

As a garnish (optional):
Fresh thyme, oregano, or marjoram sprigs

To prepare the *sofregit*: In a large skillet or, preferably, a shallow flameproof clay casserole, heat oil and add pancetta; cook over low heat for 5 minutes. Add garlic and onion; cook until soft, about 10 minutes. Add tomatoes and pepper flakes; cook until dry. Add stock and wine, increase heat to medium, and cook until liquid is reduced by half.

To prepare the *picada*: Heat oil in a small skillet, add bread slice, and fry over medium heat until golden on both sides. In a food processor, finely grind bread with almonds, red pepper (or pimiento), and herbs.

To assemble the dish: Drain snails under running water. Add them and *picada* to *sofregit* in the skillet and cook, stirring, for 5 minutes. Taste for seasoning. Serve warm, garnished with fresh herb sprigs and plenty of crusty bread to dip in the flavorful sauce.

Wine Recommendation: A crisp, young dry white wine—or the same red wine used for the *sofregit*, such as a Mediterranean wine made of the classic Catalan varieties Garnacha and Cariñena.

SOUPS
SOPES

I n Catalunya—and Spain—soup is invariably a first course, never a meal on its own, as it sometimes is here. And it is more often part of the evening meal, which in Spain is generally lighter than the midday meal. At home, we would have some kind of soup almost every evening. In winter, it was a bowl of heart-warming Thyme and Garlic Soup (p. 52) or a vegetable soup with everything good from the garden, such as Kitchen Garden Soup (see below); in summer, seasonal soups were often served chilled.

The best wine to serve with soup is always a white, and maybe a *fino* sherry. But if you want to serve only one wine and a red is more suitable with the main course, don't worry about having two wines—the red alone will do.

Kitchen Garden Soup

Puré de l'Hort

Serves eight.

This is a homey, down-to-earth, definitely good-for-you soup that Rosalia used to make all the time, in winter as well as in summer, often using some produce from our own kitchen garden. Not only is it delicious; it can be made ahead, it freezes well, and ingredients may be changed to suit availability and taste. Like Rosalia, I like to garnish it with homemade croutons (diced bread sautéed in a little olive oil until golden crisp).

2 tablespoons olive oil
1/4 pound pancetta, diced small
2 large garlic cloves, minced
1/4 cup minced shallots
2 leeks (about 1 pound), chopped with one third of green part
1 pound unpeeled carrots, trimmed and chopped
3/4 pound mushrooms, chopped
1 cup dry white wine
1 pound shelled fava beans, or two 10-ounce packages frozen lima beans
2 bay leaves
10 parsley sprigs
2 fresh thyme sprigs (or a pinch dried)
1-1/2 teaspoons salt, or to taste
1/2 teaspoon freshly ground black pepper, or to taste

In a large flameproof casserole or a stock pot, heat oil and sauté pancetta for 5 minutes. Add garlic and shallots; cook over low heat until very soft and golden. Stir in leeks, carrots, and mushrooms; sauté for 10 minutes. Pour in wine; increase heat to medium high and cook for 5 minutes. Add remaining ingredients and 2 quarts water. Bring to a boil; reduce heat to low and simmer, uncovered, for 1 hour. During this time, periodically remove scum and fat that rises to the surface.

Remove and discard thyme stems and bay leaves. Transfer vegetables from broth to a blender or food processor and purée. Strain through a medium sieve back into the broth. Taste for seasoning. Serve warm.

Thyme and Garlic Soup

Sopa d'All i Farigola

Serves six to eight.

If you like garlic, you will find this combination of flavors delicious. It was one of my favorite soups at home, another specialty of Rosalia's; she made it with fresh thyme from our garden whenever she had leftover bread.

6 large 1/2-inch-thick slices (about 6 ounces total) day-old white bread
2 tablespoons olive oil
1/3 cup minced garlic (16 large cloves)
1/2 cup minced shallots
1/4 cup (packed) fresh thyme leaves, finely chopped
1 teaspoon salt

1/2 teaspoon freshly ground black pepper
1 teaspoon paprika
8 cups Chicken Stock (p. 18)
1/2 cup flavorful dry Spanish sherry, such as *amontillado*

Optional, as a garnish:
Fresh thyme sprigs

Preheat oven to 400° F. Toast the bread for about 15 minutes, or until golden on both sides. Grind finely in a food processor.

In a large pot, heat oil and sauté garlic and shallots over low heat for 10 minutes, or until very soft. Stir in thyme and bread, salt, pepper, and paprika; sauté for 2 minutes, stirring. Add stock; bring to a boil, turn heat to low, and simmer, covered, for 30 minutes. Stir in sherry and taste for seasoning.

Serve hot in individual soup bowls, garnished with an optional sprig of fresh thyme.

Wine Recommendation: A fine oak-aged Chardonnay is the ideal accompaniment to this soup.

Cream of Fennel Soup

Crema de Fonoll

Serves six.

This is a soup I serve, warm or cold, whenever I can find fresh fennel bulbs in the market.
The recipe comes from a delightful inn high in the Catalan Pyrenees. Nestled on the outskirts of the little town of Martinet, Can Boix presents the cuisine and dishes of that area, La Cerdanya, and many of their dishes exemplify the mountain-style cooking of Catalunya.
When serving this soup chilled, I substitute yogurt for the cream; it adds a special tang—and cuts down on the calories, too.

4 tablespoons butter
1 teaspoon minced garlic
2 medium onions, minced
2 heads fennel (about 2 pounds), stems and leaves trimmed, chopped
4 cups Chicken Stock (5 cups, if served cold) (p. 18)
1 tablespoon minced orange zest (see p. 10)
1/2 cup heavy cream (or yogurt, if served cold)
1 tablespoon salt, or to taste
1/2 teaspoon freshly ground white pepper, or to taste

In a large pot, melt butter and sauté garlic with onions over low heat for 10 minutes. Add fennel and cook for 30 minutes, stirring occasionally. Add chicken stock and orange zest. Bring to a boil, reduce heat, and cook over very low heat, covered, for 30 minutes, or until vegetables are very tender.

Purée in a blender or food processor and strain through a medium sieve. Stir in cream and season with salt and pepper. Reheat and serve warm. (If served cold, add yogurt when chilled.)

Tomato-Zucchini Purée with Mint and Almonds

Sopa de Tomàquet i Menta amb Ametlles

Serves six.

This rustic tomato and zucchini purée suffused with fresh mint was inspired by a soup I loved from the moment I tasted it at the outstanding restaurant El Racó d'en Binu in Argentona, near Barcelona.

4 tablespoons butter
2 medium onions, finely chopped
1 pound unpeeled zucchini, grated
1 pound ripe tomatoes, peeled, seeded, and puréed
5 cups Chicken Stock (p. 18)
1 teaspoon salt, or to taste
1/2 teaspoon freshly ground white pepper, or to taste
1 teaspoon chopped fresh mint leaves
1/4 cup sliced toasted almonds (see p. 11)

In a medium-large skillet, heat butter and sauté onions over very low heat until soft and golden, about 20 minutes, stirring from time to time. Add zucchini and cook until tender, about 15 minutes. Purée in a food processor. Transfer to a large saucepan. Stir in tomato purée and stock. Heat soup and, before it comes to a boil, turn off heat. Add salt, pepper, and mint; taste for seasoning.

Serve warm, with sliced toasted almonds sprinkled over each serving.

Wine Recommendation: This soup is ideal with a Gewürztraminer or Muscat-Gewürztraminer blend.

SALADS
AMANIDES

n Catalunya and the rest of Spain, salads are rarely served as a side dish; they are considered first courses. And the idea of a salad as lunch on its own is practically unknown, except at the few American-influenced restaurants that have adopted this idea.

The most common salad in Catalunya is, of course, *amanida catalana*, a "Catalan salad" of lettuce greens, firm tomatoes, carrots, and onions, with Catalan cold cuts. These may include *botifarra de Vic* (a mild cooked white pork sausage), cured salami-type or smoked sausages, mountain-cured hams, etc.

Other Catalan classics are Fava Bean Salad with Cured Ham and Mint (p. 56); *Xatonada*, Tuna Salad with Anchovies, Olives, and Romesco Sauce (p. 57); and *Esqueixada*, Shredded Salt Cod Salad with Tomatoes, Peppers, and Onions (p. 58). Though they sound quite substantial, all of these would be served as a first course, while *Amanida Russa*, a "Russian" cooked vegetable salad (p. 56), is more typically served as a *tapa*. Also included in this chapter are a few personal recipes that I particularly enjoy in America.

Orange and Celery Salad with Mint

Amanida de Taronja, Api, i Menta

Serves six to eight.

This refreshing and unusual salad, quite easy to prepare, can be served either as a light first course or as a palate-freshener just before dessert.

For the dressing:
1/3 cup extra virgin olive oil
2 tablespoons fresh lemon juice, or to taste
1/4 teaspoon salt, or to taste
1/2 teaspoon freshly ground black pepper, or to taste

For the salad:
2 large oranges
1/4 pound small young carrots, scraped and thickly grated
2 inner celery stalks (about 6 ounces), cut thinly crosswise
1 head Boston lettuce, cut into small pieces
2 tablespoons fresh mint leaves, cut into thin strips

In a small bowl, mix all ingredients for the dressing. Taste for seasoning.

Peel oranges, removing all the white pith, and cut them into wedges, discarding membrane. (If they are large, cut sections in two.) Just before serving, toss all salad ingredients in a bowl with the dressing.

Red Cabbage Salad with Anchovies

Amanida de Col Llombarda amb Seitons

Serves eight.

Two Catalan favorites, cabbage and anchovies, here appear in a salad adapted from a dish I have enjoyed at the Barcelona restaurant L'Olivé. Owner Josep Olivé makes his version with seitons *(*boquerones *in Castilian), tiny pale fish, less pungent than anchovies, that are pickled in vinegar. Here, the anchovies virtually melt into the dressing.*

Start preparation 1 day ahead.

2 pounds red cabbage, finely shredded
6 tablespoons sherry wine vinegar or red wine vinegar, or to taste
2 teaspoons salt

One 2-ounce can flat anchovy fillets, drained
1/2 cup olive oil
6 tablespoons chopped fresh parsley leaves
Freshly ground black pepper to taste

In a large saucepan, combine cabbage with vinegar, salt, and 2 cups water. Bring to a boil, reduce heat to medium-low, and cook, covered, for 15 minutes. Let stand, covered and unrefrigerated, for about 24 hours.

Purée anchovies in a food processor or blender with the olive oil. Drain and squeeze excess moisture from cabbage. In a large bowl, toss cabbage with the anchovy-olive oil mixture and parsley. Taste for seasoning and sprinkle with pepper to taste. Serve cold or at room temperature.

"Russian" Vegetable Salad with Endive in a Fresh Tarragon Dressing

Endívies amb Amanida Russa

Serves eight.

Amanida russa *(*ensaladilla rusa *in Castilian) is a familiar* tapa *at bars in Catalunya and all over Spain. It is always a mix of blanched vegetables and potato, diced very small and dressed with mayonnaise. I find that scooped onto individual endive leaves, it makes a delightful appetizer as well as a great buffet salad or first course.*

For the salad:
1/2 pound thin young green beans, cut into 1/4-inch lengths
1 cup (6 ounces) shelled green peas, fresh or frozen (petite size)
1/2 pound thin young carrots, peeled and cut into 1/4-inch dice
1 pound new potatoes, peeled and cut into 1/4-inch dice
1/4 pound pimiento-stuffed green Spanish olives, quartered (3/4 cup)
1/4 pound cornichons (pickled gherkins), stemmed and cut into 1/4-inch dice (3/4 cup)
1 pound Belgian endives, ends trimmed and leaves separated

For the dressing:
1 tablespoon minced shallots or green onions
1 tablespoon chopped fresh tarragon leaves, or 1 teaspoon dried
1 egg yolk
1 tablespoon Dijon-style prepared mustard
1/4 cup fresh lemon juice
2 tablespoons sherry vinegar or red wine vinegar, or to taste
1/2 teaspoon salt, or to taste
1/4 teaspoon freshly ground black pepper, or to taste
Pinch of cayenne
1/2 cup extra virgin olive oil

In a large saucepan, bring abundant salted water to a boil and blanch separately beans, peas (if frozen, just thaw), carrots, and potatoes; they should be slightly undercooked. Toss with olives and cornichons in a large bowl.

Arrange large endive leaves in a circle on a large platter, or fanned out on 8 individual plates. Dice smaller inner leaves; toss with the salad.

In a blender or food processor, combine all dressing ingredients except olive oil. With motor running, gradually add oil in a thin stream. Taste for seasoning. Toss dressing with vegetables; arrange salad in middle of the endive leaves circle, or at the base of the endive fan.

Fava or Lima Bean Salad with Cured Ham and Mint

Amanida de Faves a la Menta

Serves eight.

The combination of fava beans with raw-cured ham and the fresh bite of mint in this refreshing salad has become a classic of Catalan cuisine, the inspiration of the late master chef Josep Mercadé. His thoughtful cooking at the restaurant Ampurdán in Figueres influenced a number of Catalunya's young chefs.

Fava beans are available in Spain much more than here, where the season is limited to a few weeks in spring; they also can be found frozen there, but not here—to my dismay! However I have found that a perfect substitute here, anytime of the year, is frozen lima beans.

For the salad:

1-1/2 pounds shelled young fava beans (about 4 to 6 pounds before shelling), or two 10-ounce packages frozen large lima beans

1/4 pound lean, good-quality prosciutto, sliced medium-thin and julienned

1 small head romaine lettuce, finely shredded

5 large fresh mint leaves, cut into thin strips

For the dressing:

2 tablespoons herbed or Dijon-style mustard

1/2 cup olive oil, preferably extra virgin

3 tablespoons sherry or red wine vinegar, or to taste

1 teaspoon freshly ground black pepper, or to taste

1/2 teaspoon salt, or to taste

In a large pot, bring abundant salted water to a boil. Add fava beans and cook until tender, 5 to 7 minutes. Drain and let cool. In a large salad bowl, toss beans with ham, lettuce, and mint.

In a small bowl, whisk all dressing ingredients together until well blended. Taste for seasoning.

Just before serving, pour dressing over salad and toss gently until lettuce is evenly coated. Serve at room temperature or slightly chilled.

Tuna Salad with Anchovies, Olives, and Romesco Sauce

Xatonada

Serves six.

Traditionally served on Ash Wednesday, this tuna salad original to the Catalan district of El Vendrell, southwest of Barcelona, is too good to eat just once a year. It is delightful as a first course for dinner or served as a light luncheon. Originally a fisherman's dish, the name xatonada *is derived from the word* xató, *the romesco sauce that is basic to the dish. Although* xatonada *traditionally uses escarole, it can also be made with other kinds of lettuces or greens.*

1 medium head escarole or another type of lettuce, or mixed greens
One 7-ounce can albacore tuna packed in olive oil, drained well
2 small Italian plum tomatoes, each cut into 6 wedges
2 hard-boiled eggs (see p. 35), each cut into 6 wedges
12 large flat canned anchovy fillets (one 2-ounce can)
3/4 cup (1/4 pound) small black olives with pits (Niçoise or dried oil-cured olives are best)
1 recipe Romesco Sauce for Salads (p. 114)

Separate, wash, and dry escarole leaves; arrange them as a bed on individual plates. In a small bowl, crumble tuna very finely with your fingers; distribute it evenly on each plate, mounding it in the center. Arrange 2 tomato wedges and 2 egg wedges on the sides of each plate; garnish each egg wedge with an anchovy fillet. Scatter olives on top.

Place a small mound of *romesco* sauce on each plate and pass remaining sauce in a bowl. Serve at room temperature.

Shredded Salt Cod Salad with Tomatoes, Peppers, and Onions

Esqueixada

Serves six to eight.

Esqueixada is a staple on menus of country-style Catalan restaurants, especially in the summertime. The basis for this intriguing salad is always hand-shredded raw salt cod, but there are many variations on the theme.
In preparing esqueixada, it is important to use a good-quality salt cod and a fine extra virgin olive oil. And to achieve esqueixada's characteristic texture, it is essential to hand shred the salt cod.

Start preparation 2 days in advance, by soaking salt cod in water.

1 pound boneless dried salt cod (see p. 7)
1 small red (or yellow or green) bell pepper, seeded and sliced into thin rings
1/2 large red onion, thinly sliced, and separated into rings
1 large ripe tomato, unpeeled and thinly sliced
3/4 cup extra virgin olive oil
1/4 cup red wine vinegar
4 large garlic cloves, minced
1/2 teaspoon freshly ground black pepper, or to taste
Salt to taste, if necessary

As a garnish:
2 ounces black unpitted olives
2 hard-boiled eggs (see p. 35), quartered

Cover salt cod with abundant cold water and soak for 48 hours, changing water 5 or 6 times. Drain and press salt cod with your hands to remove excess water. Discard any skin or bones. With your fingers, shred cod into thin strips.

In a salad bowl, toss shredded salt cod with pepper, onion, and tomato. In a small bowl combine oil, vinegar, garlic, and black pepper, beating to blend well. Pour over the salad and, with your hands, toss to coat salt cod and vegetables. Taste for seasoning.

Arrange on a platter or in a bowl and garnish attractively with olives and hard-boiled eggs.

Shredded Monkfish and Tomato Salad with a Creamy Sherry Dressing

Trinxat de Rap

Serves six.

One hot summer day, I ordered this dish for lunch at the Eldorado Petit, the first restaurant Lluis Cruanyas opened in 1976 next door to his father's café in Sant Felíu de Guixols, in the heart of the Costa Brava—and I always remembered it. A few years later, when Lluis and his wife Lolita opened a second Eldorado Petit, this time in one of Barcelona's most fashionable neighborhoods, I asked him for the recipe. Eldorado Petit quickly established itself as one of the best restaurants in the city—and all of Spain—and two years ago the Cruanyas family made the big leap by opening a third Eldorado Petit in Manhattan.

Start preparation 2 to 4 hours in advance.

For the fish:
2 pounds fresh monkfish, in whole pieces
1 tablespoon sherry wine vinegar
1 bay leaf
6 black peppercorns

For the dressing:
1 pound ripe tomatoes, peeled, seeded, and diced very small by hand
1/4 cup snipped fresh chives
1/2 cup heavy cream
1 tablespoon dry flavorful Spanish sherry, such as *amontillado*
3 tablespoons sherry wine vinegar, or to taste
2 teaspoons salt, or to taste
1 teaspoon freshly ground white pepper, or to taste

For the salad:
2 large ripe tomatoes, peeled and thinly sliced
1/2 small red onion, very thinly sliced
1/2 large English cucumber (1/2 pound), peeled and thinly sliced

To cook the fish: Place monkfish in a pan with vinegar, bay leaf, and peppercorns. Add water to cover, bring to a boil and immediately reduce heat to low; simmer for 10 to 12 minutes, or until fish is just cooked. Drain.

To prepare the dressing: In a nonreactive bowl, combine all dressing ingredients and let stand for at least 30 minutes.

To assemble the salad: Press fish with your hands to squeeze out as much water as possible. Remove loose grayish skin and membranes from the fish. With your fingers, shred it very finely. Once more squeeze water out of it with your hands. Toss fish with the dressing in the bowl and refrigerate for 1 to 3 hours, until serving time.

To serve: Arrange a bed of the thinly sliced tomatoes, onion, and cucumber, and place a mound of fish salad on top.

Veal Sweetbreads and Liver Salad

Amanida de Pedrerets i Fetge

Serves eight.

In Catalunya I have had this salad with fresh calves' brains rather than sweetbreads, but in this country those are not only hard to find—they seem to be too strong an experience for some people. However, if you have never tried brains before and can find them fresh, they are a real delicacy. Their soft, moist texture combines beautifully with the other ingredients in this recipe.

Start preparation 2-1/2 hours in advance, by soaking sweetbreads in water.

3/4 pound fresh veal sweetbreads
1 tablespoon fresh lemon juice
2 or 3 tablespoons olive oil
1/2 teaspoon salt
1/2 teaspoon freshly ground black pepper
3/4 pound fresh calves' liver, sliced thinly and cut into 1-1/2-inch strips
1 cup (6 ounces) shelled green peas (petite size, if frozen)
1 heart of romaine lettuce, finely shredded
1 pound firm ripe tomatoes, peeled, seeded, and diced by hand
1/2 cup (3 ounces) pine nuts, toasted (p. 11)

For the dressing:
1 tablespoon Dijon-style prepared mustard
3 tablespoons sherry wine vinegar or red wine vinegar, or to taste
1/2 teaspoon freshly ground black pepper, or to taste
1/4 teaspoon salt, or to taste
1/3 cup extra virgin olive oil

To prepare the sweetbreads: Soak sweetbreads in cold water to cover for 2 hours, changing the water 3 times during this period. Drain and place them in a medium saucepan. Cover with cold water and add lemon juice. Bring to a boil, reduce heat to low, and simmer for 5 minutes. Drain sweetbreads and immediately plunge them into a bowl of cold water; this will make them firmer. After a few minutes, drain them and separate lobes, removing tubes and connecting tissue. The pieces should be approximately bite size. Pat dry with paper towels.

To cook the sweetbreads: In a skillet that will accommodate all the sweetbreads in a single layer, heat 2 tablespoons oil and add sweetbreads. Sprinkle with 1/4 teaspoon *each* salt and pepper. Cook over medium-high heat, without stirring, for about 3 minutes. Turn them and sauté quickly until lightly browned, about 3 more minutes. With a slotted spoon, remove sweetbreads from skillet and set them aside.

Add liver to same skillet; add some more oil if necessary. Sprinkle with remaining 1/4 teaspoon *each* salt and pepper. Sauté liver quickly over high heat, so it browns on the outside but it still is pink on the inside. Drain on paper towels.

Blanch green peas in abundant salted water for about 3 minutes; drain and set aside. (If peas are frozen, it is not necessary to blanch them; just thaw and pass them through warm water in a colander.) Keep peas, lettuce, tomatoes, and pine nuts in bowls in the refrigerator until the last minute.

To prepare the dressing: Combine all ingredients except oil in a blender or food processor. In a thin stream, whirl in oil. Taste for seasoning.

To assemble the salad: Just before serving, heat dressing in a small pan. Combine cold ingredients in a large bowl and arrange them as a bed on each plate. Mound warm sweetbreads and liver on top, and pour warm vinaigrette over each salad. Serve at once.

FISH AND SHELLFISH
PEIX I MARISC

he Mediterranean offers outstanding seafood—plump Costa Brava prawns, razor clams, spiny lobsters, thumb-sized squid and cuttlefish, the coveted tiny lobsters called in Catalan *escamerlans*, small red mullet, delicate *rap* or monkfish, and so on. Larger fish come from the Bay of Biscay on the north coast of Spain.

Venture into the fish section of Barcelona's fabulous La Boqueria market, and female fishmongers will call out, "Hey, beautiful one, won't you buy some fish from me? Here, take it home to your husband. He'll love you forever if you cook him these prawns." Decked out in dainty lace aprons, a full coiffure, and makeup, these women can nevertheless fillet a fish with a professional flash of the knife. The lavishly arranged stands display fish whole, only hours from the sea, and the fishmongers cut it all to order. Lobsters stray from their baskets, crayfish are still wriggling, and some of the fish are alive when they arrive at the market. The price is never cheap for these freshly caught delicacies, but Catalans are crazy about fresh seafood and are willing to pay for it.

The recipes included in this chapter are all main courses; you'll find other fish and shellfish recipes in the first course and salad chapters. For more seafood recipes, check the "Earthy Country Stews" and "Paellas and Paella-style Rice Dishes" sections, too.

Broiled Scallops on a Bed of Caramelized Onions

Petxina de Pelegrí

Serves eight as a first course,
six as a main course.

*For dinner at home we often enjoyed
seafood in a light bechamel sauce,
broiled in a natural seashell. We called
them* petxinas *(conchas in Castilian)
or "shells." But on special occasions,
we would have impeccably fresh scallops—coral still attached—simply
broiled with lemon juice and oil. Since
such a delicacy is practically impossible to find here, I devised this recipe
for our bay scallops. I serve these
broiled as a light main course, or, in
smaller portions, as a first course. (You
can purchase the natural shells at a
well-stocked cookware store.)*

3 tablespoons olive oil
6 large garlic cloves, minced
  (2 tablespoons)
3 large onions, thinly sliced
1/2 cup dry white wine
1/2 teaspoon salt
1/4 teaspoon freshly ground white
  pepper

2 pounds large bay scallops
2 tablespoons sherry wine vinegar
3 to 4 tablespoons fine commercial
  bread crumbs
2 or 3 tablespoons olive oil
3 tablespoons chopped fresh parsley
  leaves

Heat oil in a medium skillet and sauté garlic with onions over low heat
for 40 to 45 minutes, or until they are golden brown and almost caramelized; stir often, especially toward the end. Add wine, increase heat to medium, and cook until wine is almost evaporated. Stir in salt and pepper;
taste for seasoning. Arrange as a bed on 6 or 8 individual shells.

In a medium bowl, toss scallops with vinegar and marinate for 15 minutes. Distribute scallops on top of onions; sprinkle with bread crumbs,
olive oil, and parsley. Meanwhile, preheat broiler.

At the last moment, place shells under broiler for 4 or 5 minutes, or until scallops are cooked through and bread crumbs are golden. Serve at once.

Wine Recommendation: Serve with an aromatic white wine such as a Riesling, Gewürztraminer, a blend of Muscat and Gewürztraminer, or a Catalan
Alella.

Braised Peas with Clams and Fresh Mint

Pesols Estofats a la Menta Fresca amb Copinyes

Serves four to six.

*The intriguing combination of peas
with mint is a traditional one from
L'Empordà region in northern Catalunya. The idea of combining peas and
mint with fresh clams comes from Sa
Punta restaurant in Pals, just east of
Girona, on the Costa Brava.
Although it is not a very soupy stew, I
do like to serve this in shallow soup
bowls, with a basket of crusty bread to
soak up the sauce.*

3 tablespoons butter
1 large onion, minced
1/2 cup finely chopped fresh mint
  leaves
2-1/2 cups (1 pound) shelled green
  peas, fresh or frozen
1/2 teaspoon salt

1/2 cup dry white wine
4 pounds live small clams (try to get
  10 to 12 per pound), shells scrubbed

As a garnish:
1 fresh mint sprig per person

In a large flameproof casserole, preferably of clay, or a skillet, heat butter
and sauté onion with mint leaves over low heat until very soft, about 20
minutes. Add peas and salt, cover, and cook until peas are tender—about
15 minutes for fresh peas, 5 minutes for frozen.

Meanwhile, in a large pot, bring wine to a boil. Place clams on a steaming rack over wine, cover pot, and steam clams until they open, 5 to 10
minutes. As they open, remove them with tongs and add them to the pea
stew. Discard any that do not open. Strain wine and juices drained from
steaming clams through a fine-mesh strainer into the stew. Taste for seasoning. Serve warm in soup bowls, garnished with a sprig of fresh mint.

Wine Recommendation: Serve with a crisp dry wine like a Sauvignon Blanc, a fresh non-oak-aged Chardonnay, a Mâcon Blanc, or a Catalan Parellada.

Snapper in a Parsley and Pea Sauce with Clams

Lluç amb Salsa Verda

Serves six

Hake in "green sauce" is a preparation of Basque origin, found all over Spain. At home we made this refreshing version in a parsley and pea sauce, without any flour, which I find much more appealing. Any firm white fish will work well, but I particularly like it with fresh snapper.

1/2 cup dry white wine
3 pounds live small clams, shells scrubbed
4 or 5 tablespoons olive oil
1 large onion, coarsely sliced
1/4 cup chopped shallots
3 large garlic cloves, minced
2 cups Fish Stock (p. 19)
1 cup (6 ounces) shelled green peas (petite size, if frozen)

1/2 cup packed finely chopped fresh parsley leaves
1/2 teaspoon freshly ground white pepper, or to taste
1/4 teaspoon salt, or to taste
2 pounds fresh snapper fillets, cut in 6 serving pieces

In a large pot, bring wine to a boil. Place clams on a steaming rack over wine, cover pot, and steam clams until they open, 5 to 10 minutes. Remove clams from shells and reserve. Discard shells, and also any clams that do not open. Strain liquid through a fine sieve and reserve.

Heat 2 tablespoons oil in a skillet and sauté onion, shallots, and garlic over low heat for about 15 minutes, until very soft and starting to color. Add fish stock and reserved clam/wine liquid; cook over medium heat for 5 minutes. Purée the mixture in a blender or food processor and return it to the pan. Stir in peas, parsley, and pepper. Taste for seasoning before adding any salt.

Heat remaining 2 or 3 tablespoons oil in a flameproof clay casserole, or in a skillet large enough to hold the fish fillets in 1 layer. Sauté the fish over medium heat, until done. Pour reserved sauce and clams over fish. Serve from the casserole, or on individual dishes.

Wine recommendation: Serve with a full-bodied white wine, such as an oak-aged Chardonnay or a flavorful Alvarinho from Galicia.

Salt Cod with Potato and Garlic

Brandada de Bacallà

Serves eight.

Salt cod has a distinct flavor—very different from fresh cod—that I enjoy very much. And this dish is one of my favorites in the Catalan repertoire of salt cod dishes. Actually, brandade de morue *is original to Nîmes in Provence, but of course that French region was linked to Catalunya and Aragón for several centuries—which explains why the dish is as popular in Catalunya as it is in Provence.*

There are a quite a few versions; the most common is just salt cod beaten to a thick paste with garlic and cream. Most of the time this version is too heavy, garlicky, and rich for my taste; I find that adding boiled puréed potato softens the flavors, and I like it much better. This recipe, by the way, is a favorite of my mother, who cannot by any means be considered a garlic lover.

Start preparation 2 days in advance, by soaking salt cod in water.

1 pound boneless dried salt cod (see p. 7)
1 pound potatoes, boiled, peeled, and finely mashed with a fork or potato ricer
4 tablespoons butter
6 garlic cloves, finely chopped (2 tablespoons)
1-1/2 cups milk, scalded
3/4 teaspoon freshly ground black pepper, or to taste
Salt to taste, if necessary
3 ounces grated Gruyère cheese (3/4 cup packed)

As a garnish:
8 triangles of white bread, crusts trimmed, fried in olive oil

Soak salt cod in abundant water for 48 hours, changing water 5 or 6 times.

Place salt cod in a medium pan, cover with cold water, and bring to just below a boil. Immediately turn heat to very low and gently simmer for 15 minutes, being careful not to let the salt cod boil. Drain salt cod. Remove any bones and skin, and crumble it finely. Add to mashed potatoes, mixing well with a fork.

Heat butter in a small skillet and sauté garlic over low heat, stirring, until soft but not golden, about 5 minutes; stir into potato and salt cod mixture. In a mixer or beating with a wooden spoon, add scalded milk gradually, incorporating it into the salt cod/potato mixture. Season with pepper; taste and add salt if necessary.

Preheat broiler. Transfer mixture to a casserole, preferably of clay. Sprinkle grated cheese on top. Place under broiler for a few minutes, until cheese turns golden. Serve immediately, garnished with triangles of fried bread.

Wine Recommendation: Serve with a dry white wine, such as a young fresh Chardonnay or a lightly oak-aged Chardonnay-Parellada blend.

Salt Cod in a Classic Catalan Sauce with Pine Nuts and Raisins

Bacallà a la Catalana amb Panses i Pinyons

Serves six.

The traditional elements of Catalan cuisine—sofregit, picada, pine nuts, and raisins—are all present in this dish, making it a classic a la catalana preparation. It is versatile enough to serve as a first course, a main course, or even as a tapa. (For an appetizer, or a tapa, cut the salt cod into smaller pieces.)

The idea for this recipe comes from Jaume de Provença, one of the most representative Catalan restaurants in Barcelona today. Owner/chef Jaume Bargués's high standards, dedication, and talent have contributed greatly to bringing my home region's cuisine to the top ranks. He's as good with old traditionals, like this one, as he is with new creations.

Start preparation 2 days in advance, by soaking codfish in water.

1 pound boneless dried salt cod (see p. 7)

For the *sofregit*:
3 tablespoons olive oil
1 large onion, finely chopped
4 large garlic cloves, minced
2 pounds ripe tomatoes, peeled and chopped
1 tablespoon chopped fresh parsley leaves
1/4 cup (1.5 ounces) pine nuts
1/4 cup raisins
1 cup dry white wine
2 cups Fish Stock (p. 19)

For the *picada*:
1 tablespoon olive oil, if necessary
1 large (1/2-inch-thick) slice white bread (1 ounce)
3 tablespoons (or 1 ounce) whole blanched almonds or hazelnuts (filberts), toasted (see p. 11)
3 large garlic cloves
1 tablespoon fresh parsley leaves
1/4 teaspoon freshly ground black pepper, or to taste
1/4 teaspoon salt, or as needed (depending on saltiness of cod)

Soak salt cod in water to cover for 48 hours, changing water 5 or 6 times. Drain and press cod with your hands to eliminate excess water. Remove any skin and bones, and cut into 6 serving pieces.

To prepare the *sofregit*: Heat 2 tablespoons oil in a large skillet or a flameproof clay casserole. Add onion and garlic and cook slowly, for 15 or 20 minutes, until quite soft. Add tomatoes and parsley and cook for 10 minutes on medium heat. Add white wine and cook until dry. Stir in fish stock and set aside.

Meanwhile, heat remaining tablespoon of oil in a small skillet and sauté pine nuts and raisins, stirring, until nuts are golden and raisins plump up. Remove them with a slotted spoon and set aside. Reserve oil in skillet.

To prepare the *picada*: Add another tablespoon of oil to small skillet if necessary, and sauté bread on both sides until golden. In a food processor, finely grind nuts with fried bread, garlic, parsley, pepper, and salt.

Bring tomato mixture to a boil, and stir in *picada*. Add salt cod and cook, uncovered, over medium-low heat for 10 minutes. Taste for seasoning. Add pine nuts and raisins. Serve warm.

Wine Recommendation: Serve with an oak-aged Sauvignon Blanc, a Viura from Rioja, or a Verdejo from Rueda.

Monkfish with Almonds, Sweet Red Peppers, and Saffron

Rap a l'Ametlla

Serves six.

At home, Rosalia used to prepare fresh monkfish in a delicate, saffron-scented almond sauce as a light dinner entrée. Since monkfish is one of the few Mediterranean fishes I can find in this country, I developed this version of her recipe. Any firm white fish, such as sea bass or snapper, works well, too.

2 pounds monkfish (angler fish), in large whole fillets (or another firm white fish)
2 tablespoons olive oil
3 large garlic cloves, minced
3 large red bell peppers, cored, seeded, and cut into strips lengthwise
1/4 pound (3/4 cup) whole almonds, toasted (see p. 11)
1/2 teaspoon (.2 gram) saffron threads

1/2 cup dry white wine
1/2 cup Fish Stock (p. 19)
1/2 teaspoon salt, or to taste
1/2 teaspoon freshly ground white pepper, or to taste

As a garnish:
1 or 1-1/2 ounces (about 1/3 cup) sliced almonds, toasted until golden (see p. 11)

Preheat oven to 350° F. Remove loose grayish skin and membranes from monkfish. Bake it in a buttered baking pan, in preheated oven, for 15 minutes. Let cool. Cut fillets into medallions and set aside. Reserve juices in pan.

In a large skillet, heat olive oil and sauté garlic and peppers over low heat for 20 minutes, stirring occasionally. Grind almonds finely in a food processor and add them to the skillet together with saffron, white wine, fish stock, reserved fish juices, salt, and pepper; cook over medium heat for 5 minutes. Transfer to a blender or food processor and purée. Return sauce to skillet, add fish medallions, and heat through. Serve immediately, with sliced almonds sprinkled on top.

Wine Recommendation: Serve with a Chardonnay-Parellada blend from Catalunya, an Alvarinho from Galicia, or a Sauvignon Blanc from California.

Fish in a Burned Garlic Sauce

Peix a l'All Cremat

Serves six.

No, this is definitely not a Catalan version of blackened redfish, but a wonderful old fisherman's dish that should be love at first taste for garlic fans. Cremat means "burnt"—and in this case it refers not to the fish but to the garlic, which is sautéed a deep mahogany brown.

1/4 cup olive oil
1 large head garlic (about 20 large cloves), peeled and thinly sliced by hand lengthwise
1/2 pound unpeeled ripe tomatoes, seeded and finely chopped

1-1/2 pounds red snapper or sea bass fillets (or any fresh, firm white fish), cut into 6 pieces
1/2 teaspoon salt

In Catalunya, this dish is always cooked and served in a clay casserole, but you can also use any flameproof casserole or nonreactive skillet with high sides that is large enough to hold the fish fillets in a single layer.

Heat oil and add garlic; cook slowly over low heat until garlic is dark brown, 10 to 15 minutes. Keep stirring so it does not turn black and burn, but it should be really dark brown (this will give color and wonderful flavor to the sauce). Add tomatoes and cook over medium-low heat until dry. Add 2 cups water, bring to a boil, and reduce by about half.

Squid Stuffed with Scallops and Shrimp in a Saffron Sauce

Calamars Farcits amb Salsa de Safrà

Serves eight.

This is an elegant and delicate recipe worthy of your most discriminating guests—as long as they like squid. During my childhood we ate squid quite often at home, and I always loved to sneak into the kitchen and help clean it. Unfortunately, my smelly hands were always a dead giveaway to my mother, who did not approve of such culinary adventures. I'm still a great fan of squid, especially since nowadays you can buy it already cleaned at some fish markets. If you've never cleaned squid, after the first try you'll see that it really is fun and easy to do, albeit a little time-consuming.

Add fish fillets in a single layer and sprinkle with salt. Reduce heat to medium and cook fish, turning it only once, 3 to 4 minutes on each side, depending on thickness of fillets. Serve immediately from the casserole.

Wine Recommendation: Serve with an oak-aged Chardonnay or a light red such as a young Pinot Noir, Merlot, or Zinfandel.

To stuff the squid:
24 medium squid (2 to 2-1/2 pounds), cleaned
1/2 pound firm white fish fillets or scallops
1/2 pound shelled cooked shrimp
1/2 cup heavy cream
2 egg whites
1/2 teaspoon salt, or to taste

For the sauce:
1 tablespoon butter

1 large tomato, peeled, seeded, and chopped
1/2 cup heavy cream
1/4 teaspoon (.1 gram) saffron threads

To cook the squid:
1 cup dry or semi-dry white wine
1 cup Fish Stock (p. 19)
Salt to taste, if necessary

To clean the squid: You can buy the squid cleaned, or do it yourself: Pull out head and discard cuttlebone and internal organs from each squid body, rinsing well under running water. Cut off tentacles from head and remove beak by pressing the tentacle base so it pops out. Remove purplish skin from body sacs. Reserve white pouches, and tentacles separately.

To stuff the squid: Pull fins off from white pouches (unless you used cleaned squid) and, in a food processor, purée the fins with fish and shrimp. With the motor running, pour in cream and egg whites. Add salt and taste for seasoning. Using a pastry bag fitted with a small tip, stuff squid bodies half full. Secure with a toothpick and set aside.

To prepare the sauce: In a small skillet, heat butter and cook tomato over medium heat until dry, about 5 minutes. Add cream and cook until reduced by about one fourth. Stir in saffron threads. Set aside.

To cook the squid: In a skillet large enough to hold squid in a single layer, bring wine and fish stock to a boil. Add squid bodies and tentacles, and bring to boil again; turn off heat, cover, and let sit for 10 minutes. Remove squid, increase heat to medium, and reduce to 1/2 cup. Stir in tomato sauce, return squid to skillet, and toss to coat. Cook to just heat through, and taste for seasoning. Serve immediately.

Wine Recommendation: Serve with an aromatic semi-dry white wine such as a Riesling, Gewürztraminer, a Muscat-Gewürztraminer blend, or a Catalan Alella.

Baked Whole Baby Salmon with a Shrimp and Olive Stuffing

Peix Farcit al Forn

Serves six to eight.

For special guests, my mother liked to serve this elegant whole baked fish as an impressive first course. She used hake, but I have found that here it works very well with salmon. And I always serve it as a main course rather than a first course.

For the filling:
1 tablespoon olive oil
1 large garlic clove, chopped
1/2 onion, chopped (1/2 cup)
3/4 cup homemade bread crumbs (see p. 10)
2 tablespoons milk
2 tablespoons *amontillado* or other flavorful Spanish sherry
1/2 pound bay shrimp or other small peeled cooked shrimp
3 ounces pimiento-stuffed green Spanish olives, chopped (about 1/2 cup)
2 hard-boiled eggs (see p. 35), chopped by hand
1 raw egg
1/2 teaspoon freshly ground black pepper
Salt to taste, if necessary

For cooking the fish:
3/4 teaspoon salt
1/2 teaspoon freshly ground black pepper
1 whole 4- to 6-pound Norwegian salmon, or a 4- to 5-pound tail section of a larger salmon, boned and butterflied (see *Note,* below)
2 large tomatoes, peeled and coarsely chopped
1 large onion, thinly sliced
1/2 pound small red-skinned potatoes, thinly sliced
2 bay leaves
1/2 cup fresh lemon juice
1/2 cup dry white wine
1/2 cup olive oil

Note: Ask your fishmonger to open the fish only on one side to remove the bone, so skin is intact on the other. The fish body or the tail section should open up like a book.

To prepare the filling: Heat oil in a small skillet. Sauté garlic and onion over low heat for 8 to 10 minutes, or until soft and dry. In a large bowl, soak bread in milk and sherry. Mix in garlic, onion, and remaining filling ingredients. Taste for seasoning. Preheat oven to 350° F.

To cook the fish: Sprinkle 1/2 teaspoon salt and 1/4 teaspoon pepper over butterflied fish, skin side down. Stuff fish with filling and sew it up with string. Arrange tomatoes, onion, and potatoes as a bed in a large casserole or ovenproof skillet, sprinkle with 1/4 teaspoon *each* salt and pepper, and place fish on top. Add bay leaves, on the sides. Pour lemon juice, wine, and oil over. Bake in 350° F oven for 30 minutes, or until fish is cooked through. Serve immediately.

Wine Recommendation: Serve with an elegant dry white wine, such as a barrel-fermented, oak-aged Chardonnay.

Prawns with Veal Sweetbreads in a Sherry Cream Sauce

Gambes amb Pedrerets de Vedella

Serves four to six.

Prawns and sweetbreads complement each other extremely well—a very Catalan combination, shellfish with a light meat—and here they are especially enhanced by the delicate flavorful sauce. I was given this recipe by one of my favorite restaurants, Racó d'en Binu, near Barcelona.

Start preparation 3 hours in advance, by soaking sweetbreads in water.

1-1/2 pounds veal sweetbreads
1 tablespoon fresh lemon juice
4 tablespoons butter
1/2 cup minced shallots
1 medium carrot, finely chopped
1 celery stalk, finely chopped
1/2 pound ripe tomatoes, unpeeled, chopped
1 bay leaf
1 tablespoon fresh (or 1 teaspoon dried) oregano, rosemary, or thyme leaves, or a mixture
1/2 cup dry, flavorful Spanish sherry, such as *amontillado*
1 cup Veal Stock (p. 18)
1/2 cup heavy cream
3/4 teaspoon salt
1/2 teaspoon freshly ground white pepper
1 pound (about 40) medium prawns, shelled
1/2 cup full-bodied brandy

To prepare the sweetbreads, follow instructions on p. 60.

Heat 3 tablespoons butter in a large skillet and sauté shallots until very soft, 8 to 10 minutes. Add carrot, celery, tomatoes, and herbs. Cook for 15 minutes over medium heat. Add sherry, increase heat, and cook until dry. Stir in veal stock and cream; heat through. Discard bay leaf. Purée in a blender or food processor and strain through a fine sieve back into the skillet.

Season sweetbreads with 1/2 teaspoon salt and 1/4 teaspoon pepper, and prawns with remaining 1/4 teaspoon *each* salt and pepper. In a large skillet, melt remaining tablespoon butter and sauté sweetbreads over high heat for 3 minutes, shaking pan. Stir in prawns; add brandy and when hot, flambé (see p. 12). Cook 2 to 3 minutes, shaking pan until flames subside. With a slotted spoon, transfer sweetbreads and prawns to skillet with the sauce. Cook brandy liquid in the other skillet over high heat until reduced to just 2 or 3 tablespoons; add to sauce. Heat through and serve immediately.

Wine Recommendation: A fine white, such as oak-aged Viura from Rioja, or a Chardonnay-Parellada or Sauvignon Blanc–Parellada blend from Catalunya.

Prawns and Chicken in a Sauce with Nuts, Herbs, and Chocolate

Gambes amb Pollastre "Mar i Muntanya"

Serves eight.

This outstanding dish, a specialty of L'Empordà region, where it originated at the beginning of this century, combines shellfish and chicken with a flavorful picada of hazelnuts, garlic, herbs—and chocolate.
A classic version is that of Eldorado Petit, the celebrated restaurant originally in Sant Felíu de Guixols in L'Empordà, then in Barcelona, and now in New York. Owner Lluis Cruanyas calls the dish mar i muntanya, *or "sea and mountain," because it combines ingredients from the two bountiful areas of L'Empordà. It is quite a rich dish, perfectly accompanied with any crusty country-style bread, such as Peasant Bread (p. 118).*

About 1-1/2 pounds prawns (2 jumbo or 3 large per person)
2 cups Fish Stock (p. 19)
1 large chicken (5 to 6 pounds), cut into 8 serving pieces (reserve chicken livers)
1 teaspoon salt
1/2 teaspoon freshly ground black pepper
2 tablespoons olive oil

For the *sofregit*:
1 pound onions, chopped
1-1/2 pounds tomatoes, peeled, seeded, and chopped
1 cup dry white wine
1/2 cup full-bodied brandy
1 bay leaf

For the *picada*:
3/4 cup (3-1/2 ounces) hazelnuts, or almonds, or a mixture, toasted (see p. 11)
1 ounce unsweetened baking chocolate
6 large garlic cloves
1/2 cup fresh parsley leaves
2 tablespoons fresh thyme, oregano, or marjoram leaves, or 2 teaspoons dried
2 tablespoons fresh lemon juice
1/2 teaspoon (.2 gram) saffron threads, or 1/4 teaspoon powdered saffron
1/4 teaspoon ground cinnamon
1/2 teaspoon salt

Peel and devein prawns, leaving tail end intact and reserving shells. In a saucepan, heat fish stock with prawn shells, and simmer gently for 1/2 to 3/4 hour, covered, while you prepare the chicken.

To prepare the chicken: Poach chicken livers in a small pan of simmering water to cover for 10 minutes; drain and reserve livers. Pat dry chicken pieces, and season with salt and pepper. In a large skillet, heat 2 tablespoons oil and sauté chicken pieces over medium heat until golden. Set them aside. Pour off fat, leaving just 1 or 2 tablespoons.

To prepare the *sofregit* and cook the chicken: Add chopped onions to the skillet and sauté over low heat until soft, 5 to 10 minutes. Add chopped tomatoes and cook over medium heat for 5 minutes. Add white wine and cook until dry. Add brandy and, when hot, flambé (see p. 12). Cook, stirring, 3 to 5 minutes or until dry.

Transfer this mixture to a large pot. Remove prawn shells from fish stock, straining them through a fine sieve and pushing them down with a spoon; discard shells. Add fish stock to the pot and bring to a boil. Add chicken pieces and bay leaf, cover tightly with a double layer of aluminum foil, place lid on top, and simmer over low heat for 20 minutes.

Remove chicken (reserve sauce) to a large serving dish; in Spain we traditionally use a clay casserole. Arrange chicken pieces decoratively, and keep warm.

To prepare the *picada*: In a food processor, grind together chicken livers with all *picada* ingredients and 2 tablespoons sauce from the pot.

To assemble the dish: Stir *picada* into sauce and add prawns. Cook for 5 minutes, or until prawns are done (depending on their size). Taste for seasoning. Remove bay leaf. Arrange prawns on serving dish, pour sauce over, and serve immediately.

Wine recommendation: Serve with a hearty Mediterranean wine, such as a Garnacha-Cariñena blend from Catalunya, a Gigondas or Châteauneuf-du-Pape from southern Rhône, or a Zinfandel from California.

POULTRY AND GAME
AUS I CAÇA

▼ ▼ ▼

Catalans are great aficionados of game and, in season, market stands proffering pheasants with their showy feathers, tasty little partridges, squab, wild duck, and *pintada* or guinea hen, attract quite a crowd. Hunting for feathered game is a favorite pastime in the country; whenever a hunter friend presented my mother with a brace of partridges, we would have Braised Partridge with Cabbage Croquettes, Empordà Style (p. 79) that night for dinner—a dish I really love. And for special occasions, my Aunt Oriola would cook Pheasant with Grapes and Walnuts (p. 76).

Finding game with the true wild taste is difficult in this country, but farm-raised game birds, although milder in flavor, can be very tasty; so I have adapted recipes to suit more widely available birds, such as game hens. Also included are a couple of my favorite recipes for domestic birds such as chicken and duck, which are very popular in Catalunya. The grain-fed ducks from L'Empordà region north of Barcelona are the best I've ever tasted anywhere. For more poultry and game recipes, check the "Earthy Country Stews" Chapter, too.

Chicken Galantine with a Classic Spanish Stuffing

Gallantina de Pollastre

Serves eight.

This recipe has been served by the women of the Torres family for years. It is a favorite of my sister-in-law, Mahle, for her buffet dinners, because it can—and should—be prepared ahead. Sliced and fanned out on a platter, garnished with sprigs of fresh herbs, it makes an impressive first course or entrée.

The most time-consuming part of making a chicken galantine is the first step: boning the chicken. But if you can't persuade your butcher to do it for you, it's not hard to do it yourself, and with a little practice it takes much less time. I have also simplified Mahle's original recipe; instead of wrapping the galantine in cheesecloth and poaching it in stock the traditional way, I find that baking it is much faster and easier. It turns out just as moist—or maybe even more so—and no chicken stock is required.

Start preparation at least 10 hours or up to 2 days ahead.

One 3-1/2- to 4-pound chicken, deboned (see instructions below) and liver reserved.
About 1/4 cup olive oil
3 large garlic cloves, minced
1 large onion, finely chopped
1/3 pound medium-ground pork
1-1/4 teaspoons salt
1 teaspoon freshly ground black pepper
1/4 cup full-bodied brandy
2 tablespoons chopped fresh oregano, marjoram, or thyme leaves, or a mixture of chopped fresh herbs
1/4 cup chopped fresh parsley leaves
1 egg, beaten
1/4 pound thinly sliced prosciutto
3 small hard-boiled eggs (see p. 35)
2 large red bell peppers, roasted, peeled, cored, and seeded (see p. 10), or 3/4 cup packed whole roasted red bell peppers from a jar, preferably the fire-roasted ones from Spain
About 16 (2 ounces) pimiento-stuffed green Spanish olives
1/2 teaspoon dried oregano

To debone the chicken: You may prevail upon your butcher to debone the chicken for you (ask him to split the chicken up the back before deboning, and not to pierce the skin on the breast). Or you can do it yourself: First cut through the backbone along both sides and remove it. Lay chicken out flat and, with a sharp boning knife, follow along the bones, pushing meat down and away from bone. Be careful not to pierce the skin. Work on legs by pushing the bone up. Cut wings off at second joint and tuck cut skin into the meat.

To prepare the stuffing: In a medium skillet, heat 2 tablespoons oil and cook garlic with onion until soft, about 10 minutes. Chop chicken liver and add it to skillet together with ground pork, 1/2 teaspoon salt, and 1/4 teaspoon pepper. Cook, stirring, for 2 minutes. Add brandy and, when hot, flambé (see p. 12); continue cooking until dry. Stir in herbs. Transfer to a bowl and, when cool, add beaten egg.

To stuff the chicken: Preheat oven to 350° F. Place chicken, skin side down, on a cutting board; tuck in meat from legs and wings, spreading it over any bare skin to form a layer of meat as even and rectangular as possible. (If necessary, cover meat with waxed paper and pound to shape it.) Sprinkle chicken with 1/4 teaspoon *each* salt and pepper.

Spread stuffing over chicken and cover it with sliced prosciutto. Arrange the 3 hard-boiled eggs along center of bird, half of peppers flat on each side of eggs, and 2 rows of olives alongside between eggs and peppers. Fold in the ends of the chicken and, beginning at one of the long sides, roll meats tightly around the eggs, trying to neatly enclose the filling. With a long thread, sew closed with string, starting at the middle. (Filling will shift somewhat; don't worry, it will come out fine.)

Shape chicken roll with your hands so it has a nicely oval form. Rub roll with dried oregano and remaining 1/2 teaspoon *each* salt and pepper, and baste it with about 2 tablespoons oil. Place chicken in a roasting pan, seam side down, and bake in the 350° F oven for 1 hour, basting it several times with fat from the pan.

Let chicken cool at least 15 minutes and preferably until it is room temperature, then cover and chill for 6 hours or overnight.

Remove strings from around the galantine and slice thinly onto a serving platter. Serve at room temperature.

Wine Recommendation: Serve with a young red like a Merlot, Zinfandel or Gamay, or an oak-aged white wine.

Chicken in a Samfaina Sauce of Mediterranean Vegetables

Pollastre amb Samfaina

Serves four to six.

Samfaina is one of the most traditional Catalan dishes or sauces. A similar version is found in Provence as rata- touille, *a heritage of the centuries that Provence was linked to Catalunya and Aragón. Slowly simmered* samfaina *marries the deep flavors of peppers, eggplant, and zucchini with those of tomatoes and onions. In the rest of Spain (and especially La Mancha), you can also find a similar mélange of vegetables called* pisto.

This chicken stew is a nurturing, home-style recipe Rosalia cooked in my childhood. And today, it is one of my standbys at home, for it is healthful and easy to make—plus it gets better after one or two days in the fridge.

Also, as with most country-style dishes, you don't need to worry too much about precise measurements or timing. Serve it with freshly made Peasant Bread (p. 118) to soak up the sauce.

One 4- to 5-pound chicken, cut into 6 or 8 serving pieces
1-1/4 teaspoons salt
1/2 teaspoon freshly ground black pepper
2 or 3 tablespoons olive oil
1 large onion, sliced
3 large garlic cloves, minced
4 large tomatoes (2 pounds), peeled, seeded, and chopped
1/2 cup dry white wine
1/2 cup full-bodied brandy
1/3 pound prosciutto or smoked ham, in one slice, cut into 1/4-inch dice

1 large red bell pepper, seeded and cut into 1/2-inch dice
1 pound eggplant (preferably the long, thin Japanese variety), unpeeled, cut into 1/2-inch dice
3/4 pound small zucchini, sliced
1/2 tablespoon chopped fresh rosemary leaves
2 tablespoons chopped fresh oregano, thyme, or marjoram leaves (or 3/4 tablespoon dried)
1 bay leaf
12 pitted flavorful black olives such as Italian-style dried oil-cured or Kalamata, halved

Pat chicken dry and season with 1/4 teaspoon *each* salt and pepper. Heat oil in a large lidded flameproof casserole and brown chicken over medium heat; be careful not to overcook breast. Remove from casserole and set aside.

Drain off most of the fat, leaving just 1 or 2 tablespoons. Add onion and garlic; cook over low heat for 5 to 10 minutes, or until soft. Add tomatoes, increase heat, and cook another 5 to 10 minutes. Add wine and cook until dry. Add brandy and, when hot, flambé (see p. 12). Cook, stirring, for 3 to 5 minutes or until dry. Add remaining ingredients, including remaining teaspoon salt and 1/4 teaspoon pepper. Return chicken to casserole, mixing with vegetables. Reduce heat to low and simmer slowly for 30 minutes, covered. Taste for seasoning. Remove bay leaf. Serve warm, with good crusty bread to dip in the sauce.

Wine Recommendation: Serve this classic Catalan dish with a medium-bodied dry red wine, such as a young Merlot or Tempranillo; or an older Pinot Noir–Tempranillo, or a Cabernet Sauvignon–Tempranillo blend.

Braised Game Hens in a Sweet and Sour Sauce

Capons a l'Agredolç

Serves eight.

The taste for sweet and sour in Mediterranean countries is a legacy from the Arabs, who lived there for centuries. In this dish the marinade of wine, sherry vinegar, and fresh herbs enhances the flavor of a mild bird such as Cornish game hen. Capons are used in Spain, but Cornish game hens are easier to find here and work just as well. And the whole garlic cloves, sweet and succulent, are a treat all on their own! Serve this dish with crusty fresh bread; the Wreath Bread with Rosemary, Raisins, and Pine Nuts (p. 120) goes especially well. I prefer to have no other accompaniment, but I find a green salad with a light vinaigrette dressing is perfect afterwards.

Start preparation 9 to 10 hours ahead or the day before, by marinating hens.

4 Cornish game hens, about 1-1/2 pounds each

For the marinade:
8 large garlic cloves, peeled
2 bay leaves
2 tablespoons chopped fresh thyme, oregano, or marjoram leaves
2 tablespoons chopped fresh mint leaves
8 cloves
1/2 cup sherry wine vinegar
1 cup dry white wine

For cooking the hens:
3 tablespoons olive oil
2 large onions, thinly sliced
1 teaspoon salt
1/2 teaspoon freshly ground black pepper
1 cup Chicken Stock (p. 18)
1/2 cup sugar
1/2 cup full-bodied brandy

Optional, as a garnish:
A few fresh mint, thyme, oregano, or marjoram sprigs

Wash and pat hens dry; remove innards and cut off wing tips. With a skewer, poke holes all over each hen. Tie legs together with string.

To prepare the marinade: Mix marinade ingredients in a non-reactive bowl; add hens, tossing them to coat. Cover and refrigerate for at least 8 hours. During this period, turn hens in the marinade several times.

Remove hens from the refrigerator 2 hours before cooking. Set aside.

To cook the hens: In a flameproof lidded casserole, large enough to hold all the hens, heat oil and sauté onions slowly for about 45 minutes, or until golden brown and almost caramelized; stir often, especially toward the end. Add hens to casserole and sprinkle with salt and pepper; pour marinade and stock over hens. Bring to a boil and immediately reduce heat to low; cover hens tightly with a double layer of aluminum foil, place lid on casserole, and simmer gently for 30 minutes.

Preheat oven to 400° F. Remove hens from casserole, reserving stock; brush off onions that cling to them and place hens in a baking pan. Brush them with olive oil and bake uncovered in the 400° F oven for 15 to 20 minutes, or until done.

Meanwhile, discard bay leaves and defat stock. In a small saucepan, caramelize (see p. 13) sugar until it turns golden brown. Pour caramelized sugar into casserole; it will hiss and solidify, but don't worry—it will soon melt. Cook sauce over high heat until reduced to about 2 cups.

To assemble the dish: When hens are baked, cut them in half, place them on a serving platter, and keep warm. Pour off fat from baking pan, deglaze (see p. 13) with brandy, and add this glaze to the sauce.

Pour sauce with onions over and around hens, and place 1 garlic clove on each plate. Garnish with optional fresh herbs.

Wine Recommendation: Serve with an oak-aged Pinot Noir, a Pinot Noir–Tempranillo blend, or a *reserva* Tempranillo from Catalunya, Rioja, or Ribera del Duero.

Pheasant with Grapes and Walnuts

Faisà amb Raïm i Nous

Serves eight.

This is a very special recipe from the best cook in the family, my Aunt Oriola. Pheasant is just as much a delicacy in Spain as it is here—except there we can get the true wild birds, which are always much tastier than the domesticated variety. I have also tried this dish, just as successfully, with Cornish game hens.

2 large (about 2-1/2 pounds each) pheasants, or 4 Cornish game hens
1 teaspoon salt
1/4 teaspoon freshly ground black pepper
3 tablespoons butter
1 tablespoon olive oil
1/2 cup fresh orange juice
1 cup semi-dry, fruity white wine, such as Muscat or Riesling
1 cup Chicken Stock (p. 18)
1/2 cup tea, brewed with 1 teaspoon black tea leaves
Pinch of cayenne
1 cup (3-1/2 ounces) walnut halves
1 pound seedless green or red grapes, or a mixture
1/4 cup sugar

Truss birds and pat them dry. Sprinkle about 1/4 teaspoon *each* salt and pepper over them. In a large flameproof casserole, heat 1 tablespoon *each* butter and olive oil. Sauté birds over medium-high heat until golden on all sides (cut up necks and brown them, too—they will add flavor to the sauce later); remove from pan and set aside. Pour off fat and stir in orange juice, wine, stock, and tea; bring to a boil, scraping with a spatula to loosen browned bits stuck to bottom. Add birds and necks; season with cayenne and remaining 3/4 teaspoon salt. Reduce heat to low, cover birds tightly with a double layer of aluminum foil, place lid on top, and simmer for 40 minutes, or until they are cooked through.

Remove birds and quarter them, discarding backbone (if using game hens, halve them). Keep warm. Discard necks, bring liquid to a boil, and cook rapidly until reduced to 1 or 1-1/2 cups. Taste for seasoning.

In a medium skillet, heat remaining 2 tablespoons butter and sauté walnuts and grapes for about 1 minute, stirring, over medium-high heat. Sprinkle with sugar, reduce heat to medium, and continue to cook, stirring, for 4 to 5 minutes. Stir walnuts and grapes, with their syrup, into sauce. Cook for another minute.

Arrange birds on a serving platter, with walnuts and grapes on top. Pour some sauce over and pass rest around in a sauceboat.

Wine Recommendation: Serve with the same wine used in its preparation—a fragrant Muscat, Riesling, or Muscat-Gewürztraminer blend; or else an elegant, medium-bodied well-aged red.

Quail with Apples and Raisins

Guatlla amb Pomes

Serves four.

Cooking poultry or meats with fruit is characteristic of Catalan cuisine—especially when nuts or raisins are included, as in this recipe and the former one. Catalans have a fondness for quail and eat it often, sometimes even as a tapa. *This is a more refined recipe, sure to make an impression on your guests.*

1/4 pound raisins, preferably a mix of dark and golden
1/2 cup full-bodied brandy
8 quail, trussed
3/4 teaspoon salt
1/2 teaspoon freshly ground black pepper
2 tablespoons olive oil
1 medium carrot, finely chopped
1 large onion, finely chopped
1 large leek, finely chopped, with about one-third of green part
1 small tender celery stalk, with leaves, finely chopped
3 tablespoons butter
2 pounds tart apples (Gravenstein, Pippin, or Granny Smith), peeled and cut in wedges
1/4 cup sugar
1 cup Chicken Stock (p. 18)
1 cup dry white wine

Soak raisins in brandy for at least 30 minutes.

Pat quail dry and season with 1/4 teaspoon *each* salt and pepper. In a large flameproof casserole, heat olive oil and quickly brown quail over medium-high heat. Remove from pan and set aside. Add carrot, onion, leek, and celery to the pan; scrape bottom with a spatula to release browned particles and cook over low heat for 20 minutes.

Meanwhile, heat butter in a medium skillet and sauté apple wedges over medium heat for 12 minutes, stirring. Add sugar, increase heat to medium-high, and cook for about 5 minutes, turning apples until they caramelize. Add raisins with brandy and when hot, flambé (see p. 12). Cook, shaking pan, for 3 to 5 minutes, or until dry. Set aside.

Add stock and wine to casserole, and season with remaining 1/2 teaspoon salt and 1/4 teaspoon pepper. Bring to a boil, add quail, turn heat down to low, cover, and simmer for 15 minutes. Transfer quail to a serving platter, arrange raisins and apples around them, and keep warm. Strain sauce in casserole through a fine sieve into skillet where apples were cooked. Increase heat to high and cook, stirring, until reduced to about 1 cup. Pour sauce over quail and serve warm.

Wine Recommendation: A fragrant, medium-dry white such as Muscat or a Muscat-Gewürztraminer blend; or a fine, mature, oak-aged Pinot Noir.

Braised Duck with Figs in an Orange Sherry Sauce

Ànec amb Figues

Serves four.

Some of the tastiest ducks I've ever eaten have come from L'Empordà, the bountiful region in northeast Catalunya, where ducks are often cooked with pears, apples, or other fruits. Agut d'Avignon, an outstanding restaurant on a narrow alley in Barcelona's Gothic quarter, features many classic specialties of L'Empordà, among them a delicious duck with figs, which inspired this recipe. I have tried this dish with both fresh and dried figs and actually favor the richer taste of the dried—just like Agut does.

Start preparation 3 hours ahead, by soaking dried figs in water.

8 ounces dried figs, stemmed
1 large (4- to 5-pound) duck, quartered (reserve liver, fat, neck and back bones; see Note, below)
1/2 teaspoon salt
1/2 teaspoon freshly ground black pepper
1 cup dry Spanish sherry, preferably *amontillado* or a dry *oloroso*
1 large orange
2 tablespoons finest-quality brandy
Pinch of ground cinnamon
1 cup Veal Stock (p. 18)

Note: You will need the duck's liver for this recipe; if there isn't one, substitute 3 chicken livers.

Cover figs with 1 cup boiling water and soak for 2 hours. Stem figs and reserve figs and water.

To cook the duck: Remove any loose skin and fat from duck quarters, neck, and backbones. Cut these in small pieces, and cut off wing tips. Pat duck quarters dry with paper towels and season with 1/4 teaspoon *each* salt and pepper. In a large, lidded flameproof casserole, heat reserved duck fat and, over medium-high heat, brown duck quarters. In the same fat, sauté duck pieces—wing tips, neck, and backbones—until they are very brown, turning them around. Set aside duck quarters and duck pieces. Discard browned skin, pour off fat, and deglaze (see p. 13) with 1/2 cup sherry. Add duck quarters, skin side down, cover them tightly with a double layer of aluminum foil, and place lid on top. Braise for 45 minutes over low heat, so duck will exude a lot of its fat.

To prepare the sauce: Meanwhile, simmer liver in 1/4 to 1/2 cup water reserved from soaking figs—just enough to cover—for 15 minutes. Drain; reserve liquid. In a blender or food processor, purée drained liver with 4 figs; add juice and minced zest of orange (see p. 10), brandy, cinnamon, remaining 1/4 teaspoon *each* salt and pepper, and liquid from simmering livers. Reserve sauce.

To assemble the dish: Set duck quarters aside and defat casserole. Deglaze with remaining 1/2 cup sherry. Stir in reserved sauce, figs and water used to soak them, browned duck pieces and duck quarters. Pour veal stock over. Bring to a boil, reduce heat to low, cover tightly with a double layer of aluminum foil, place lid on top, and braise for 20 minutes.

Remove duck quarters and figs to a serving platter and keep warm. Discard brown duck pieces. Reduce sauce, if necessary, to desired consistency. Taste for seasoning. Pour some sauce over duck and pass remaining sauce in a sauceboat.

Wine Recommendation: Serve with a mature Pinot Noir–Tempranillo or a Cabernet–Tempranillo blend, or an oak-aged *reserva* Tempranillo from Catalunya, Rioja, or Ribera del Duero.

Braised Partridge or Game Hens with Cabbage Croquettes, Empordà Style

Perdiu amb Farcellets de Col a L'Empordanesa

Serves eight.

Partridge is prepared in many different ways all over Catalunya, but partridge with cabbage is a classic that can be traced back to the fifteenth century. The dish is a classic from the bountiful Empordà region north of Barcelona, and this recipe is based on a very old one given to me by my friend, the gastronomic historian Manuel Martínez-Llopis.

While partridge is always used in Catalunya for this dish because it is a very popular game bird there, I have also made it with Cornish game hens and I like it just as much. Since they are larger than partridges, you will need only 4 Cornish game hens.

1 large head green cabbage, preferably Savoy, quartered and cored
2 cups Chicken Stock (p. 18)

For the birds:
8 partridges, or 4 Cornish game hens
1/2 pound pancetta, sliced medium thick (8 slices)
Salt, pepper, and nutmeg for seasoning birds
2 tablespoons olive oil
4 large garlic cloves, finely chopped
1 medium onion, minced
1/4 cup finely chopped shallots

1 pound carrots, peeled and finely chopped
1 tablespoon *each* chopped fresh oregano leaves and thyme leaves (or other fresh herbs)
4 whole cloves
1-1/2 cups medium-bodied dry red wine
1/4 cup full-bodied Spanish brandy

For the *farcellets*:
Cooked cabbage leaves
2 eggs, beaten
Flour for coating *farcellets*
Abundant olive oil for frying

Place cabbage in a medium pot and add stock; bring to a boil, reduce heat to low, cover, and cook for 20 minutes. Drain cabbage on a strainer over a saucepan and set aside cabbage and stock.

To cook the birds: Pat birds dry and truss them. Loosen skin covering their breasts and slide 1/2 slice pancetta (1 for game hens) under skin of each bird. Cut remaining pancetta in small strips and reserve. Sprinkle salt, pepper, and a grating of nutmeg over each bird on all sides.

Heat oil in a large, lidded flameproof casserole. Add reserved pancetta strips and sauté over low heat for 5 minutes. Increase heat to medium-low and add garlic, onion, shallots, and carrots; sauté for 30 to 45 minutes, decreasing heat at end, until vegetables are very soft and golden. Add herbs, cloves, wine, and reserved chicken stock. Bring to a boil, place birds on top, and cover with cabbage leaves. Reduce heat to low, cover birds tightly with a double layer of aluminum foil, place lid on casserole, and simmer gently for 1 hour (30 minutes for game hens).

Preheat oven to 400° degrees F. Remove cabbage leaves from casserole, drain, and set aside. Remove birds from casserole, reserving stock and vegetables; brush off vegetables that cling to them and place birds in a baking pan. Brush them with olive oil and bake in the 400° F oven, uncovered, for 15 to 20 minutes, or until done.

Meanwhile, remove cloves from casserole, purée stock and vegetables in a blender or food processor, and return to casserole.

Transfer birds to a serving platter and keep warm (if using game hens, cut them in half). Deglaze (see p. 13) pan with brandy and add glaze to sauce.

To prepare the *farcellets*: While birds are baking in the oven, form cabbage leaves into 2-inch dumplings: Don't roll leaves, just press with the palms of your hands to shape them into tight balls. Put eggs and flour in separate bowls. Dip each ball first into eggs and then into flour to coat. Have a deep, heavy skillet ready with hot oil (340° F) to a depth of 1 inch and, over medium-high heat, sauté cabbage dumplings until golden. Drain on paper towels.

To assemble the dish: Ladle some sauce on each plate, place 1 partridge (or half a game hen) on top, and 1 or 2 *farcellets* on the side. Pass remaining sauce in a sauceboat.

Wine Recommendation: Serve with a mature red wine: a fine oak-aged Cabernet, a *reserva* Tempranillo from Rioja or Penedès, or an elegant old Pinot Noir.

Rabbit in an Herb and Garlic Sauce

Conill a l'All

Serves eight.

Rabbit is one of my favorite meats, and in Catalunya it is a typical offering at country-style restaurants, often simply grilled over charcoal and served with an allioli *sauce. I have the fondest memories of summer evenings spent with friends laughing, drinking wine, and stuffing ourselves with this down-to-earth dish. You will relish this recipe if you like rabbit and garlic. And despite the generous amount of garlic used, you won't find it at all overpowering—just very flavorful.*

5 or 6 tablespoons olive oil
2 large heads garlic (about 40 cloves), peeled and thinly sliced lengthwise
2 rabbits, about 2-1/2 pounds each, quartered
1 teaspoon salt
1/2 teaspoon freshly ground black pepper

1/4 cup full-bodied brandy
1/2 cup dry white wine
1 cup Chicken Stock (p. 18)
1 tablespoon chopped fresh rosemary leaves
1 tablespoon chopped fresh thyme leaves, or 1 teaspoon dried
1 bay leaf

In a large, lidded flameproof casserole, heat oil and sauté garlic over medium heat until golden, being careful not to burn it. With a slotted spoon, remove garlic and drain, spreading slices on paper towels; discard any burnt pieces. Reserve about 1/4 cup for garnish.

Pat rabbit pieces dry and season with 1/2 teaspoon salt and 1/4 teaspoon pepper. Brown in same oil in casserole, over medium-high heat. Set rabbit aside. Add brandy and deglaze (see p. 13). Add white wine, stock, rosemary, thyme, bay leaf, remaining 1/2 teaspoon salt and 1/4 teaspoon pepper, and garlic slices. Bring to a boil and return rabbit to casserole, placing larger pieces on bottom. Reduce heat to low, cover rabbit tightly with a double layer of aluminum foil, place lid on top and simmer for 30 minutes or until meat is tender.

Transfer rabbit and garlic to a serving plate and keep warm. Discard bay leaf. Increase heat to high and cook sauce until reduced to 1 or 1-1/2 cups. Taste for seasoning, pour sauce over rabbit, and sprinkle reserved garlic on top.

Wine Recommendation: Serve with a full-bodied Mediterranean red wine, such as Garnacha-Cariñena blend from Catalunya, a Garnacha blend from southern Rhône, or a mature California Zinfandel.

Roast Turkey Stuffed with Dried Fruits, Nuts, and Sausage

Gall Dindi Farcit a la Catalana

Serves eight, with leftovers.

We don't eat turkey very often in Spain, but in Catalunya it is traditional at Christmas. At home we always make it using this recipe, a classic Catalan preparation that is quite unusual in this country. I often thought it is so delicious we should eat it other times of the year—and all by itself. At Christmas, you see, the turkey comes after the substantial Grandmother's Pot of Meats, Sausages, and Vegetables (p. 104). And by that time I'm so full I am never really able to appreciate it! There is a consolation, though: the traditional and utterly irresistible rice made the next day with all the turkey leftovers, called arròs de Sant Esteve *(Saint Stephen's rice), because his feast day is December 26.*

Before turkey arrived from the New World in the sixteenth century, this dish was prepared with a rooster (gall in Catalan), a tradition documented as early as the thirteenth century. Hence turkey became known as gall dindi *in Catalan, the last word a contraction meaning "from the Indies."*

Start preparation about 7 hours in advance.

One 10- to 12-pound turkey (reserve neck, liver, and giblets)

For the stock:
1 large onion, chopped
2 medium unpeeled carrots, chopped
1 small celery stalk, chopped
3 parsley sprigs
2 bay leaves
1 fresh thyme sprig, or a pinch of dried thyme
6 cups Chicken Stock (p. 18), preferably, or water

For the stuffing:
3/4 pound pitted prunes
1/2 pound dried apricots
1/2 cup dark raisins
1/4 cup olive oil
1-1/2 pounds mild Italian sausage, cut in 1/2-inch slices
1-1/2 cups pine nuts, toasted until golden (see p. 11)
1 pound Pippin or Granny Smith apples (2 large), peeled and cut into 3/4-inch dice
1 teaspoon salt
1/2 teaspoon freshly ground black pepper

For the turkey and its sauce:
2 teaspoons salt
1 teaspoon freshly ground black pepper
1/2 cup full-bodied brandy

To prepare the stock: Combine neck, liver, and giblets from turkey in a large pot with all stock ingredients. Bring to a boil, immediately reduce heat to very low, and cook, partially covered, for 2 hours. Strain stock and reserve. Discard neck and innards.

To prepare the stuffing: While stock is cooking, put prunes, apricots, and raisins in a bowl and cover with boiling water. Soak them for about 2 hours. Drain and reserve. Discard water.

Heat oil in a large skillet and, over low heat, sauté sausage until cooked. Add pine nuts, prunes, apricots, raisins, and apples; cook, stirring, for about 5 minutes. Stir in salt and pepper. Remove stuffing to a bowl. Pour in 1/2 cup of stock and deglaze pan (see p. 13). Stir this glaze into stuffing in bowl.

To cook the turkey: Preheat oven to 350° F. Season inside of turkey with 1 teaspoon salt and 1/2 teaspoon pepper. Stuff it with fruits, nuts, and sausage filling. Truss.

Place turkey, breast side up, in a baking pan without a rack. Pour 1 cup reserved stock over turkey and bake in the 350° F oven for 2 or 2-1/2 hours, or until the internal temperature of the meat reaches 165° F on a meat thermometer. Baste with stock from time to time, adding more as needed (you may end up using it all, especially if you have an electric oven).

To prepare the sauce: Remove turkey to a cutting board and pour pan juices into a saucepan. Add brandy to roasting pan and deglaze it, scraping sides with a wooden spatula to release any bits stuck to the pan.

Pour this glaze into saucepan with turkey juices, and add any remaining stock that was not used for basting. Reduce to desired sauce consistency, if necessary—2 or 3 cups. Season with remaining teaspoon salt and 1/2 teaspoon pepper, or to taste. Strain sauce and pass in a sauceboat.

Wine Recommendation: Serve with a flavorful oak-aged Chardonnay or an elegant medium-bodied red (Tempranillo, Pinot Noir, Merlot), preferably a mature one.

PORK, LAMB, VEAL, AND BEEF
PORC, XAI, VEDELLA, I VACA

Catalans not only cook poultry and game with peaches or grapes, but they also like to combine meats with fruit. In this chapter, you'll find recipes for whole apples or peaches filled with a savory meat stuffing and served as a main course. Pork and lamb, both Catalan specialties, may turn up with a subtly flavored stuffing, too. And while we may not grill as much as Californians, we do quite a bit of cooking outdoors, usually over an open fire. One of the best examples of a festive outdoor meal is Grilled Leg of Lamb and Mediterranean Vegetables with Romesco Sauce (p. 88). Or it might be as simple as a mixed grill of chops, chicken, and sausages. And for a buffet dinner, one of my favorite recipes is the Braised Veal with Small Caramelized Pears in a Pear Brandy Sauce (p. 89).

Veal Sweetbreads in a Honey and Sherry Sauce

Pedrerets a la Salsa de Mel i Xerès

Serves four to six.

Sweet and sour sauces like this one, flavored with honey and sherry vinegar, are characteristic of the south of Spain, where the Arab presence was longest. But the Arabs actually had a great influence on cooking all over the Mediterranean. In this recipe from Toya Roqué, the owner of Azulete restaurant in Barcelona, the balance of sweet to sour is just right. And it goes especially well with Rice with Saffron Threads (p. 96).

Start preparation 2-1/2 hours in advance, by soaking sweetbreads in water.

For the sweetbreads:
2-1/2 pounds fresh veal or lamb sweetbreads (see *Note,* below)
1 tablespoon fresh lemon juice
2 tablespoons butter
2 tablespoons olive oil
1/2 teaspoon salt
1/2 teaspoon freshly ground black pepper

For the sauce:
2-1/2 tablespoons sherry wine vinegar, or to taste
1/4 cup *fino* sherry, or another flavorful dry Spanish sherry
1/3 cup finely chopped shallots
1/3 cup finely chopped onions
2 cups Veal Stock (p. 18)
1 tablespoon honey

Note: Lamb sweetbreads are delicious if they can be found fresh. I have made this dish with both lamb and veal, and it comes out just as well with either; most important is that the sweetbreads be fresh. Lamb sweetbreads are smaller and firmer than veal.

To prepare the sweetbreads follow instructions on p. 60.

To cook the sweetbreads: In a skillet that will accommodate all sweetbreads in a single layer, heat butter and oil. When butter is melted and oil is hot, add sweetbreads. Sprinkle with salt and pepper. Cook over medium-high heat, without stirring, for about 3 minutes. Turn them and cook quickly until golden, about 7 more minutes. Set sweetbreads aside.

To prepare the sauce: Deglaze skillet (see p. 13) with vinegar and sherry. Reduce heat to low and add shallots and onions; sauté for about 5 minutes, until soft. Add veal stock and cook over high heat until reduced to about 1-1/2 cups. Stir in the honey and taste for seasoning.

To assemble the dish: Return sweetbreads to the pan and turn to coat with the sauce. Serve immediately.

Wine Recommendation: Serve with an oak-aged Chardonnay or a fine, mature medium-bodied red such as a Pinot Noir or a Pinot Noir–Tempranillo blend.

Baked Apples Stuffed with Pork, Ham, and Pine Nuts

Pomes Farcides al Forn

Serves six.

This is a favorite recipe from my late friend Ramón Cabau, the flamboyant genius of Catalan cooking who died in the late eighties. His great Barcelona restaurant, Agut d'Avignon, is still one of the best in the city and features most of his original dishes. These savory stuffed apples, with their filling of pork, ham, and pine nuts, are typical of Girona, the region north of Barcelona that is home to the famed Costa Brava.

6 large thick-skinned baking apples, such as Rome Beauties or Pippins (about 1/2 pound each)
2 tablespoons olive oil
1/4 cup (1.5 ounces) pine nuts
1 medium onion, minced
3 large garlic cloves, minced
3/4 pound boneless lean baked ham, chopped finely by hand
3/4 pound medium-ground pork
1/2 cup homemade bread crumbs (see p. 10)
1 teaspoon salt
1/2 teaspoon freshly ground black pepper
2 eggs
1 cup dry white wine
2 cups Veal Stock (p. 18), or more as needed
4 tablespoons sugar

With the stem side down, cut top quarter off each apple. With a small knife or melon-ball scoop, remove and discard seeds and hard core, without going all the way through to bottom of apple. With a knife, enlarge opening, shaping it like a funnel; chop apple pieces and set aside.

Preheat oven to 350° F. Heat oil in a large skillet and sauté pine nuts until lightly golden. Add onion and garlic, and sauté over low heat until soft, 10 to 15 minutes. Add chopped apple pieces; stir and cook until tender, about 10 to 15 minutes. Off heat, add ham, pork, bread crumbs, salt, and pepper; stir and set aside. Beat eggs lightly in a large bowl; add meat mixture and use your hands to distribute egg evenly throughout.

Pack stuffing into apples, mounding it on top; they should look like giant mushrooms. The stuffing will shrink during baking, so don't worry if they look too big; use up all the stuffing. Place apples in an ungreased baking dish, pour wine around them, and bake in the 350° F oven for 1-1/4 to 1-1/2 hours. (Baking time will depend on the size and kind of apples; a 1/2-pound Rome or Pippin apple will take about 1-1/2 hours.) Test apples with a fork, knife, or needle; they should feel soft and pierce easily without resistance. While baking, there should always be a little liquid in the pan; check periodically and add stock if needed, to make sure juices don't burn (especially if you have an electric oven).

Remove apples to a serving platter. Add veal stock to baking dish. Reduce over high heat to desired consistency; it should be a rather light sauce. Meanwhile, caramelize sugar (see p. 13) until it turns an amber color; pour over apples. Serve apples surrounded with the sauce.

Wine Recommendation: Serve with a fairly young, oak-aged, medium-bodied red wine, such as a Tempranillo from Rioja, Catalunya, or Ribera del Duero.

Braised Peaches with a Pork and Almond Filling in a Brandy and Muscat Sauce

Préssecs Farcits

Serves six.

At the height of summer, when peaches are at their best, my mother served this intriguing dish of braised peaches with a meat filling. The idea of serving fruit as a main course rather than a dessert may be new to Americans, but it is very old in Catalunya.

6 large, firm fresh peaches (about 1/2 pound each), unpeeled

For the filling:
1/3 cup whole almonds, toasted (see p. 11)
1/4 pound medium-ground pork
1/4 cup homemade bread crumbs (see p. 10)
1 egg, beaten
1/2 teaspoon salt
1/4 teaspoon freshly ground black pepper
1/8 teaspoon ground cinnamon

For the peaches:
2 tablespoons olive oil
2 tablespoons butter
1 to 2 tablespoons flour
1/4 cup full-bodied brandy
1/4 cup sweet muscat wine
5 whole cloves
2 cups Veal Stock (p. 18)
Salt to taste, if necessary

With the help of a knife and melon-ball scoop, carefully remove pits from whole peaches without cutting them in half. Reserve pits.

To prepare the filling: Grind almonds finely in a food processor. Mix them in a medium bowl with all filling ingredients, and stuff peaches with mixture.

To cook the peaches: Heat oil and butter in a large skillet. Put flour on a dish and dip the stuffed side of each peach into flour; sauté peaches over medium heat, stuffing side down, until golden.

Transfer peaches to a large, lidded flameproof casserole, stuffed side up. Remove fat from skillet; deglaze with brandy (see p. 13) and pour into casserole. Add muscat wine, cloves, and veal stock. Bring liquid to a boil, reduce heat to medium, add reserved pits, and simmer peaches, partially covered, for 35 to 40 minutes.

Arrange peaches on a platter, stuffing side up, and keep warm. Discard pits. Reduce sauce, if necessary, to 3/4 or 1 cup. Taste for seasoning. Pour sauce over peaches and serve immediately.

Wine Recommendation: Serve with an oak-aged Cabernet, or a Cabernet-Merlot or Cabernet-Tempranillo blend.

Braised Potatoes, Onions, and Artichokes with a Pork and Herb Stuffing

Verdures Farcides

Serves four.

I think of this old-style country dish as Catalan soul food. Perfect for damp winter days, the golden brown vegetables simmering in their sauce are a heartwarming sight. Rosalia made it at home as a first course, but I think the meat filling makes it substantial enough to serve as a main course for a lunch or light supper.

4 small white or yellow onions (about 1/4 pound each), peeled
4 red-skinned new potatoes, same size and weight as onions
4 medium artichokes (about 1/2 pound each)

For the stuffing:
2/3 cup homemade bread crumbs (see p. 10)
1/2 cup milk
3/4 pound medium-ground pork
1 tablespoon full-bodied brandy
1 egg
1 teaspoon finely chopped fresh thyme, oregano, or marjoram leaves
1 tablespoon finely chopped fresh parsley leaves
4 large garlic cloves, minced
1/2 teaspoon paprika
1/2 teaspoon salt
1/4 teaspoon freshly ground black pepper

To cook the vegetables:
1/4 cup olive oil
1 or 2 tablespoons flour
1/2 cup full-bodied brandy
3 cups Chicken Stock or Veal Stock (p. 18)
1/2 teaspoon salt
1/8 teaspoon freshly ground black pepper, or to taste

With a large melon baller, scoop out a medium hole from the upper part of the potatoes and onions. Cut a thin slice from the bottom so they sit flat. Cut off top third of artichokes; remove tough outer leaves and cut stems close to bottom. Scoop out some inner leaves and the furry choke, leaving a shell to fill.

To prepare the stuffing: In a medium bowl, soak bread in milk. Add remaining stuffing ingredients and mix well, mashing with a fork. Fill holes in potatoes, onions, and artichokes with stuffing, piling it on top.

To cook the vegetables: Heat oil in a large, flameproof lidded casserole. Spread flour on a dish. Dip vegetables, stuffing side down, in flour and, over medium heat, sauté them until stuffing is golden. Set vegetables aside.

Pour off fat from casserole and deglaze with brandy (see p. 13). Add stock and bring to a boil. Add vegetables, stuffing side up. Return to a boil, season with salt and pepper, reduce heat to low, cover, and simmer for 1 hour, or until vegetables are tender.

Transfer vegetables to a serving platter; keep warm. Over high heat, reduce sauce to about 1 cup. Taste for seasoning. Pour sauce over vegetables.

Wine Recommendation: Serve with a medium-bodied dry red, such as a young Tempranillo, Merlot, or Zinfandel.

Grilled Leg of Lamb and Mediterranean Vegetables with Romesco Sauce

Xai a la Brasa amb Escalivada i Romesco

Serves eight.

Spring is a great time for outdoor barbecues, and this festive meal is perfect for the occasion because both the marinated spring lamb and the vegetables are best when grilled over charcoal. I marinate the lamb for 3 days to give it even more flavor, but 2 also will do. And you can improvise the escalivada *with any combination of eggplant, pepper, potato, onion, or tomato. I accompany the dish with a romesco sauce, definitely my favorite of all the Catalan sauces. Any of the half a dozen* romesco *recipes in this book will go well here, but I like the Romesco Sauce for Grilled Seafood, Meats, and Vegetables (p. 114) best because it is simple and colorful. Be sure to make it a few hours ahead of time to allow the flavors to develop. Grill the vegetables first, and while you peel them, cook the lamb. Don't worry about the vegetables getting cold; they're delicious at room temperature.*

Start preparation 3 days ahead, by marinating lamb.

For the lamb marinade:
2 cups full-bodied dry red wine
1/2 cup sherry vinegar or red wine vinegar
1/4 cup olive oil
3 large garlic cloves, minced
1 medium onion, sliced
2 tablespoons chopped fresh rosemary leaves
1 tablespoon chopped fresh thyme, oregano, or marjoram leaves
2 teaspoons salt
1 teaspoon freshly ground black pepper
One 5- to 6-pound leg of lamb, boned and butterflied (3 to 3-1/2 pounds of meat)

For the *escalivada*:
About 2 tablespoons olive oil
2 pounds young, small eggplants (preferably the narrow Japanese variety, see p. 34) cut in half lengthwise
4 large red bell peppers, cut in quarters lengthwise, cored, and seeded
1/4 teaspoon salt, or to taste
1/4 teaspoon freshly ground black pepper, or to taste
1 tablespoon chopped fresh parsley leaves
1 recipe Romesco Sauce for Grilled Seafood, Meats, and Vegetables (p. 114)

To prepare the marinade: In a large non-reactive bowl, mix all ingredients for marinade and toss lamb in it. Cover and refrigerate for 3 days, turning lamb at least once each day.

To cook the lamb and the *escalivada*: Light a charcoal fire in a grill with a cover. Rub vegetable skins with about 1 tablespoon oil. Drain lamb and place on grill over red-hot coals; place vegetables skin side down around lamb. Grill lamb and vegetables for 25 to 30 minutes. Remove from grill to a plate and let rest for 10 minutes before serving.

While meat rests, peel eggplant and peppers. With your fingers, tear them into very thin strips and arrange on a serving platter. Season vegetables with salt and pepper, drizzle about 1 tablespoon oil over, and sprinkle with parsley. Serve with Romesco Sauce.

Wine Recommendation: Serve with a full-bodied red wine, which may be the same used in the marinade, such as an oak-aged Zinfandel, a Cariñena-Garnacha or Garnacha-Monastrell blend from Catalunya or southern Rhône, or a mature Tempranillo from Ribera del Duero.

Braised Veal with Caramelized Pears in a Pear Brandy Sauce

Vedella amb Peres

Serves six.

This is another of Rosalia's cherished recipes, a very Catalan dish of meat cooked with fruit. Here tender veal is stewed with small whole baking pears.

In this country, such small baking pears may be hard to find unless you shop at the local farmers' market or have your own pear tree, but any type of pear can be substituted. I have used Winter Nellis, small Bosc, or even Bartlett pears successfully. I always cook and serve this dish in a shallow clay casserole.

6 small pears, peeled and cored, leaving stems intact, whole or halved
6 tablespoons pear brandy or full-bodied brandy
3 pounds boneless veal stew meat, cut into 1-1/2- to 2-inch pieces
3/4 teaspoon salt
3/4 teaspoon freshly ground black pepper
About 6 tablespoons olive oil
3 medium onions, minced
6 large garlic cloves, minced
1/2 cup (3 ounces) pine nuts
1/2 cup dry white wine
2 bay leaves
6 tablespoons sugar

Place pears in a large bowl and pour brandy over them, tossing gently. Cover and marinate at room temperature for at least 30 minutes.

Season veal with 1/4 teaspoon *each* salt and pepper. In a large, lidded, skillet, heat 4 tablespoons olive oil and, over medium-high heat, sauté veal briefly, in small batches, to sear in juices. Set veal aside. Add more oil to skillet if necessary and sauté two thirds of the chopped onions and garlic until soft, about 10 minutes. Add veal and its pan juices, cover, and cook over very low heat for 30 minutes. Season with remaining 1/2 teaspoon *each* salt and pepper.

Meanwhile, in a lidded, flameproof casserole large enough to hold the pears, sauté pine nuts in 2 tablespoons oil until golden. Remove with a slotted spoon and drain on paper towels. Add remaining onion and garlic and sauté over low heat until soft, about 10 minutes. Add pears, stem side up, with their marinade, wine, bay leaves, and pine nuts; stir gently, bring liquid to a boil, and turn heat to very low. Cover and simmer for 20 minutes. Push pears to the sides of the casserole and pour in veal with its sauce. Cover and simmer for another 30 minutes.

Remove veal and pears to a serving platter, mounding meat in the center with pears surrounding it. Discard bay leaves. Cover and keep warm. Over high heat, reduce sauce until thickened to desired consistency. Taste for seasoning. Pour over veal.

In a small pan, caramelize sugar (see p. 13) until it turns an amber color. Pour over pears. Serve immediately.

Wine Recommendation: Serve with an elegant oak-aged Pinot Noir, a Pinot Noir–Tempranillo blend, or a mature medium-bodied Zinfandel.

Flank Steak Roll with a Green Bean Omelet and Sausage Filling

*Tall Rodó Farcit
de Truita i Salsitxa*

Serves eight.

This recipe was one of my mother's summertime favorites, especially on Sundays when she knew we'd return from the beach for lunch as late as 4 or 5 P.M. The flank steak with its colorful stuffing is as good at room temperature as it is warm. For that reason it is perfect for buffet dinners and picnics—and it makes great leftovers! But I actually do prefer it warm, especially with the sauce. My mother accompanied it with mashed potatoes to soak up the delectable sauce (and fill up our ravenous stomachs).

For the omelet:
3 tablespoons olive oil
1 large onion, finely chopped
1 pound thin green beans, trimmed and cut into 3/4-inch lengths
5 eggs
1/2 teaspoon salt
1/4 teaspoon freshly ground black pepper

For the meat roll:
2 pounds flank steak, in one piece
1/2 teaspoon salt, or to taste
3/4 teaspoon freshly ground black pepper, or to taste
2 flavorful pork sausages, about 3 ounces each
3 tablespoons olive oil
1/4 cup full-bodied Spanish brandy
1 pound ripe tomatoes, unpeeled, chopped
1 large onion, sliced
1 cup dry white wine
2 bay leaves

To prepare the omelet: In a small skillet, heat 1 tablespoon oil and sauté onion until soft, about 10 minutes. Blanch green beans in boiling water for 4 to 5 minutes; drain. Beat eggs in a bowl with salt and pepper; mix in onion and beans. In an 8- or 10-inch nonstick skillet, heat remaining 2 tablespoons oil. When quite hot, pour in bean mixture and turn heat down to low. Cook, shaking skillet occasionally, until omelet is set on the bottom and halfway through, about 10 minutes. Cover pan with a plate and invert omelet onto it; slide omelet back into pan. Cook another 2 to 3 minutes, or until omelet is firm. Set aside.

To cook the meat roll: Butterfly steak by slicing it almost through horizontally so that it opens like a book to form about a 10-inch square. Sprinkle 1/4 teaspoon *each* salt and pepper over meat. Slide omelet onto it and arrange sausages on top, down the center. Roll up meat with omelet/sausage filling and tie at 1-inch intervals, sewing the ends.

In a large, lidded flameproof casserole, heat oil and, over medium-high heat, brown meat roll on all sides. Remove meat, add brandy, and deglaze (see p. 13). Stir in tomatoes and sliced onion, add wine, and bring to a boil. Add bay leaves, place meat on top, and turn heat down to low. Cover and cook for 2 hours, turning meat occasionally.

Remove meat to a cutting board and keep warm. Remove bay leaves from casserole, transfer remaining contents to a blender or food processor, and purée. Strain through a fine sieve back into casserole; cook over high heat until reduced to about 1-1/2 cups, and season with remaining 1/4 teaspoon salt and 1/2 teaspoon pepper, or to taste.

To serve, cut meat roll into 1/2-inch-thick slices; pour about 3 tablespoons sauce on each plate and place 1 or 2 slices on top.

Wine Recommendation: Serve with a fine oak-aged Cabernet or Merlot, or a mature Zinfandel.

Beef Tenderloin with Dried Figs, Apricots, and Prunes in a Cream Brandy Sauce

*Filet de Bou
amb Fruites Seques*

Serves six.

Here is a classically Catalan combination of meat and dried fruits, a simple yet inspired idea from Francesc Fortí's great restaurant, Racó d'en Binu. With its cream brandy sauce, it is worth every calorie and sure to win the admiration of your guests. I prefer to serve it without any vegetable or accompaniment, just by itself with the dried fruits; or at the most, with white rice or crusty fresh bread.

Start preparation 3 hours ahead, by soaking dried fruits in water.

6 dried figs (about 3 ounces)
18 dried apricots (about 3 ounces)
12 pitted prunes (about 3 ounces)
Six 6-ounce slices of beef tenderloin, each about 3/4 inch thick, cut from the center of the loin
1-1/2 tablespoons crushed green peppercorns
1-1/2 teaspoons salt
2 tablespoons butter
1/2 cup full-bodied brandy
1/2 cup heavy cream
1 cup Veal Stock (p. 18)

Place figs, apricots, and prunes in a saucepan and cover with boiling water. Let them soak for about 2 hours.

Meanwhile, cut away fat from sides of beef steaks and tie string around each piece to give it a round shape. Cover both sides of the steaks with peppercorns, and sprinkle them with 1 teaspoon salt. Let them sit, unrefrigerated, for an hour.

Remove fruits from soaking water and cut them into 1/4-inch slices. Over medium-high heat, reduce liquid in saucepan to 1/3 cup.

In a skillet large enough to hold all of the steaks, heat butter and, over medium-high heat, sauté them for 1 minute on each side. Add brandy and flambé (see p. 12). Set steaks aside on a serving platter, remove strings, and keep warm. Add fruits, reduced liquid in saucepan, cream and veal stock to the skillet. Increase heat and reduce sauce by one third, or to desired consistency. Add remaining 1/2 teaspoon salt or to taste. Pour sauce with fruits over steaks and serve immediately.

Wine Recommendation: Serve with a fine, mature oak-aged Cabernet or Zinfandel, or a *gran reserva* Tempranillo from Rioja or Ribera del Duero.

ACCOMPANIMENTS
ACOMPANYAMENTS

I n this section I have grouped together the dishes I make most often to accompany the main courses given so far. The first three recipes, Peppers and Zucchini Sautéed with Garlic (below) Charcoal-grilled Mediterranean Vegetables (p. 93), and Charcoal-grilled Catalan-style Leeks (p. 94) can be served as a first course as well. Of all the dishes in this chapter, the Potato and Onion Cake with Fresh Rosemary Leaves (p. 96) and the Glazed Onion Relish (p. 95) are the two I use the most. And do try the Rice with Saffron Threads (p. 97) and the Brown Rice with Pine Nuts and Raisins (p. 97). They may seem basic, but the results are so good you'll make them again and again.

Peppers and Zucchini Sautéed with Garlic

Pebrots i Carbaçons a l'All

Serves six as a first course, eight as an accompaniment.

This dish works as an accompaniment to many entrées, but it also can be served as a light first course or at a picnic—at room temperature in that case.

1/2 cup olive oil
15 large garlic cloves, minced (5 tablespoons)
2 large red bell peppers (about 1 pound), cored, seeded, and cut into strips
2 large yellow bell peppers (about 1 pound), cored, seeded, and cut into strips
1 large green bell pepper (about 1/2 pound), cored, seeded, and cut into strips
1 teaspoon salt

3/4 teaspoon freshly ground black pepper
3 medium zucchini (about 1 pound), trimmed and sliced about 1/4 inch thick

Optional, if served at room temperature:
2 tablespoons extra virgin olive oil
2 tablespoons balsamic vinegar
1 tablespoon finely chopped fresh parsley leaves

Heat 1/4 cup oil in a large skillet and, over medium heat, sauté 3 tablespoons garlic until golden brown, stirring, being careful not to burn it. Stir in peppers, 1/2 teaspoon salt, and 1/4 teaspoon pepper; reduce heat to medium-low and cook, stirring occasionally, until peppers are soft, about 15 minutes.

Meanwhile, heat remaining 1/4 cup oil in another large skillet and sauté remaining 2 tablespoons garlic until it starts to turn golden. Add zucchini slices in one layer (you will probably need to make 2 batches);

sprinkle remaining 1/2 teaspoon *each* salt and pepper (1/4 teaspoon on each batch), and cook over medium heat until golden on bottom. Turn each slice with tongs and cook until the other side is golden. Remove with tongs and drain on paper towels.

Arrange vegetables on a plate: zucchini in center, surrounded by peppers. If served cold as a first course, drizzle olive oil and vinegar over, and sprinkle zucchini with parsley.

Charcoal-grilled Mediterranean Vegetables

Escalivada

Serves four to six.

Escalivar is the Catalan word meaning "to cook over hot embers." Vegetables rubbed with olive oil and grilled over charcoal (or baked) are called escalivada *and are very popular in summertime, the peak season for sweet red peppers, vine-ripened tomatoes, and flavorful narrow eggplants (similar to the Japanese eggplants available here).* Escalivada *can be made with just eggplant and peppers, or with any or all of the vegetables in this recipe. Artfully arranged on a platter, it is a perfect accompaniment for grilled meats or fish, roasts, and barbecued chicken. Grilled Leg of Lamb with Escalivada and Romesco (p. 88) makes a festive outdoor meal. (If you're not planning to grill, you can also bake the vegetables in a hot oven, although the flavors are particularly wonderful when cooked over charcoal.)* Escalivada *can also be served as an appetizer or first course. Toast thin slices of Peasant Bread (p. 118), top with a little* escalivada, *and you may garnish with an anchovy fillet.*

2 large tomatoes, halved crosswise
1 pound small eggplants, preferably the narrow Japanese variety (see p. 34)
2 large red bell peppers
2 large white onions, unpeeled
2 baking potatoes, halved lengthwise
About 4 tablespoons olive oil

1/2 teaspoon salt, or to taste
1/4 teaspoon freshly ground black pepper, or to taste

As a garnish:
2 tablespoons chopped fresh parsley leaves

Light a charcoal fire in a grill with a cover (or preheat oven to 350° F).

Rub all vegetables with about 2 tablespoons oil. Place them on the grill over red-hot coals (or on a baking sheet in the oven); tomatoes and potatoes should go cut side up. Grill (or bake) about 15 minutes for tomatoes, 45 minutes to 1 hour for eggplant and peppers, 1 hour for onions and potatoes; turn eggplant, peppers, and onions occasionally. Cooking time depends on size of vegetables and distance from coals.

Peel eggplants and peppers. With your fingers, tear them into very thin strips, discarding core. Peel onions and separate the layers. Arrange all vegetables on a large platter. Season with salt and pepper, drizzle about 2 tablespoons oil over, and sprinkle with parsley. Serve warm or at room temperature.

Charcoal-grilled Catalan-style Leeks

Ceballots

Serves six.

Springtime, when the tender young onions called ceballots *or* calçots *are harvested, is the occasion for a special feast in Valls, near Tarragona. About the size of leeks, the* ceballots *are bundled together and charred over the embers of fast-burning grapevine cuttings.*

In the old days, a grill was often improvised from iron bedsprings. Sunday parties called calçotadas *are organized around this very simple, seasonal delicacy. The idea is to peel away the charred skins, douse the grilled onions with a tangy* romesco *sauce—and feast away.*

Until someone decides to grow ceballots *here, I improvise with leeks, which I have found work almost as well. Of course, they taste better cooked on an outdoor charcoal grill, but they are also delicious cooked on an indoor grill or baked in the oven.*

3 bunches young leeks, trimmed of all but 2 or 3 inches of green part
About 1/2 cup olive oil

1/2 recipe Romesco Sauce for Grilled Seafood, Meats, and Vegetables (p. 114)

Cut leeks in half lengthwise down to within 1 inch from bottom, or root end. Rub them quite generously with olive oil and cook them (over a covered charcoal grill, on an indoor grill, or in a preheated 425° F oven) until they are very tender and golden. Depending on their size and cooking method, they may take from 30 to 60 minutes. Turn them over occasionally while cooking.

Serve leeks warm, with *romesco* sauce on the side.

Glazed Onion Relish

Confit de Cebes

Serves four to six.

I rely very often on this unbeatable on-ion relish to accompany roast meat or poultry. Served at room temperature, it is equally good with pâtés, cold meats, and sausages. The recipe comes from a delightful Barcelona restaurant that owner Mercedes Navarro named Roig Robí, after the ruby red color of fine red wine.

4 tablespoons butter
2 pounds onions, thinly sliced
1-1/2 cups (1/2 bottle, or 375 ml.) medium-bodied dry red wine
1/2 cup sherry wine vinegar or red wine vinegar
1/4 teaspoon salt, or to taste
2 tablespoons honey

Heat butter in a deep skillet. Add onions and cook over low heat, very slowly, until soft and golden; it should take about 45 minutes to 1 hour. Stir onions occasionally, especially toward the end. Add wine, vinegar, and salt; cook over medium heat until liquid evaporates. Add honey and cook slowly until mixture begins to caramelize, about 15 minutes. Taste for seasoning. Serve warm or at room temperature.

Sautéed Spinach with Pine Nuts and Raisins

Espinacs a la Catalana

Serves four.

Spinach sautéed with pine nuts and raisins couldn't be more Catalan. The idea is quite simple, yet ingenious and very tasty; you can also make this dish with Swiss chard. It is always a good accompaniment for pork or game.

4 small bunches spinach (about 3 pounds), washed and stemmed
2 tablespoons olive oil
1/2 cup (3 ounces) pine nuts
1/4 cup dark raisins or black currants
1/4 teaspoon salt, or to taste
1/4 teaspoon freshly ground black pepper, or to taste

Rinse spinach well and place in a large saucepan. Cook over medium heat, covered, with only the water that clings to leaves, just until wilted, about 10 minutes. Toss spinach with 2 spoons from time to time. Drain and squeeze dry. Chop coarsely.

Heat olive oil in a large skillet. Add pine nuts and raisins; sauté over medium-high heat until pine nuts are golden and raisins plump up, 3 or 4 minutes. Add spinach, salt, and pepper; gently toss until well mixed. Taste for seasoning. Serve warm.

Sorrel and Potato Timbales

Pastissets d'Agrella

Serves six (makes six 1/2-cup timbales).

These timbales complement almost any meat entrée. The potato not only adds an interesting texture; it makes the timbales lighter and more healthful than the traditional cream-based version, while softening the lemony tang of the sorrel. Though you can also make them with spinach, I find the sorrel version more intriguing.

1/2 pound potatoes
2 tablespoons butter
1/2 cup chopped onion
1 large bunch sorrel (about 1 pound), stemmed and chopped
1/2 cup (2 ounces) freshly grated Parmesan or Gruyère cheese
2 eggs, beaten
1/4 cup milk
1/2 teaspoon salt
1/4 teaspoon freshly ground black pepper, or to taste
About 1/4 cup finely grated Parmesan cheese

Boil, peel, and mash potatoes well with a potato ricer, masher, or fork (don't use a food processor or blender). While still warm, mix in 1 tablespoon butter with a fork.

In a skillet large enough to hold sorrel, sauté onion in 1 tablespoon butter until soft. Add sorrel and cover; cook until wilted, about 3 minutes. Do not drain, but coarsely chop. Transfer to a large bowl and combine with mashed potatoes, grated cheese, eggs, milk, salt, and pepper. Mix well with a fork; taste for seasoning.

Preheat oven to 350° F. Oil muffin tins or individual timbale molds. Flour lightly and shake out excess; sprinkle generously with some Parmesan cheese. Fill with sorrel and potato mixture.

Place molds inside a larger pan filled with boiling water halfway up the molds. Bake in the 350° F oven until mixture puffs up, about 30 minutes. Remove from oven and let cool.

Preheat broiler. Run a knife around edges of timbales and unmold onto a flameproof serving platter. Sprinkle remaining Parmesan over tops. Place under broiler for a few moments, until golden. Serve immediately.

Potato and Onion Cake with Fresh Rosemary Leaves

Pastís de Patata amb Romaní

Serves eight to ten.

This is another recipe I make again and again because it is so versatile. It is a great complement to any of my recipes for poultry, game, or meat dishes braised with fruit, and also works well as a light luncheon entrée with a seafood salad.

6 tablespoons butter
3 large onions, thinly sliced
2 pounds new potatoes, thinly sliced by hand
1 teaspoon salt
1/2 teaspoon freshly ground black pepper
3 tablespoons coarsely chopped fresh rosemary leaves
1 cup half-and-half

In a large skillet, heat butter and sauté onions over low heat for about 30 minutes, stirring occasionally, until very soft and lightly golden but not brown.

Preheat oven to 350° F. Butter a 9- or 10-inch round baking dish or pie plate. Arrange potatoes in a thin layer, sprinkle with some salt and pepper, cover with a thin layer of onions, and sprinkle some rosemary over. Continue to alternate layers, ending with rosemary. Pour half-and-half over and around.

Cover with aluminum foil and bake in the 350° F oven for 1 hour. Remove foil and bake another 20 to 30 minutes, or until top turns golden. Serve immediately.

Rice with Saffron Threads

Arròs al Safrà

Serves eight.

This lovely saffron-stained rice is a fine complement to many Catalan fish, poultry, or meat recipes, and very easy to make if you have flavorful home-made chicken stock on hand. Be sure to use a good-quality Spanish saffron (see p. 6).
To accompany main dishes with a sauce, I like to shape it in individual molds as described here.

4 tablespoons butter
1 large onion, minced
3 large garlic cloves, minced
3 cups Chicken Stock (p. 18)
1/2 teaspoon (.2 gram) saffron threads, or 1/4 teaspoon powdered saffron
1 teaspoon salt
1/4 teaspoon freshly ground black pepper
1-1/2 cups short-grain rice (see p. 6)

Heat butter in a large saucepan. Sauté onion and garlic over low heat until soft, 10 to 15 minutes. Meanwhile, bring stock to a boil in a small saucepan; stir in saffron, salt, and pepper. Add rice to onion mixture and cook for 1 minute over medium heat, stirring. Add boiling stock; bring liquid to a boil again, reduce heat to low, cover and simmer for 18 minutes. Remove from heat and let stand for 5 to 10 minutes before serving or shaping into molds.

To prepare the individual molds: Rinse a 1/3- or 1/2-cup flan mold or individual muffin tin in cold water and pack the rice firmly in it, up to 1/4 inch from top. Invert mold onto a serving platter and tap against surface; it will come out in a neat mound. Repeat until you use up all the rice, rinsing mold each time; arrange rice molds attractively on a platter. Before serving, cover with aluminum foil and warm in the oven.

Brown Rice with Pine Nuts and Raisins

Arròs amb Panses i Pinyons a la Catalana

Serves six.

This is a very traditional "Catalan-style" rice, with the requisite pine nuts and raisins. Since I've been living in California, I've found that I like it even better made with brown rice. This dish is not only attractive; the flavor is so good you don't have to use a stock.
It is a great accompaniment to any meat or poultry dish, especially those cooked with fruits.

2 tablespoons butter
1/4 cup (1.5 ounces) pine nuts
6 tablespoons raisins
1 teaspoon salt
1-1/2 cups short-grain brown rice (see p. 6)

In a medium lidded saucepan, heat butter and sauté pine nuts with raisins over medium-low heat, stirring, until raisins plump up and pine nuts turn golden. Meanwhile, in a medium saucepan, bring 4 cups water to a boil with salt. Add rice to pine nuts and raisins; stir and scrape bottom to get the brown bits attached to the pan.

Pour boiling water over rice; reduce heat to low and cook, covered, for 40 minutes. Taste for seasoning. Turn off heat, cover, and let sit for 10 to 15 minutes, or until liquid has evaporated. (This rice is just as good made ahead and warmed, or even a day later.)

n this section I have included a diverse group of recipes, from a homey chicken stew and several remarkable fish stews to an unusual rabbit dish with a touch of chocolate in the sauce. Based on traditional old-style recipes, some of these dishes are quite substantial, such as Grandmother's Pot of Meats, Sausages, and Vegetables with the Broth Served as a Pasta Soup (p. 104), which is really a meal in itself, but any of them can be served on their own. With so many ingredients simmered together, all these earthy country stews have wonderful sauces, so be sure to provide plenty of good crusty bread to soak them up.

Catalan-style Fava or Lima Bean Stew with Sausages and Fresh Mint

Faves a la Catalana

Serves eight.

This succulent mélange of beans simmered with sausages is a classic Catalan peasant dish, often served in winter as a first course. I consider it more of a hearty main dish, ideal for buffet dinners—and for hearty appetites. I never worry about making too much; it is even better reheated the next day, and it freezes perfectly. Of course, in order to make it here I have had to make some substitutions for the traditional Catalan sausages. And since fresh fava beans are not widely available, I either freeze them during their short season for later use, or substitute frozen lima beans.

4 cups shelled fava beans, butter beans, or lima beans (4 to 6 pounds unshelled) or two 10-ounce packages frozen lima beans
2 tablespoons olive oil
1/2 pound pancetta, julienned
2 medium onions, chopped
4 large garlic cloves, minced
1 pound mild pork sausage (such as sweet Italian)

1 pound pork blood sausage, such as Italian blood pudding or French *boudin noir*
3 tablespoons chopped fresh mint leaves
1 large or 2 small bay leaves
1 cup dry white wine
3 cups Chicken Stock (p. 18)

Shell fava beans. (If, when you open pod, the small husk attached to pod is black, the beans are not young. In that case, blanch them for 2 or 3 minutes and peel before using.)

In a large, flameproof lidded casserole (preferably of clay), heat oil and cook pancetta over low heat for about 10 minutes. Remove it and set aside. Add onions and garlic to casserole and sauté until golden, about 20 minutes. Add fava beans and toss for 4 or 5 minutes.

Pour about 1/2 cup water in a large skillet and add sausages. Pierce them with a fork and cook over medium-high heat for 3 to 5 minutes, until water evaporates and sausages are lightly browned. Cut them into 1-inch slices and add to fava beans. Add pancetta, 1 tablespoon chopped mint, bay leaf, and wine. Add stock, bring to a boil, reduce heat to low, and cook, partially covered, for 1 hour or more, until beans are quite soft. If you find sauce too thin, uncover and cook for another 15 minutes, or until sauce reaches desired consistency; the stew should be rather soupy. Taste for seasoning. At the last minute, stir in remaining 2 tablespoons chopped mint and serve.

Wine Recommendation: Serve with a heart-warming Mediterranean red, such as a Catalan, oak-aged Cariñena-Garnacha blend, a Côtes-du-Rhône, or a California Zinfandel.

Tarragona-style Fish Stew with Sweet Dried Peppers and Almonds

Romesco de Peix

Serves six to eight.

Tarragona and the nearby district of El Vendrell are the home of romesco, *the rustic sauce of sweet red peppers, tomatoes, and almonds derived from the fish stew of the same name. Today most of the restaurants in the area serve* romesco *as a sauce, but only a few serve the marvelous local dish* romesco de peix. *Essential to this dish are the dried* nyoras, *a type of pepper found all along the Mediterranean coast of Spain. They are small, round, dark red, and extremely flavorful, with just a trace of heat. Unfortunately they are not available here, but I have found that dried* ancho *or* pasilla *chiles (also called* poblanos *or* pisados) *work quite well; they are available at most Mexican or Latino groceries, as well as in fine markets. Or substitute another mild dried chile pepper.*

2 dried *ancho* chile peppers, or another type of dried sweet-mild chile pepper
3 to 5 tablespoons olive oil
2 large (1/2-inch-thick) slices of white bread (2 ounces total)
4 large garlic cloves, finely chopped
1 medium onion, finely chopped
1 cup dry white wine
1/2 cup (2-1/2 ounces) whole almonds, toasted (see p. 11) and finely ground

2 cups Fish Stock (p. 19)
1 teaspoon salt, or to taste
1/4 teaspoon freshly ground black pepper, or to taste
3 pounds fresh fish fillets, cut into 18 pieces (you may use one or more types of fish: red snapper, cod, sea bass, and so on)

Place chiles in a small saucepan and cover them with water. Bring water to a boil, reduce heat to low, and simmer for 10 minutes. Turn off heat, cover, and soak chiles for 45 minutes. Remove from pan and drain; reserve 1 cup soaking water. Stem, seed, and peel chiles. Set aside.

Heat 2 or 3 tablespoons oil in a large skillet and fry bread until golden. Set bread aside.

Meanwhile, in a medium skillet, sauté garlic and onion in 1 or 2 tablespoons oil over very low heat, stirring occasionally, until soft and golden, at least 20 minutes. Add wine, increase heat, and cook briskly until dry. Purée in food processor with the chiles, almonds, bread, 1 cup water reserved from soaking chiles, fish stock, 1/2 teaspoon salt, and pepper.

Pour sauce into a large skillet and heat through. Season fish with remaining 1/2 teaspoon salt, add to sauce, and turn to coat. Reduce heat and cook over low heat, covered, for about 10 minutes, or until fillets are done. Taste for seasoning. This is a rather soupy stew. Serve with lots of bread to dip in the sauce!

Wine Recommendation: Serve with an oak-aged Chardonnay or with a medium-bodied, fairly young red such as a Tempranillo or Merlot.

Costa Brava–style Fish Stew with Potatoes and Garlic Mayonnaise

Suquet de Peix

Serves six.

Every Catalan cook has a different way of making this subtly flavored fish and potato stew from the Costa Brava, the rugged seacoast north of Barcelona. The name suquet *is the diminutive of the word* suc, *which means "juice." And that's because this is a very soupy fish stew. As is traditional with many fisherman-style dishes, this one is served with pungent garlic mayonnaise (allioli) on the side.*

For the *sofregit*:
1/4 cup olive oil
4 large onions, minced
2 large red bell peppers, cored, seeded, and minced
1 pound ripe tomatoes, peeled, seeded, and chopped

For the fish and potatoes:
3 tablespoons olive oil
2 pounds fresh firm white fish fillets, such as red snapper, cut into pieces
Flour for coating fish
3 large garlic cloves, minced
2 tablespoons chopped fresh parsley leaves
1/2 cup full-bodied brandy
4 cups Fish Stock (p. 19)
1 pound white potatoes, peeled and sliced thin
1 teaspoon salt, or to taste
1/2 teaspoon freshly ground black pepper, or to taste

For the *picada*:
1 tablespoon olive oil
1 thin slice of white bread (about 1/2 ounce)
1/4 cup (1-1/4 ounces) whole almonds, toasted (p. 11)
2 large garlic cloves, coarsely chopped

As an accompaniment:
1 recipe Garlic Mayonnaise (p. 116)

To prepare the *sofregit*: In a large flameproof casserole (preferably of clay) heat oil and sauté onions with peppers over medium-low heat. The secret to this dish is in sautéing onions and peppers for a very long time, 45 minutes to an hour, until onions are almost caramelized. Toward the end, reduce heat to low and stir often. You may have to add a little water so vegetables don't burn, but they must be golden brown. Add tomatoes and cook until dry.

To cook the fish and potatoes: Heat oil in a skillet large enough to accommodate all fish fillets. Flour fish and sauté it over medium heat very briefly on both sides. Set fish aside, draining on paper towels. Add garlic and parsley to same skillet and sauté until garlic is soft. Add brandy and cook over high heat until almost dry. Transfer contents of skillet to casserole with vegetable mixture; add fish stock and potatoes. Bring to a boil and cook over medium-low heat for about 20 minutes or longer, until potatoes are tender. Season with salt and pepper.

To prepare the *picada*: In a small skillet, heat olive oil and fry bread slice until golden on both sides. In a food processor, grind very finely almonds, fried bread, and garlic.

When potatoes are tender, stir in *picada*. Add fish fillets and cook about 7 more minutes, just until fish is done.

Serve warm, passing Garlic Mayonnaise ("*allioli*") around in a sauceboat.

Left: Mercè Navarro, owner-chef of Roig Robí restaurant in Barcelona, using a hot iron to brown the sugar topping on the classic Catalan Caramel Custard (p. 124).

Right: Chef Jaume Bargués, from Jaume de Provença restaurant in Barcelona, making *allioli* (Garlic Mayonnaise, p. 116) in his kitchen.

Right: Shellfish *Paella* in a Clay Casserole (p. 110) at Els Perols de L'Empordà restaurant in Barcelona.

Left: Harvesting grapes at the Torres vineyards in Penedès.

Below Left: Winemaker Miguel Torres, Jr., and Jacques Bergeret, one of Miguel's former professors of oenology in Burgundy, tasting wines at the Torres winery in Penedès.

Right: Lluis Cruanyas at his Eldorado Petit restaurant in Barcelona with three of his dishes: Peppers Stuffed with Salt Cod, Pheasant with Grapes and Walnuts (p. 76), and *"Mar i Muntanya"* (Prawns and Chicken in a Sauce with Nuts, Herbs, and Chocolate, p. 70).

Below: A typical Penedès landscape with the renowned Montserrat mountains in the background.

Above: A selection of Catalan wines lined up at El Celler del Penedès, a rustic country restaurant near Vilafranca del Penedès.

Left: Chef Mercè Giralt holding a tray of desserts at her Agut d'Avignon restaurant in Barcelona: Pears in Red Wine with a Fresh Cheese Filling and Strawberry Sauce (p. 127), Classic Flan, Baked Apples, and variations on *Panellets* (p. 132).

Opposite: A fishmonger in Barcelona's exuberant La Boqueria market just off the famous Ramblas, in the city's gothic quarter near the sea.

Right: Picturesque stand offering all manner of salt cod in one of Barcelona's turn-of-the-century covered markets.

Left: Marimar shopping at one of the artfully arranged cascades of fruits and vegetables at La Boqueria market.

Left: Marimar buying fish at La Boqueria market.

Below: People bidding at a fish auction in the seaside village of Vilanova i la Geltrú, just south of Barcelona and Sitges.

Left: *Xatonada* (Tuna Salad with Anchovies, Olives, and *Romesco* Sauce, p. 58), *Escalivada* (Charcoal-grilled Mediterranean Vegetables, p. 93), and *Cargols Picants* (Snails in a Piquant Sauce of Tomatoes, Herbs, and Almonds, p. 50) at El Celler del Penedès.

Below left: *Romesco de Peix* (Tarragona-style Fish Stew with Sweet Dried Peppers and Almonds, p. 99) at Casa Isidre in Barcelona.

Below right: *Pa amb Tomaquet* (Bread with Tomato, p. 41), one plate topped with Costa Brava anchovies, the other with raw-cured *serrano* ham, at the restaurant L'Olivé in Barcelona.

Wine Recommendation: Serve with an oak-aged Chardonnay or Viura (Rioja), a flavorful Alvarinho, or a Chardonnay-Parellada blend from Catalunya.

Barcelona-style Shellfish Stew with Tomatoes, White Wine, and Saffron

Sarsuela de Marisc

Serves six.

According to a Catalan saying, "Pinch a man on the streets of Barcelona—if he doesn't cry out in pitch he's not Catalan." Our love of music and food combine in sarsuela, *an extravagant shellfish stew that takes its name from the Catalan term for light opera or operetta. And with its wealth of ingredients, the dish is indeed a colorful production worthy of Gilbert and Sullivan.*

Sarsuela (zarzuela in Castilian) is a specialty of seafood restaurants along the beach in Barceloneta, the seaside quarter of Barcelona, and in villages surrounding the city. One of my favorites is Peixerot, a delightful old restaurant in the fishing village of Vilanova i la Geltrú, south of Barcelona, where I have spent many a lovely summer evening feasting on their excellent sarsuela *and other seafood dishes. Another thing I like about this recipe (and about country stews in general, really) is that you can substitute or make additions to suit your taste. Quantities need not be precise, either.*

1/4 cup olive oil
2 large onions, minced
2 large red (or green) bell peppers, cored, seeded, and cut into thin strips lengthwise
2 ounces lean prosciutto, julienned
3 pounds tomatoes, peeled, seeded, and chopped
4 large garlic cloves, minced
1/2 cup whole almonds, toasted (see p. 11), and finely ground
1/2 teaspoon (.2 gram) saffron threads
3 bay leaves
1 tablespoon chopped fresh thyme leaves, or 1 teaspoon dried
1 teaspoon chopped fresh rosemary leaves, or 1/3 teaspoon dried

2 teaspoons salt, or to taste
1/2 teaspoon freshly ground black pepper, or to taste
1/2 teaspoon hot red pepper flakes
1 cup dry white wine
3 cups Fish Stock (p. 19)
1 tablespoon fresh lemon juice
12 small live clams, scrubbed
12 small live mussels, scrubbed
6 large prawns in their shells
1 pound scallops
1-1/2 pounds squid, cleaned (see Note, p. 67), bodies cut into rings, and tentacles whole

As a garnish:
6 lemon wedges

In a large, lidded flameproof casserole, preferably of clay, heat oil and sauté onions and peppers for 10 minutes, or until soft. Stir in prosciutto and cook for a few minutes. Add tomatoes and cook rapidly until dry. Stir in garlic, almonds, saffron, bay leaves, thyme, rosemary, salt, pepper, pepper flakes, wine, fish stock, and lemon juice. Bring to a boil. Add clams and mussels; cover, reduce heat to moderate, and cook 10 minutes. Add prawns, scallops, and squid, and cook 5 more minutes. Taste for seasoning and serve from the casserole, garnished with lemon wedges.

Wine Recommendation: Serve with an oak-aged Chardonnay or Sauvignon Blanc, or a flavorful Alvarinho from Galicia.

Rosalia's Chicken Stew with Mushrooms, Onions, and Carrots in an Almond-Saffron Sauce

Pollastre Estofat de Rosalia

Serves four to six.

This was the family's favorite chicken recipe of Rosalia, my parents' cook—maybe her best. The sauce derives its earthy flavors from the picada *of saffron, almonds, and egg yolks.*

One 4- to 5-pound chicken, cut into 6 or 8 serving pieces
1-3/4 teaspoons salt
3/4 teaspoon freshly ground black pepper
2 tablespoons olive oil
16 small boiling onions, peeled
3/4 pound carrots, peeled and sliced into 1-inch rounds
1/2 pound medium mushrooms
8 small unpeeled red potatoes
1 bay leaf

1 cup dry white wine
1 cup Chicken Stock (p. 18)

For the *picada*:
1/2 cup (2-1/2 ounces) whole almonds or (hazelnuts)
3 large garlic cloves, coarsely chopped
1/2 teaspoon (.2 gram) saffron threads, or 1/4 teaspoon powdered saffron
3 hard-boiled eggs, halved

Pat chicken dry and season with 1/4 teaspoon *each* salt and pepper. Heat oil in a large skillet and, over medium-high heat, brown chicken pieces on all sides. Transfer them to a large, lidded flameproof casserole. Add onions, carrots, and mushrooms to skillet and cook them over medium heat, stirring, until they start to brown, 5 to 10 minutes. Add them to casserole and arrange potatoes around chicken. Nestle bay leaf in the middle and sprinkle with remaining salt and pepper.

Remove most of the fat in skillet used to brown chicken, add wine, and deglaze (see p. 13). Pour glaze over chicken in casserole. Add stock and bring to a boil. Reduce heat to very low, cover, and simmer for 30 minutes. Discard bay leaf.

To prepare the *picada*: In a food processor, finely grind almonds with garlic; add saffron and egg yolks (reserve whites). Stir in enough liquid from casserole to form a paste.

To assemble the dish: Whisk *picada* into casserole and cook for another 5 minutes. Taste for seasoning. Chop egg whites by hand and sprinkle over as a garnish.

Wine Recommendation: Serve with a medium-bodied young red, such as a Tempranillo from Catalunya, Rioja or Ribera del Duero, a fresh Zinfandel, or a Merlot.

Rabbit Stewed in Red Wine with Tomatoes, Chocolate, and Herbs

Estofat de Conill al Vi Negre

Serves eight.

This hearty rabbit stew combines a touch of chocolate and almonds with rosemary, thyme, oregano, and bay: the classic quartet of Catalan herbs. The recipe comes from my Aunt Oriola, the great cook in my family.

Start preparation at least 8 hours ahead or the day before, by marinating rabbit.

For the marinade:

1 (750 ml) bottle full-bodied dry red wine
3 large garlic cloves, minced
2 bay leaves
1/4 cup (packed) finely chopped mixed fresh herb leaves, such as oregano, rosemary, and thyme (or 1 tablespoon dried)
1/3 cup minced shallots

For the rabbit stew:

2 rabbits (about 5 pounds total), cut into serving pieces
2 tablespoons olive oil
1/3 cup full-bodied brandy
One 3-inch cinnamon stick
1 ounce unsweetened baking chocolate, grated
2-1/2 pounds tomatoes, puréed
1/2 teaspoon salt, or to taste
1/2 teaspoon freshly ground black pepper, or to taste
2 tablespoons fresh lemon juice
1/2 pound small red-skinned potatoes
1/2 pound carrots
1/2 pound medium mushrooms
1 pound small boiling onions, peeled and trimmed

As a garnish:

1/4 pound (3/4 cup) sliced almonds, toasted (see p. 11)

To prepare the marinade: In a large non-reactive bowl, mix together wine, garlic, bay leaves, herbs, and shallots. Add rabbits and marinate for at least 6 hours, covered and refrigerated. Turn pieces occasionally. Drain, pat rabbits dry, and reserve marinade.

To cook the rabbits: Heat oil in a large, lidded flameproof casserole. Brown rabbit pieces over medium heat. Set them aside.

Deglaze (see p. 13) casserole with brandy. Add marinating liquid with herbs and bring to a boil. Stir in cinnamon stick, chocolate, tomatoes, salt, and pepper. Reduce heat to very low and return rabbit to casserole. Add vegetables, cover stew tightly with a double layer of aluminum foil, place lid on top, and simmer over low heat for 1 hour, turning rabbit pieces occasionally.

To assemble the dish: Transfer rabbit to a serving platter and keep warm. Discard cinnamon stick and bay leaves. Increase heat to high and cook sauce until reduced by half. Stir in lemon juice. Taste for seasoning. Pour sauce over rabbit and sprinkle almonds on top just before serving.

Wine Recommendation: Serve with an earthy oak-aged red such as a Catalan Cariñena-Garnacha blend, a Syrah from California, or a French Côtes-du-Rhône.

Grandmother's Pot of Meats, Sausages, and Vegetables with the Broth Served as a Pasta Soup

Escudella i Carn d'Olla

Serves eight, with leftovers.

In the old days, this Catalan meal-in-a-pot was the staple dish on farms in the countryside. I remember my grandmother, who was a grape farmer, telling us that when she was young they had escudella i carn d'olla five or six times a week! Related to boiled dinners like the French pot-au-feu and the Italian bollito misto, today escudella is traditionally served in Catalunya on Christmas day.

The essence of the dish is to gently simmer a variety of meats and sausages with winter vegetables; the rich broth is served as a first-course soup with pasta, usually the large shell-shaped pasta called galets in Catalan. Then come the meats and vegetables—including the pilota, or meatball, which may be the best part—served as the main course, with a little extra virgin olive oil drizzled over. And on Christmas, if you can believe it, after that we have the turkey!

Start preparation the day before, by soaking beans overnight, or use canned beans. Preparation time: 5 hours.

For the stock:

1/2 pound dried or one 1-pound can garbanzo beans (chick-peas)
2 tablespoons olive oil
1/2 pound pancetta, diced small
6 large garlic cloves, chopped
1/4 cup chopped shallots
1 pound leeks, coarsely sliced, with one third or more of green part
3 celery stalks, coarsely chopped
1 pound veal or beef knuckle bones (with marrow, if possible), cut up
One 1-pound ham hock, cracked into small pieces
1 pound stewing beef, cut into 1-inch cubes
1 whole stewing hen or large chicken, fat trimmed (see *Note*, below)
1 teaspoon salt
1 teaspoon freshly ground black pepper

For the meatball:

1 pound medium-ground pork
1 cup homemade bread crumbs (see p. 10)
2 eggs, beaten
3 tablespoons chopped fresh parsley leaves
3 large garlic cloves, minced
1/4 cup (1.5 ounces) pine nuts
1/2 teaspoon salt
1/2 teaspoon freshly ground black pepper
1/8 teaspoon ground cinnamon
3 or 4 tablespoons flour for coating meatballs

For the stew:

8 small turnips, peeled
8 small red-skinned potatoes
1 small head green cabbage, cored and quartered
1 pound carrots, peeled and cut into 1/2-inch-thick diagonal slices
2 pounds assorted flavorful pork sausages
1/4 pound large shell pasta

As a garnish:

Extra virgin olive oil

Note: If you can find it, a stewing hen is best for the dish; otherwise, try to get a 5- to 6-pound roasting chicken. The stewing hen should simmer for 2-1/2 hours, whereas the chicken should not cook more than 1-1/2 hours.

In a bowl, cover dried garbanzo beans with water and soak overnight. Drain and reserve water. (If you use canned beans, discard water.)

In a very large, lidded flameproof casserole or a stockpot, heat oil and sauté pancetta over low heat until golden, about 10 minutes. Add garlic, shallots, leeks, and celery; cook 15 minutes. Add remaining stock ingredients, dried garbanzo beans and their water (if using canned beans, add them later), and water to cover. Bring to a boil, reduce heat to low, cover and simmer gently for 2 hours. (If using a chicken, remove it after 1-1/2 hours.) Skim off periodically scum and fat that rise to surface.

To make the meatball: Mix all ingredients except flour in a large bowl. Divide meatball mixture in half and shape it into 2 cylinders about 3 inches in diameter. Sprinkle flour on a board and roll cylinders in it, coating them with flour all over.

To finish the stew: After 2 hours of simmering, add turnips, potatoes, cabbage, carrots, sausages, and meatball cylinders (and canned beans if you are using them). If necessary, add more boiling water to cover. Simmer for another 30 minutes.

Remove meats and vegetables from broth and arrange them separately on 2 platters; keep warm. Strain broth through a fine sieve back into pot, and cook pasta in broth at a rapid boil until tender, about 15 minutes. Taste for seasoning.

Serve broth and pasta as a soup, followed by vegetables and meats with extra virgin olive oil drizzled over.

Wine Recommendation: Serve with a fine oak-aged Cabernet, Zinfandel, or a mature Merlot throughout the meal. You can also serve an elegant white wine or a *fino* sherry with the soup and vegetables.

PAELLA AND PAELLA-STYLE RICE DISHES
PAELLES I PLATS D'ARRÒS

Paella, the intricate rice dish studded with shellfish, meat, and sausages, is Spain's best-known dish. Its birthplace was in Valencia, around the area called La Huerta, or "the vegetable garden," for the small, fertile gardens along the coast. Named after the iron skillet in which it is cooked, *paella* is actually not very old—two hundred years at the most; it evolved from a Lenten dish made with local vegetables, salt cod, and snails. Some inventive cook decided to add a little chicken or a couple of pimiento-stained sausages, and restaurants began to improvise with more sophisticated ingredients such as shellfish and even lobster. Originally it was cooked outdoors over a fire of vine cuttings and served right from the paella pan.

The region of Valencia (along with the Balearic Islands, which include Mallorca, Ibiza, and Menorca) is considered part of the *Països Catalans,* or Catalan homelands. So *paella* is in fact a Catalan dish; even its name is Catalan, derived from the Catalan word for skillet.

And it is the pan that sets *paella* apart from rice dishes cooked in other parts of the Països Catalans. The *cassola,* a shallow earthenware casserole that can be used on top of the stove or in the oven, originated in Catalunya and is the precursor of the iron *paella* pan developed in Valencia (see p. 15). The *cassola* is widely used all over Catalunya for the kind of rice dishes that would be cooked in a *paella* pan in Valencia and invariably would be called *paella* there, rather than *arròs a la cassola,* the Catalan "rice in a casserole." Because a *cassola* is deeper than a *paella* pan and not totally flat, the rice cooks a little differently—it takes longer and is usually less dry. In fact, in Valencia they call this "soupy" rice.

In Spain, the rice dishes in this chapter are often served as a first course, but in this country I always serve them as a main course, by themselves.

Paella with Chicken and Shellfish, Rosemary and Saffron

Paella Mixta de Pollastre i Marisc

Serves eight, with leftovers.

At home, my favorite paella was the one prepared by Adriana, my grandmother's cook; she used only the extremely flavorful seafood from the Mediterranean. Most restaurants, however, add some meats like chicken, pork, and chorizo, which contribute a lot of flavor, and call it paella mixta; that's what I find works best here. I developed this "perfect" paella recipe shortly after I came to live in the United States, and it has been a hit with my guests ever since. The secret is to use the freshest produce available, and real chicken stock instead of water.

2 large red bell peppers, cored and seeded
2 tablespoons olive oil
One 3- or 4-ounce firm lean *chorizo* or *linguiça* sausage, or other spicy pork sausage with paprika, removed from casing and crumbled
One 3- or 4-pound chicken, cut into 8 serving pieces
3 teaspoons salt
2 teaspoons freshly ground black pepper
1 pound pork, cut into medium dice (or 1-1/2 pound pork chops, cut up with bones)
16 large prawns or shrimp, in their shells
1-1/2 pounds squid, cleaned (see Note, p. 67), bodies cut into rings, and tentacles whole
6 large garlic cloves, finely chopped
3 pounds ripe tomatoes, peeled, seeded, and chopped
16 live mussels or clams, scrubbed
About 6 cups Chicken Stock (p. 18), preferably, or water
1 pound green beans, trimmed and cut into 1-inch pieces
2 teaspoons finely chopped fresh rosemary leaves
3 cups short-grain rice (see p. 6)
1 teaspoon (.4 gram) saffron threads, or 1/2 teaspoon powdered saffron
8 lemon wedges

Cut half a pepper into thin strips lengthwise and finely chop the rest. In a *paella* pan or large shallow skillet, heat oil and sauté pepper strips over medium heat until golden; drain and set aside. Add *chorizo* and sauté over low heat for 5 minutes; remove with a slotted spoon and set aside. Pat chicken dry and season with 1/2 teaspoon *each* salt and pepper. Brown chicken pieces in *paella* pan or skillet over medium-high heat; remove and set aside. Season pork with 1/4 teaspoon *each* salt and pepper; sauté until golden; remove and set aside. Add prawns and sauté, turning over once, until they just turn color; remove and set aside. Pat squid dry, season with 1/4 teaspoon *each* salt and pepper, and sauté briefly until they just turn color, 2 to 3 minutes; remove and set aside. Add garlic and sauté until soft. Add tomatoes and chopped peppers; cook over high heat for about 20 minutes, or until dry.

Meanwhile, in a large pot, bring about 1 cup water to a boil. Steam mussels or clams on a rack over water until they open, 4 to 5 minutes for mussels and 5 to 10 for clams. Strain broth through a fine-mesh strainer. Reserve broth and mussels or clams, discarding any that do not open.

Add green beans and rosemary to *paella* pan or skillet and cook, stirring, for 5 minutes. Stir in rice, remaining 2 teaspoons salt and 1 teaspoon pepper, *chorizo*, pork, and squid. Add chicken pieces, pressing them down into rice.

Preheat oven to 350° F. Measure reserved broth and add enough stock or water to equal 7 cups. In a saucepan, bring liquid to a boil; stir in saffron. Add to *paella* pan or skillet and cook over medium heat for 10 minutes. Transfer to 350° F oven and cook another 10 minutes (rice should be slightly underdone and a little soupy).

Remove pan from oven and arrange shellfish on top of rice. Place a cloth over pan and let it sit for 10 minutes. Arrange lemon wedges around pan and garnish with reserved pepper strips. Serve immediately. As the Spanish saying goes, rice doesn't wait for you—*you* wait for it!

Wine Recommendation: Almost any wine will do, because of the variety of ingredients. A dry rosé, a full-bodied white, a young red—use your imagination!

Barcelona-style Paella with Pork, Chorizo, and Vegetables, with a Grated Cheese Topping

Arròs Barcelonès

Serves eight.

One of my favorite rice dishes at home, arròs barcelonès *is a specialty of Barcelona, the capital of Catalunya. Lombardy and its capital, Milan, were Spanish possessions from the mid-sixteenth century until the early eighteenth century. That explains the Italian idea of grated cheese topping this Barcelona specialty.*

2 or 3 tablespoons olive oil
1/4 pound thickly sliced pancetta, julienned
One 4- or 5-ounce firm, lean *chorizo* sausage (or a flavorful spicy pork sausage with paprika), removed from casing and crumbled
1/2 pound lean boneless pork, diced
1 large red bell pepper, cored, seeded, and cut into thin strips lengthwise
1 medium green or yellow bell pepper, cored, seeded, and cut into thin strips lengthwise
3 large garlic cloves, chopped

2-1/2 pounds ripe tomatoes, peeled, seeded, and chopped
3 cups short-grain rice (see p. 6)
2 pounds fresh green peas, shelled (about 2 cups), or one 10-oz. package frozen peas
1/2 teaspoon paprika
1-1/2 teaspoons salt
1/2 teaspoon freshly ground black pepper
1/2 teaspoon (.2 gram) saffron threads, or 1/4 teaspoon powdered saffron
6 cups Chicken Stock (p. 18), boiling
1/4 pound Gruyère cheese, grated (1 cup)

In a *paella* pan, large skillet, or shallow flameproof clay casserole, heat 2 tablespoons olive oil and sauté pancetta over low heat for a couple of minutes. Add *chorizo* and cook 5 minutes. Add pork and cook another 5 minutes. With a slotted spoon, remove meats from pan and set aside. Add peppers and cook 12 to 15 minutes; remove from pan and set them aside.

Preheat oven to 350° F. Add remaining tablespoon oil to pan or casserole, if necessary; sauté garlic and tomatoes until dry. Stir in rice, peas, reserved meats and peppers, paprika, salt, and pepper. Add saffron to boiling stock and pour in pan or casserole; stir and bring to a boil again. Cook over medium heat for 10 minutes. Sprinkle cheese on top and bake in 350° F oven for another 10 minutes. Remove from oven, cover with a cloth, and let sit for 10 minutes. Serve immediately.

Wine Recommendation: Serve with a red wine with lots of fruit and flavor, such as a young Cabernet, Zinfandel, or Tempranillo.

Black Rice with Squid and Shrimp Cooked in the Squid's Ink

Arròs Negre

Serves eight to ten.

When rice is cooked with squid and its ink in this dish, each grain of rice is coated with the intensely flavored sauce stained with the squid's own ink. Originally from the district of L'Empordà in northern Catalunya, arròs negre or "black rice" is found all along the Mediterranean coast of Spain.

I used to have to buy extra squid to get enough ink sacs to really color the sauce (Spanish squid have more ink, since they are caught with bait). But now you can buy small (1 teaspoon) packets of squid ink, and it works perfectly! The packets are dated and should be used within 2 years. (They are available from some wholesale seafood suppliers.)

Six 4-gram packets squid ink (about 1 teaspoon each)
8 cups Fish Stock (p. 19)
2 tablespoons olive oil
3 large garlic cloves, minced
1 large onion, minced
2 pounds unpeeled ripe tomatoes, chopped
2 large red bell peppers, cored, seeded, and chopped
1/8 teaspoon hot red pepper flakes
1 bay leaf
1/2 cup dry white wine
1-1/2 teaspoons salt, or to taste
1/2 teaspoon freshly ground black pepper, or to taste
2 pounds squid, cleaned (see *Note*, p. 67), bodies cut into rings and tentacles whole
3/4 pound small or medium prawns in their shells
2-1/2 cups short-grain rice (see p. 6)

As an Accompaniment (optional):
1/2 recipe Garlic Mayonnaise (p. 116) (make whole recipe and use half)

In a small bowl, dissolve ink in 1 cup fish stock, and set aside.

To prepare the *sofregit*: In a *paella* pan, large skillet, or shallow flame-proof clay casserole, heat oil and sauté garlic with onion over low heat for 10 minutes, or until soft. Stir in tomatoes, red peppers, pepper flakes, and bay leaf; cook over medium heat for 15 minutes. Add white wine, salt, and pepper; cook until dry, stirring occasionally (lower heat toward the end).

Cut squid bodies (with fins attached) into rings. Stir squid body rings and tentacles, reserved fish stock with ink, and 1 cup more of fish stock into *paella* pan or skillet and cook for 15 minutes over medium-low heat. Add prawns and cook for 5 more minutes, turning them over once. Taste for seasoning. Remove bay leaf and prawns, and shell them; discard shells and reserve prawns.

Preheat oven to 350° F.

Bring remaining 6 cups fish stock to a boil. Stir rice into pan and add boiling liquid. Cook over medium heat for 10 minutes; gently move rice around so it cooks evenly throughout. Transfer to 350° F oven and cook for another 10 minutes. Remove pan from oven, push prawns down into rice, and cover pan with a cloth for 10 minutes. Serve immediately; if you let it sit any longer, rice will overcook. It should not absorb all the liquid. If desired, pass Garlic Mayonnaise separately in a sauceboat.

Wine Recommendation: Serve with an oak-aged Chardonnay or Sauvignon Blanc, a *reserva* Viura from Rioja, or a flavorful Alvarinho from Galicia.

Shellfish Paella in a Clay Casserole

Arròs a la Cassola amb Marisc

Serves eight.

I never thought a true shellfish paella could successfully be made in America, until I tried this dish at Els Perols de L'Empordà. This small, very Catalan restaurant in Barcelona specializes in the cuisine of L'Empordà district; unfortunately, many of their dishes use ingredients not easily adapted to those we have here—like the wonderful Catalan sausages typical of that area. But when Juli Serrat gave me this recipe, I thought it was worth a try—and it really works, as long as you get the freshest produce available, use a homemade fish stock, and are patient enough to spend an hour making the old-style sofregit. *Traditionally, this fisherman-style rice dish is prepared in a shallow clay casserole (a 12-inch cassola is perfect). It should be a little soupy and is typically served with a dab of garlic mayonnaise* (allioli) *on the side.*

For the *sofregit*:
1/3 cup olive oil
2 pounds red onions, minced
2-1/2 pounds ripe tomatoes, peeled, seeded, and chopped

For the *picada*:
2 large garlic cloves, coarsely chopped
2 tablespoons fresh parsley leaves
1/2 teaspoon (.2 gram) saffron threads, or 1/4 teaspoon powdered saffron
3/4 teaspoon salt, or to taste
3/4 teaspoon freshly ground white pepper, or to taste

For the rice and shellfish:
16 small live clams, scrubbed
16 small live mussels, scrubbed
2 tablespoons olive oil
2 pounds squid, cleaned (see Note, p. 67), bodies cut into rings and tentacles whole
1-1/2 cups short-grain rice (see p. 6)
About 4 cups Fish Stock (p. 19)
16 large prawns in their shells
1/2 pound large scallops

As a garnish:
8 lemon wedges
1/2 recipe Garlic Mayonnaise (p. 116) (make whole recipe and use half)

To prepare the *sofregit*: Heat oil in a shallow flameproof clay casserole, or in a large skillet. Add onions and sauté slowly over low heat, stirring from time to time, until onions are brown and almost caramelized; it will take 45 minutes to 1 hour (add small amounts of water if necessary, so onions don't burn). Add tomatoes and increase heat to medium; cook until dry.

To prepare the *picada*: In a food processor, finely grind all ingredients. Set aside.

To prepare the clams and mussels: In a large pot, bring about 1/2 cup water to a boil. Steam clams and mussels on a rack over boiling water until they open, 4 to 5 minutes for mussels and 5 to 10 minutes for clams. Set them aside, discarding any that do not open. Strain broth through a fine-mesh strainer. Reserve.

To cook the rice and shellfish: Preheat oven to 350° F. In a medium skillet, heat oil; add squid rings and tentacles. Sauté for 2 or 3 minutes, stirring. Add sautéed squid and their juices to casserole or skillet with *sofregit*. Stir in rice and *picada*.

Measure reserved broth and add enough fish stock to equal 4-1/2 cups. Bring to a boil in a medium saucepan. Add to casserole or skillet and cook over medium heat for 10 minutes; gently move rice around so it cooks evenly throughout. Add prawns and scallops, pushing them down into rice so they are covered with broth.

Transfer casserole or skillet to 350° F oven and cook another 10 minutes, or until rice is slightly underdone. Remove casserole from oven, and arrange mussels and clams on top. Cover casserole or skillet with a cloth and let it sit for 10 minutes.

Serve immediately, garnished with lemon wedges, and pass the Garlic Mayonnaise in a sauceboat.

Wine Recommendation: Serve with an oak-aged Sauvignon Blanc, a Verdejo from Rueda, or a Chardonnay–Parellada blend from Catalunya.

Summer Paella with Sausages and Vegetables Baked in a Clay Casserole

Arròs Passejat d'Estiu

Serves eight.

In the old days when few households had ovens, this baked rice was dubbed arròs passejat, *or "walked rice," because women would walk their casseroles over to the local baker, who cooked them in his oven after the bread was finished. I particularly like this recipe because there is no compromise in taste when it is made with American ingredients. The ideal utensil to bake it in is a 12-inch shallow clay casserole.*

The recipe comes from one of my favorite restaurants in the region: Galbis, located in L'Alcudia de Carlet, a little town 20 miles south of Valencia. Juan Carlos Galbis is famous for preparing a paella *so enormous it broke all existing records. He used a huge* paella *pan some thirteen feet across that fed twenty-five hundred people, requiring over a ton of firewood and about five hundred pounds of rice!*

3 tablespoons olive oil
1/4 pound pancetta, finely diced
One 3- or 4-ounce firm, lean *chorizo* or *linguiça* sausage, or another spicy pork sausage with paprika, removed from casing and crumbled
1/2 pound pork blood sausage, such as Italian blood pudding or French *boudin noir*, removed from casing and cut into 1/2-inch rounds
4 large garlic cloves, minced
2 large red bell peppers, cored, seeded, and cut lengthwise into thin strips

2 pounds ripe tomatoes, peeled but unseeded, and chopped
1 pound green beans, trimmed and cut into 1-inch lengths
One 10-ounce package frozen baby green peas
2 cups short-grain rice (see p. 6)
1 teaspoon paprika
1 teaspoon ground turmeric
1/2 teaspoon (.2 gram) saffron threads, or 1/4 teaspoon powdered saffron
1 teaspoon salt
1 teaspoon freshly ground black pepper

In a large pan, heat 1 tablespoon olive oil and add pancetta, *chorizo*, and blood sausages. Cook over low heat for 10 minutes.

Heat remaining 2 tablespoons oil in a large skillet. Add garlic and peppers; cook over medium heat for 10 minutes, or until peppers are soft. Add tomatoes and cook briskly until dry. Transfer to pan with sausages. Add green beans and 4 cups water. Bring to a boil, reduce heat to low, and cook for 10 minutes, uncovered. Drain through a colander into a large shallow flameproof casserole (preferably of clay). Measure liquid into a medium saucepan and if it is less than 4 cups, add enough water to equal 4 cups; set aside. Stir remaining ingredients into casserole.

(One of the good things about this dish is that it can be prepared ahead of time up to this point. As Juan Carlos Galbis told me, you do it "in the morning, before you go to the beach; and then when you come home, just add the water, put it in the oven, let it cook by itself and it is ready to eat!")

Preheat oven to 400° F. Bring the 4 cups of liquid to a boil. Add to casserole and place in 400° F oven for 30 minutes. Remove rice from oven, cover with a cloth, and let it sit for 10 minutes. Serve immediately.

Wine Recommendation: Serve with a young, fruity red such as a Beaujolais or Gamay, a Merlot, or a Tempranillo from Catalunya or Rioja.

Mountain-style Rice with Rabbit and Rosemary in a Rich Broth

Arròs Caldós de Muntanya

Serves six to eight.

Named "mountain rice" because the main ingredients—rabbit, rosemary, and snails—all come from the mountains, this rice dish is typically more soupy than a regular paella. *I love it made with fresh snails, but have left these optional, because the canned commercial variety doesn't contribute that much flavor to the dish; unless you can find them fresh, I recommend omitting them. And when I haven't found rabbit at the market, I have successfully substituted chicken. This is a versatile recipe!*

1 rabbit, cut into small serving pieces
2 teaspoons salt, or to taste
1 teaspoon freshly ground black pepper, or to taste
1/4 cup olive oil
1 pound mushrooms, thinly sliced
1 pound green beans, trimmed and cut into 1-inch lengths
1-1/2 pounds tomatoes, peeled, seeded, and chopped
3 large garlic cloves, minced
1 teaspoon finely chopped fresh rosemary leaves
1 teaspoon paprika
1/2 teaspoon (.2 gram) saffron threads, or 1/2 teaspoon powdered saffron
2 cups short-grain rice (see p. 6)
2 dozen fresh snails in the shell (optional)
8 cups Chicken Stock (p. 18), preferably, or water

Pat rabbit pieces dry, and season with 1/2 teaspoon salt and 1/4 teaspoon pepper. Heat oil in a shallow flameproof clay casserole, *paella* pan, or large skillet and sauté rabbit over medium heat until golden. Remove rabbit and set aside. Add mushrooms to casserole or pan and sauté for 5 minutes. Add beans and cook another 5 minutes. Add tomatoes and garlic, increase heat, and cook quickly until dry. Stir in rosemary, paprika, saffron, and remaining 1-1/2 teaspoons salt and 3/4 teaspoon pepper. Taste for seasoning.

Stir in rice and optional snails, and return meat to casserole or pan. Bring stock or water to a boil and pour it in. Return to a boil, reduce heat to medium-low, and cook for 20 minutes, or until rice is just slightly underdone. Let rice sit for 5 minutes, or until cooked to the right consistency.

Since this dish is meant to be soupy, it should be served immediately or the rice will overcook.

Wine Recommendation: Serve with a rich full-bodied Mediterranean red, such as a Châteauneuf-du-Pape, Gigondas, Bandol or Catalan Cariñena–Garnacha blend.

ROMESCO AND ALLIOLI SAUCES
ROMESCOS I ALLIOLIS

▼ ▼ ▼

omesco, the ruddy sauce of tomatoes, red peppers, garlic, and hazelnuts or almonds, is indigenous to the city of Tarragona and its surroundings. Every cook has a different way of making this popular sauce, and at the beginning of summer, they all compete in the annual *romesco* festival for the title of *Mestre Major Romescaire,* or Grand Master Romesco Maker.

The origin of this wonderfully tasty sauce is a dish called *Romesco de Peix* (Tarragona-style Fish Stew with Sweet Dried Peppers and Almonds, p. 99). Fishermen all along the coast from Vilanova i Geltrú, south of Barcelona, to Valencia, made this fish stew in a strongly flavored sauce, which became known as *romesco.* Later on, the sauce became popular all on its own and today is served most often alongside grilled, poached, or deep-fried fresh fish.

In this chapter, I have included a half dozen of my favorite *romesco* recipes. Make them at least 4 hours ahead to allow flavors to mingle. Use them with salads, grilled fish, meats or vegetables, even pasta or rice. To accompany grilled or fried fish, restaurants in Catalunya usually serve a small bowl of *romesco* along with a pungent *allioli* (Garlic Mayonnaise, p. 116) (the same sauce that goes by the name *aïoli* in Provence) and often both sauces are blended together.

Romesco Sauce
for Salads

Xató

Makes about 2-1/2 cups.

Traditionally served with xatonada *(Tuna Salad with Anchovies and Olives, p. 57),* xató *is a sharp and nutty* romesco *sauce, smooth as butter—and wonderful with just about anything.*

1 medium red bell pepper
1 cup (5 ounces) whole almonds, toasted (see p. 11)
1 large garlic clove, coarsely chopped (1 teaspoon)
1 tablespoon fresh parsley leaves

1/2 teaspoon salt
1/4 teaspoon freshly ground black pepper
1/2 cup red wine vinegar
3/4 cup extra virgin olive oil

Roast red pepper over a flame or in oven (see p. 10) until skin starts to blacken; peel, seed, and coarsely chop.

Grind almonds finely in a food processor. Purée with red pepper, garlic, parsley, salt, and pepper. Add vinegar, whirling to form a smooth paste. With motor running, gradually add oil in a thin stream. Taste for seasoning. The sauce should have a thick consistency and very sharp flavor. Depending on the strength of the vinegar used, you may need more or less oil.

Romesco Sauce for
Grilled Seafood, Meats,
and Vegetables

Salbitxada

Makes about 2-1/2 cups.

Typically served with ceballots *(Charcoal-grilled Catalan-style Leeks, p. 93), this version of* romesco *boasts a lovely terra-cotta color and rich harmonious flavors. It is great with other grilled vegetables, too, such as* escalivada *(Charcoal-grilled Mediterranean Vegetables, p. 92) and with grilled fish, meats, and poultry, especially Grilled Leg of Lamb (p. 88).*

1 tablespoon olive oil for frying
1 large (1/2-inch-thick) slice white bread (1 ounce)
1/2 cup (2-1/2 ounces) whole almonds, toasted (see p. 11)
1/4 teaspoon hot red pepper flakes
1 large garlic clove, coarsely chopped (1 teaspoon)
2 medium red bell peppers (about 12 ounces total), cored, seeded, and cut up, or 4 ounces (1/2 cup packed) whole roasted red bell peppers or pimientos from a jar, preferably fire-roasted ones from Spain

1/2 pound ripe tomatoes
1/4 teaspoon paprika
1/4 teaspoon salt, or to taste
1/2 teaspoon freshly ground black pepper, or to taste
1/4 cup red wine vinegar
1/2 cup extra virgin olive oil

Heat 1 tablespoon oil in a small skillet and, over medium heat, fry bread slice until golden on both sides.

Grind toasted almonds finely in food processor, together with bread, pepper flakes, and garlic. Add red peppers, tomatoes, paprika, salt, and pepper; purée to form a smooth paste. Whirl in vinegar. With motor running, add oil slowly, in a thin stream. Taste for seasoning.

The following two *romesco* sauces use *nyoras*, the Mediterranean dried red peppers somewhat similar to our dried *ancho* or *pasilla* chiles, and both hazelnuts and almonds, which provide earthy, full-bodied flavors. The first recipe comes from L'Olivé, a tiny and very popular Barcelona restaurant; Josep Olivé adds onion and paprika to his recipe for a rounder, milder taste. Isidre Gironés from Casa Isidre, a restaurant specializing in classic Catalan cuisine, contributed the second recipe; he first bakes the tomato and garlic for a sweeter, tangier flavor.

Both sauces are excellent with roasted lamb, barbecued pork or chicken, or any other grilled meats and sausages.

Romesco Sauce with Dried Red Peppers, Onion, and Paprika

Romesco de L'Olivé

Makes about 3 cups.

2 medium dried *ancho* (*pasilla*) chile peppers*
1 tablespoon olive oil for frying
1 large (1/2-inch-thick) slice of white bread (1 ounce)
1/2 cup (2-1/2 ounces) whole almonds, toasted (see p. 11)
1/2 cup (1-3/4 ounces) hazelnuts (filberts), toasted (see p. 11)
1 large garlic clove, coarsely chopped (1 teaspoon)
1/2 cup chopped onion
1/2 pound unpeeled ripe tomatoes, cut up
2 teaspoons Spanish paprika
3/4 teaspoon salt
1/4 teaspoon freshly ground black pepper
2 tablespoons red wine vinegar, or to taste
1/2 cup extra virgin olive oil

Cover chiles with water in a small saucepan. Bring to a boil and cook for 10 minutes over medium-low heat. Turn off heat, cover, and steep for 30 minutes. Remove stems and seeds, and discard water. (You should have 1/4 cup packed peppers.)

Heat 1 tablespoon oil in a small skillet and, over medium heat, fry bread slice until golden on both sides.

In a food processor, grind almonds and hazelnuts finely with garlic and bread. Add chiles, onion, tomatoes, paprika, salt, and pepper. Purée to form a smooth paste. Add vinegar and whirl. With motor running, pour in oil slowly, in a thin stream. Taste for seasoning.

*Available in Latino markets and some international groceries.

Romesco Sauce with Sweet Dried Peppers and Baked Garlic

Romesco de Casa Isidre

Makes about 2 cups.

2 medium dried *ancho (pasilla)* chile peppers*
1 large head garlic
1 large unpeeled ripe tomato
1 tablespoon olive oil for frying
1 large (1/2-inch-thick) slice white bread (1 ounce)

1/4 cup (1-1/4 ounces) whole almonds, toasted (see p. 11)
1/4 cup (1 ounce) hazelnuts (filberts), toasted (see p. 11)
1/4 teaspoon hot red pepper flakes
1/4 cup red wine vinegar
1/2 teaspoon salt
1/2 cup extra virgin olive oil

Preheat oven to 350° F. Cover chiles with water in a small saucepan. Bring to a boil and cook 10 minutes over medium-low heat. Turn off heat, cover, and steep for 30 minutes. Remove stems and seeds; you should have 1/4 cup (packed) peppers. Reserve 2 tablespoons of water.

Bake whole head of garlic for 45 minutes and tomato for 20 minutes on an ungreased baking sheet in the 350° F oven. Cut off top quarter of garlic head and squeeze pulp out. Peel tomato.

Heat 1 tablespoon oil in a small skillet and, over medium heat, fry bread until golden on both sides. Grind it finely in a food processor, together with nuts and pepper flakes. Add tomato, garlic pulp, and chiles; whirl to form a smooth paste. Whirl in vinegar, salt, and 2 tablespoons reserved water from cooking chiles. With motor running, add oil slowly, in a thin stream. Taste for seasoning.

Garlic Mayonnaise

Allioli

Makes about 1-1/2 cups.

Purists in Catalunya insist on making their allioli *in a mortar and pestle— but I always use a food processor and it takes me only a few minutes to make it. While I prefer to use olive oil in my mayonnaise, you can also make it with half olive oil, half vegetable oil. And it is best to prepare this sauce the day before, to allow flavors to mingle and mellow out.*

1-1/2 tablespoons minced garlic
1 egg, at room temperature
1-1/2 cups fruity olive oil
1 to 1-1/2 tablespoons fresh lemon juice, to taste

1/2 teaspoon salt
1/4 teaspoon freshly ground white pepper

In a blender or a food processor, purée garlic with egg. Mix oil with lemon juice in a pouring jar. With motor running, add oil mixture slowly, in a thin stream. Add salt and pepper and whirl an additional 10 seconds. Taste for seasoning. Transfer to a bowl, cover, and refrigerate.

If mixture separates or does not thicken, correct it as follows: Pour all but 1 tablespoon of separated mayonnaise into another container. Add 1 tablespoon water to remaining tablespoon of mayonnaise in food processor. With motor running, add separated mayonnaise slowly; mixture should regain right consistency—if not, try again. It will work!

*Available in Latino markets and some international groceries.

Honey Garlic Mayonnaise

Allioli de Mel

Makes 1-1/2 cups.

I tasted this and the next allioli *recipe at chef Montse Guillén's celebrated restaurant in Barcelona, which she ran before she moved on to New York and Japan to open new ventures. The honey and the apple add a "new" note to an old Catalan recipe such as* allioli. *Serve either of these sauces as accompaniments to lamb chops and other grilled meats.*

1 egg
2 tablespoons minced garlic
1 cup fruity olive oil

3 tablespoons honey
1/2 teaspoon salt

In a blender or food processor, purée egg with garlic. With motor running, gradually add oil in a thin stream until it thickens like a mayonnaise. Add honey and salt, whirl to mix, and taste for seasoning. Keep refrigerated until serving time.

Apple Garlic Mayonnaise

Allioli de Poma

Makes 2-1/2 cups.

I find this apple allioli *goes very well with the Terrine of Rabbit and Pork with Prunes, Carrots, and Herbs (p. 39), as well as with cold meats, such as ham.*

1 pound tart cooking apples, such as
  Pippin or Granny Smith, peeled,
  cored, and cut into 1-inch pieces
1 teaspoon minced garlic

2/3 cup olive oil
1/4 teaspoon salt, or to taste
1/4 teaspoon freshly ground white
  pepper, or to taste

Place apples in a saucepan and cover with water. Bring to a boil, reduce heat to low, cover, and simmer until tender—30 to 45 minutes. Drain apples and place them in a blender or food processor. Add garlic and purée finely. With motor running, gradually add oil in a thin stream. Add salt and pepper, and taste for seasoning. Keep refrigerated until serving time.

Good bread always has a place on my table, and very often it is bread I make myself. My basic bread is Peasant Bread (below), a round country loaf with a golden crust. It may sound like a lot of work, but with a food processor it takes only minutes to mix and knead enough dough for two loaves.

For all breads and doughs, I prefer unbleached flour over the bleached flour developed for commercial bread baking, since chemicals are used in the bleaching process. And for bread making, I particularly recommend hard wheat flours such as those from Manitoba or Deaf Smith in Texas; their high-gluten content gives an elastic, supple dough.

When measuring flour, scoop it into a measuring cup and gently slide a knife across the top to remove any excess. I don't bother to sift the flour beforehand, since the moisture content of flour can vary so much. Despite careful measurement, it may be necessary to adjust the flour or liquid to achieve a dough with the right consistency.

Peasant Bread

Pa de Pagès

Makes 2 small loaves.

Pa de pagès is to Catalunya what sourdough is to San Francisco: the familiar daily loaf. It is very simple to make with a food processor, and well worth the small amount of time and effort to put a loaf of homemade bread on the table.

2 packages (4 teaspoons or 1/2 ounce) active dry yeast	1 tablespoon salt
1 tablespoon sugar	5-1/2 cups unbleached all-purpose flour
2 cups warm (105° to 115° F) water	

In a food processor bowl, dissolve yeast and sugar in warm water; don't stir, just let it sit for 5 to 10 minutes to activate yeast (when yeast starts popping to the top, that means it is ready to work). Immediately add salt and 1/2 cup flour; whirl to combine well. Add all remaining flour; process for 2 minutes. Oil a bowl and place dough in it, turning to coat all sides with oil. Cover with a cloth and put bowl in a warm place for about 1 hour, or until dough has doubled in size.

Punch down dough to release the air and let it rest for 3 or 4 minutes. Oil a large baking sheet. Divide dough in half and shape each into a rounded mound; place them on baking sheet. Using a razor blade or a very sharp knife, make 3 parallel slashes on the tops. Cover again with a cloth and let rise in a warm place for 20 to 30 minutes, or until rounds again double in size.

Preheat oven to 400° F. Place a pan of hot water on bottom of oven, or on bottom rack if oven is electric. Just before baking, spray dough with water to obtain a harder crust. Bake for 30 minutes, or until loaves are golden and sound hollow when thumped on the bottom. Remove to a rack and let cool.

Bread Rings Basted with Olive Oil

Rotllos de Pa

Makes 12 medium bread rings.

It's always fun to make these skinny bread rings. Get the kids into the act, rolling the dough into ropes and forming them into circles.

2 packages (4 teaspoons or 1/2 ounce) active dry yeast
1 tablespoon sugar
1 cup warm (105° to 115° F) water
2 tablespoons olive oil
1 teaspoon salt

2-1/2 cups unbleached all-purpose flour

For finishing loaf:
About 3 tablespoons olive oil
1 or 2 teaspoons coarse salt

In a food processor bowl, dissolve yeast and sugar in warm water; don't stir, just let it sit for 5 to 10 minutes, to activate yeast (when yeast starts popping to the top, that means it is ready to work). Immediately add olive oil, salt, and 1 cup flour; whirl for 1 minute. Add remaining flour and whirl until a ball forms or dough pulls away from sides of bowl. Continue to whirl for 1 minute. If it doesn't form a ball, don't worry; even if dough is sticky, don't add any more flour.

Oil a bowl and place dough in it, turning to coat all sides with oil. Cover with a cloth and let rise in a warm place until doubled in size, about 1 hour.

Punch dough down to release the air. Divide it into quarters, then divide each quarter into 3 equal pieces. Work with 1 piece at a time and keep remaining dough covered. With your hands, roll each piece of dough into a 12- to 14-inch-long rope. Press edges together to form a ring. Place rings on 2 oiled baking sheets, setting them 2 inches apart. Cover them with a cloth and let rise in a warm place for another 30 minutes. Preheat oven to 375° F.

Bake rings in 375° F oven for 5 minutes. Brush with olive oil and bake for 10 more minutes. Brush with oil again and sprinkle with salt. Bake for another 5 to 10 minutes, or until rings are golden brown. Remove to a rack and let cool.

Wreath Bread with Rosemary, Raisins, and Pine Nuts

Pa de Romaní

Makes 1 large wreath.

Flavored with the Catalan trio of rosemary, raisins, and pine nuts, this wreath-shaped bread makes a spectacular centerpiece for your table. And the aromatic pungency of the rosemary blends particularly well with poultry or meat dishes cooked with fruit, such as Pheasant with Grapes and Walnuts (p. 76) or Beef Tenderloin with Dried Figs, Apricots, and Prunes (p. 91). Serve the bread on a large round wooden board decorated with fresh rosemary sprigs.

2 packages (2 teaspoons or 1/2 ounce) active dry yeast
1 teaspoon honey
1 cup warm (105° to 115° F) water
1 cup milk
2 tablespoons coarsely chopped fresh rosemary leaves
1/2 cup dark raisins
1/4 cup (1.5 ounces) pine nuts, lightly toasted (see p. 11)
5-1/2 cups unbleached all-purpose flour
2 tablespoons fruity olive oil, preferably extra virgin
1-1/2 teaspoons salt

As a garnish (optional):
Bouquet of fresh rosemary sprigs

In a food processor bowl, dissolve yeast and honey in warm water; don't stir, just let it sit for 5 to 10 minutes to activate yeast (when yeast starts popping to the top, that means it is ready to work). Meanwhile, heat milk in a small saucepan until warm (115° F); set aside. In a small bowl, toss chopped rosemary, raisins, and pine nuts with 1/2 cup flour; set aside.

As soon as yeast is activated, mix in warm milk (it should be at 105° to 115° F), olive oil, salt, and 1 cup flour; whirl for 1 minute. Add remaining 4 cups flour and process until dough starts to pull away from the sides. (It may be sticky, but don't overwork it, as it will be kneaded further.) Turn dough out onto a floured board and knead in rosemary, raisins, and pine nuts with their flour. Continue to knead until these are evenly distributed throughout dough and the surface is shiny and elastic.

Oil a bowl and place dough in it, turning to coat all sides with oil. Cover with a cloth and let rise in a warm place until doubled in size, about 1 hour.

Oil a pizza pan. Punch dough down to release the air. Lift it and, holding it in both hands, punch your thumbs through the middle of the dough and pull it apart to make a large doughnut-shaped bread about 12 inches in diameter. Be sure to make hole in center quite large; it will close up as bread bakes. Place on oiled pizza pan and slash it around the edges with a sharp knife or razor blade to make it resemble a braided wreath. Brush top with olive oil and let it rest for 5 minutes.

Place loaf in a cold oven, turn oven to 400° F, and bake for 35 minutes, or until crust is browned and bread sounds hollow when tapped on the bottom.

Let bread cool on a rack. Serve on a wooden board surrounded with rosemary sprigs, if desired.

Three Kings' Sweet Bread with Orange Almond Filling

Tortell de Reis amb Sorpresa

Serves eight. Makes 1 (12-inch) ring.

Tortells *are a popular dessert in Catalunya; they are round, shaped like a doughnut, and filled with anything rich and sinful—whipped cream, chocolate, pastry cream. At home we had them often on Sundays; after mass we would head for the pastry shop, which was invariably crowded at that hour. In Spain nobody makes* tortells *at home; they always come from a pastry shop.*

Tortell de Reis *is probably the one* tortell *eaten not only in Catalunya but elsewhere in Spain (where it is known as* Roscón de Reyes*) on January 6, which is Epiphany, or Three Kings' Day. The tradition of eating this* tortell *dates back to the fifteenth century, in France as well as in Spain. The celebration was also called Festa de la Fava or feast of the fava bean, because a dried fava bean was hidden in the filling. Whoever found the fava bean was the king or queen of the festival! Even today, it is traditional to hide a fava bean and/or a little prize or goody inside the filling.* Tortell *can be served as a dessert or as a teatime cake, and it is also superb for breakfast with a little sweet butter. For this to be a true* tortell de reis*, you must have a little "surprise" (sorpresa) to insert in the filling!*

Start preparation at least 6 hours in advance, or the day before.

For the dough:
2 packages (4 teaspoons or 1/2 ounce) active dry yeast
1/2 cup sugar
1/4 cup warm (105° to 115° F) water
3/4 cup (1-1/2 sticks) unsalted butter, at room temperature
3 eggs
1/2 teaspoon salt
1 teaspoon vanilla extract
2 tablespoons minced orange zest (see p. 10)
2-1/2 cups all-purpose flour

For the filling:
1/2 pound blanched almonds, finely ground
2/3 cup sugar
6 tablespoons fresh orange juice
1/4 teaspoon almond extract

For the garnish:
1 egg
1/2 cup sliced almonds

To prepare the dough: In a small bowl, dissolve yeast and 1/4 cup sugar in warm water; don't stir, just let it sit for 5 to 10 minutes to activate yeast (when yeast starts popping to the top, that means it is ready to work). Meanwhile, in a food processor or mixer, combine remaining 1/4 cup sugar with butter, eggs, salt, vanilla, and orange zest. Add yeast as soon as it is ready, and mix well. Add 1 cup flour and work dough vigorously. Add remaining 1-1/2 cups flour and mix well.

Transfer to a bowl, cover with a cloth and allow dough to rise in a warm place until doubled in size. It may take as long as 2 hours.

Stir down dough with a spoon or your fingers (this is a sticky dough) to release the air. Refrigerate for at least 2 hours (it will continue to rise in the refrigerator).

To prepare the filling: In a food processor, finely grind almonds and sugar. Add orange juice, gradually, and almond extract.

To assemble the sweet bread: Stir down the dough again. Flour your hands and a board, and roll dough into a 30-inch-long log. Pat log flat to about 5 inches wide. Spread filling all the way down the center of the log, to within 1 inch of the side edges. At this point, remember to insert a little "prize" inside the filling!

Pinch sides of dough up and over the filling. Pinch log ends together to form a circle. Place bread, seam side down, on a buttered pizza pan or a large square baking sheet.

To garnish the *tortell*: Beat egg in a small bowl and brush top of the bread with it. Pat sliced almonds all over. Allow bread to rise, uncovered, for 20 minutes. Preheat oven to 400° F.

Bake bread in 400° F oven for 25 minutes. Serve warm.

DESSERTS, ICE CREAMS, AND AFTER-DINNER TREATS
POSTRES, GELATERIA, I DOLÇOS PER A PICAR

t's no mistake that this is the largest chapter in the book. I love desserts and wanted to include every one of my favorite recipes—which of course was not possible. I should explain that in Catalunya, most meals at home conclude with seasonal fresh fruit rather than a sweet. Even restaurants will offer, along with their sweet desserts, a selection of fresh fruit such as pineapple, a tangy fruit salad, tiny wild strawberries, or even a plain glass of freshly squeezed orange juice. Other simple yet classic Catalan desserts are *mel i mató,* fresh white cheese with honey, or *postre de músic,* a plate of dried fruits and nuts.

More elaborate desserts are reserved for special occasions. On Sundays, at home we would often buy a fancy dessert from the pastry shop. And whenever my mother had a dinner party, she loved to make the desserts herself (always more than one!). In fact, the women in my family contributed some of the best recipes in this chapter. And you will see that, as befits our heritage, most of their recipes feature at least a dash of brandy.

Caramelized Apple Flan Scented with Cinnamon and Brandy

Flam de Poma al Caramel

Serves eight.

A favorite from my mother's recipe file, this flan features chunks of apples in a silken custard enhanced by a dash of fine brandy.

For the caramel:
1/3 cup sugar

For the flan:
3 tablespoons butter
2 pounds Pippin or Granny Smith apples, peeled, cored, and coarsely chopped
1/2 cup finest-quality brandy
6 eggs
1/2 cup sugar
1 teaspoon ground cinnamon
1 cup half-and-half

As a garnish:
1 cup heavy cream
2 tablespoons powdered sugar
1/2 teaspoon vanilla extract
1/4 teaspoon ground cinnamon

To prepare the caramel: In a small, heavy saucepan, dissolve sugar in water. Cook over medium-high heat until sugar melts and turns medium to dark brown. Don't stir; just shake pan. Immediately pour caramel into a

8- or 9-cup mold. With oven mitts on both hands, rotate mold gently, swirling caramel to cover bottom and part of sides; continue turning mold until caramel is almost set.

To prepare the flan: Preheat oven to 350° F. In a heavy, medium skillet with a lid, heat butter and cook apples over medium-low heat, covered, for 15 minutes. Add brandy; when hot, flambé (see p. 12). Cook for 2 or 3minutes, shaking skillet. In a large bowl, beat eggs with sugar and cinnamon. Stir in half-and-half and apples.

Pour apple mixture into caramelized mold and place in a larger pan filled with boiling water halfway up the mold. Bake in 350° F oven, uncovered, for 50 minutes, or until a cake tester comes out clean.

To prepare garnish and assemble the dish: Whip cream with powdered sugar and vanilla. As soon as flan is cool enough to handle, unmold it onto a serving platter. Spoon caramel over flan. Mound cream in center of flan, sprinkling top with cinnamon. Serve warm or at room temperature.

Fresh Blackberry Flan with a Blackberry-Cassis Sauce

Flam de Móres amb Salsa de Móres

Serves six to eight.
Makes one 5-cup flan.

If you like blackberries and can get them fresh during their short season, don't miss making this flan, a creation of the great chef Jean-Louis Neichel, who owns Neichel, one of the best restaurants in Barcelona. Light and airy in texture, with the intense flavor of fresh blackberries, this flan is easy to prepare and quite foolproof.

For the flan:
1 cup milk
1 teaspoon vanilla extract
1/2 cup sugar
4 egg yolks
1 envelope (1/4 ounce) unflavored gelatin
1/2 cup crème de cassis liqueur

1 pound fresh blackberries
1 cup heavy cream

For the sauce:
1/2 pound fresh blackberries
1/3 cup sugar
2 tablespoons crème de cassis liqueur

To prepare the flan: In a heavy, medium saucepan, combine milk, vanilla, sugar, and egg yolks. Heat gently and cook over low heat, stirring constantly, until custard thickens and coats the back of a spoon, about 15 minutes.

In a small saucepan, dissolve gelatin in cassis liqueur, stirring over low heat until gelatin is dissolved. Stir into custard. Refrigerate custard until it begins to set, about 45 minutes.

Meanwhile, with a fork or potato ricer, crush 1/2 cup blackberries and mix it with remaining whole berries. Whip cream until it forms stiff peaks. Remove custard from refrigerator; carefully fold in blackberries and cream. Pour mixture into a 5- to 7-cup flan or ring mold. Refrigerate for at least 3 or 4 hours before serving.

To prepare the sauce: In a blender or food processor, purée blackberries with sugar and cassis liqueur. Strain through a fine sieve.

To assemble the dish: Unmold flan by dipping it into a pan or sink filled with hot water for 5 or 6 seconds. Invert mold onto a serving platter and pour some sauce around flan. Pass remaining sauce in a sauceboat. Serve chilled.

Catalan Caramel Custard

Crema Catalana

Serves six to eight.

A delicious custard with a burnt sugar crust, crema catalana *is very often served in restaurants and also at home, especially on St. Joseph's day (March 19). I remember Rosalia making it every year on that traditional day. The best part is the caramelized crust on top, made by sprinkling sugar over the individual custards and searing it with a red-hot iron plate, about 3 inches in diameter, with a handle.*

These days such iron plates are sold commercially in Catalunya, but are still rather hard to find in this country. Instead, you can use a flat metal spatula heated over a gas burner. Or you can place the ovenproof ramekins briefly under a preheated broiler to caramelize the sugar. In Catalunya, crema catalana *is usually served in shallow individual* cassoletas, *ceramic or earthenware ramekins 5 to 6 inches across—as Roig Robí, one of my favorite restaurants, does.*

1-1/2 tablespoons cornstarch
1 quart milk
Peel of 1 lemon
1 cinnamon stick

12 eggs
3/4 cup sugar, plus sugar for caramelizing custard tops

In a small bowl, dissolve cornstarch in 2 tablespoons milk; set aside. In a medium saucepan, scald remaining milk with lemon peel and cinnamon; just before it comes to a boil, turn off heat, cover, and set aside.

In a large, heavy saucepan, beat eggs, sugar, and cornstarch/milk mixture with a whisk. Remove lemon peel and slowly add milk to egg mixture, whisking constantly. Cook over low heat (with cinnamon stick), stirring constantly, just until mixture thickens, about 10 minutes. Remove cinnamon stick. Immediately strain through a fine sieve into a large pouring jar, then pour into individual earthenware *cassoles* or ovenproof ramekins (or onto a serving platter). Refrigerate until serving time.

To burn the custard top: Shortly before serving, heat a special iron plate or a metal spatula to red hot over a gas flame. Sprinkle about 1 tablespoon sugar over top of each custard and touch surface of sugar with the red-hot metal just long enough to caramelize it. (Or place serving dish under a preheated broiler for a few minutes to brown the sugar.)

Dried Fruit Tart with a Topping of Mixed Nuts

Pastís de Músic

Serves eight.
Makes one 10-inch round tart.

Postre de Músic, *or "musician's dessert," is one of Catalunya's simplest desserts: nothing more than a mixture of dried fruits and nuts. The name comes from the old days when musicians, often young and poor, traveled around the countryside to perform. They were rarely paid much but were always offered some food in exchange for their music, and if they played really well, a dessert treat such as raisins, hazelnuts, almonds, pine nuts—whatever the farmer had on hand.* Pastís de músic *is a sophisticated version of that humble dessert made into a delicious tart, with a rich filling and a topping of toasted nuts, perfect as a Thanksgiving or Christmas dessert.*

(Note: *Store leftover pastry dough in the freezer; it is wonderful for small individual tartlets, which you can serve with any filling as an appetizer. I often fill them with tiny bay shrimp tossed in a light lemon vinaigrette with fresh snipped chives.*)

For the pastry shell:
1-1/2 cups unbleached all-purpose flour
1/2 cup (1 stick) chilled unsalted butter, cut into 1-inch cubes
1 egg

For the filling:
12 ounces mixed dried fruits of your choice, such as figs, apricots, prunes, pears, raisins, and dates
2 egg yolks
1/4 cup finest-quality brandy, or to taste
1 tablespoon unsalted butter
1/2 tablespoon flour
1/2 cup cold milk
1/2 cup sugar
3 tablespoons fresh lemon juice, or to taste

For the topping:
1/3 cup hazelnuts (filberts) toasted (see p. 11)
1/3 cup blanched almonds, toasted (see p. 11)
1/3 cup walnut halves
1/3 cup pine nuts

As a garnish:
1 cup heavy cream
1 tablespoon finest-quality brandy, or to taste
2 tablespoons sugar, or to taste

To make the pastry shell: Preheat oven to 425° F. In a food processor, pulse flour and butter together until mixture acquires consistency of cornmeal. Add egg and whirl until a ball forms. Keeping pastry at room temperature for ease in pressing, press it into a 10-inch removable-rim tart pan to height of 1 inch; form a thin layer, especially on the sides. (You will have some pastry left over, which can be frozen. See *Note*, below left.) Refrigerate for at least 15 minutes before baking; this will keep it from shrinking during baking.

Place a piece of aluminum foil over pastry and fill foil with pie weights or beans. Bake in 425° F oven for 25 minutes, or until golden. Remove rim of tart pan. Lower oven temperature to 375° F.

To prepare the filling: In a medium saucepan, combine dried fruits with 1 cup water. Bring to a boil, reduce heat to low, cover, and cook for 10 minutes. Uncover, increase heat to medium-high, and cook, stirring occasionally, until there is no liquid left in pan. Chop fruit coarsely by hand.

In a small bowl, beat egg yolks with brandy; set aside. In a medium saucepan, melt butter; over medium heat, stir in flour. Add cold milk and sugar, stir, and cook for 1 minute. Add egg yolks and brandy and cook over low heat, stirring constantly with a whisk, until custard thickens, about 10 minutes. Stir in chopped fruits and lemon juice; taste to see if you would like more lemon juice or brandy. Pour into prepared crust.

To prepare the topping: Sprinkle hazelnuts, almonds, walnuts, and pine nuts over tart, and pat them down with your hand. Bake in 375° F oven for 45 minutes, or until nuts and pie crust are golden. Let cool on a rack before unmolding.

To prepare the garnish: In a deep bowl, beat cream to soft peaks. Mix in brandy and sugar.

Serve at room temperature or slightly warm, accompanying each slice with a dollop of cream.

Bread Pudding with Dried Fruits and Orange Liqueur

*Púding de Fruites Seques
al Licor de Taronja*

Serves six to eight.

This homey bread pudding, a recipe from my Aunt Oriola, combines the richness of dried fruits with a generous dollop of orange liqueur. It is a perfect winter dessert, ideal for Christmas, also very easy and quick to make.

For the caramel:
1/3 cup sugar

For the pudding:
2 cups milk
2 tablespoons unsalted butter
1/2 pound mixed dried fruits: 2 ounces each apricots or peaches, figs, dates, and raisins, or a mixture of your choice
6 ounces day-old white bread, crusts trimmed (4-1/2 ounces after trimming crusts), thinly sliced

4 to 5 tablespoons orange liqueur, to taste
2 teaspoons minced orange zest (see p. 10)
3 eggs, beaten

As a garnish:
1 cup heavy cream, whipped with 2 teaspoons sugar

To prepare the caramel: Caramelize a 5-cup mold with sugar, proceeding as directed in recipe for Caramelized Apple Flan Scented with Cinnamon and Brandy, p. 123.

To prepare the pudding: Preheat oven to 350° F. Bring milk to a boil and add butter, stirring until it melts. Coarsely chop dried fruits by hand and place them in a medium bowl. Pour milk/butter mixture over and add bread in chunks; let it steep for 15 minutes. Add liqueur and orange zest, and mash with a fork to mix well. Stir in beaten eggs. Pour into prepared mold.

Place mold inside a larger pan filled with boiling water 2 inches up the sides of the mold. Bake in 350° F oven for 40 minutes, or until a cake tester comes out clean.

To assemble the dish: Let cool 10 or 15 minutes before unmolding onto a serving plate. Garnish with whipped cream.

Wine Recommendation: Serve with a luscious sweet dessert wine.

Aunt Oriola's Pears in Red Wine with a Fresh Cheese Filling and Strawberry Sauce

Peres al Vi Negre Oriola

Serves six.

Whole pears cooked in red wine is a Catalan dessert classic, but these may be the best ever, with a sweet fresh strawberry sauce played against the natural tartness of the wine.

For the pears:
6 large ripe but firm pears, such as Bartlett or Bosc
One 750-ml bottle full-bodied dry red wine
1/2 cup sugar
Two 2-1/2-inch cinnamon sticks

For the filling:
3 ounces cream cheese, at room temperature
1/4 cup sugar
1/4 cup heavy cream, whipped
Dash of finest-quality brandy

For the sauce:
3/4 pound fresh strawberries, stemmed
1/4 cup sugar

To prepare the pears: Peel pears and core them whole, from bottom to top, making a cylindrical hole with a melon-ball scoop or a small knife. In a pan large enough to hold pears, bring wine, sugar, and cinnamon to a boil. Turn heat to low and simmer pears in wine, uncovered, for about 30 minutes, or until they are very tender but not mushy. As they simmer, baste pears with wine from time to time, so that they will take on the color of the wine. Remove pears from pot and discard cinnamon sticks. Bring liquid to a boil and reduce it to 3/4 or 1 cup. Set aside.

To prepare the filling: Mix cream cheese with sugar in a blender or food processor. Transfer to a small bowl and fold in whipped cream. Stir in dash of brandy, to taste.

With a pastry bag, pipe filling into pears. Place them in a serving bowl. Pour reduced wine over. Chill.

To prepare the sauce: Purée strawberries with sugar in a blender or food processor until sugar dissolves completely. Chill.

To assemble the dish: Just before serving, cover pears with strawberry purée, or pass sauce in a sauceboat.

Grandma Pepeta's Apple Fritters Scented with Anise

Bunyols de Poma de l'Avia Pepeta

Serves six.

This is a taste from my childhood, one of the few recipes I have from my grandmother, who was not a cook, but enjoyed making desserts. And if I happened to be really good, she would let me help fry these bunyols—*that was the best part!*

The anise liqueur I use in the preparation is an old Spanish favorite called Anís del Mono, *a brand popular since the late 1800s and now owned by the Sherry firm of Osborne.* Anís del Mono *is available in some parts of the United States, and if you can find it, it is best, for both this recipe and for any other occasion requiring an anise liqueur. If you can't get it, substitute the French Pernod liqueur.*

3/4 cup anise liqueur, preferably
  Anís del Mono, or Pernod
1 pound (2 large) apples (see Note, below)

For the batter:
2 eggs
1 cup flour
1/4 cup milk
1 tablespoon olive oil
1/4 cup sugar
1/4 teaspoon salt
1/3 cup reserved marinade
1 teaspoon baking powder

For finishing the fritters:
Abundant olive oil (preferably light)
  for frying
1/4 cup powdered sugar
1 teaspoon ground cinnamon

Note: The apples we use in Spain are Golden Delicious, which you can find here. I have tried it with other kinds of apples, such as Pippins and Rome Beauties, and these also work; they just provide a different texture. I prefer Golden Delicious because they are more crisp and sweet, but you can follow your personal preference.

Pour liqueur into a wide, shallow glass or ceramic bowl. Peel, core, and slice apples into 1/2-inch-wide crescents. Place them in bowl with liqueur and let them marinate for 1 hour or more, turning apples occasionally.

To prepare the batter: In a large bowl, beat together all batter ingredients baking powder. Let sit for at least 1 hour, at room temperature.

Scoop out 1/3 cup liqueur from marinade and stir into batter mixture together with baking powder.

In an electric deep fryer or in a deep, heavy pan, heat oil to 340° F. There should be about 1 inch of oil in the pan. Remove apples from marinade with tongs and dip them in the batter. Slide them, a few at a time, into hot oil. Cook quickly, turning often, until crescents turn golden. Remove to paper towels to drain.

Mix powdered sugar and cinnamon together in a small bowl and sprinkle over apples. Serve immediately, while still hot.

Frozen Orange Soufflé with Orange Liqueur

Soufflé de Taronja Gelat

Serves six.

This is a "double-orange" soufflé I always relished at home—especially when prepared with our orange brandy liqueur, Gran Torres.

Start preparation 12 hours ahead.

Minced zest of 3 oranges (3 loose tablespoons) (see p. 10)
3/4 cup sugar
1 cup freshly squeezed orange juice, strained
7 eggs, separated
1/4 cup orange liqueur
1 cup heavy cream, whipped to stiff peaks

As a garnish:
1 orange, 1 peach, 1 nectarine, peeled and cut into wedges (orange without membrane)

Chill a 5- or 6-cup soufflé dish in the freezer.

In a large saucepan, combine orange zest, sugar, and orange juice. Bring to a boil and cook until syrup reaches thread consistency or registers 230° F on a candy thermometer. Meanwhile, beat egg yolks in a blender or food processor. With motor running, add syrup to egg yolks in a thin stream. Continue whirling for 5 minutes. Blend in liqueur. Transfer to a large bowl. Beat egg whites until stiff and fold them into egg yolk mixture. Gently fold in whipped cream, using a spatula or a balloon whisk. Pour into chilled soufflé dish and freeze until firm, about 10 hours.

To unmold, pass a knife around edge of soufflé dish and dip it for 5 seconds into a pan or sink filled with hot water. Invert mold onto a serving platter, garnish with fresh fruit wedges around the soufflé and serve immediately.

Wine Recommendation: Serve with a glass of the orange liqueur used in this soufflé's preparation.

Sherbets and Ice Creams

Sorbets i Gelateria

Homemade ice cream or sherbet is always a special treat. On summer afternoons in Spain my brother Miguel and I would crank the old-fashioned machine to make all sorts of wonderful ice creams, imagining with every turn of the handle just how good it would taste.

With today's commercial machines, making ice cream is a breeze. It no longer requires an entire afternoon; once the basic custard is made, you can have homemade ice cream in less than a half hour. It is also an ideal dessert to make ahead.

In the following recipes, I have assumed that you have an ice cream maker; but if you don't, here's how to make ice creams and sherbets without one: Refrigerate mixture in a bowl until completely chilled. Freeze until firm about 1 inch from the edge of the bowl. Beat with an electric mixer to blend thoroughly. Cover and freeze until partially firm. Repeat process twice more. Freeze until set.

Today we can get such wonderful commercial ice creams that it hardly seems worth the effort any more to make them at home. So I've selected from my repertoire only a few outstanding recipes.

Red Wine Sherbet with Orange, Lemon, and Mint

Xarrup de Vi Negre a la Menta

Makes about 5-1/2 cups.

I always enjoyed this unusual sherbet at Cal Joan, a country restaurant in Vilafranca del Penedès, the home of my familys' winery. The owner, Joan Samsó, used to make this sherbet with our Coronas wine, and this is what I use for this recipe. You could also substitute any dry medium-bodied red wine without aggressive tannins; coarse, or tannic, reds will give the sherbet an unappealing harsh taste.

1 cup sugar
5 or 6 fresh mint leaves
One 750-ml bottle fine medium-bodied dry red wine

1/2 cup fresh orange juice
3 tablespoons fresh lemon juice

In a small saucepan, combine sugar and mint leaves with 1/2 cup water. Bring to a boil and boil for 1 minute. Let cool and remove mint leaves.

Pour wine into a nonreactive bowl. Add mint-infused sugar syrup, orange and lemon juice, and stir. Chill and make into sherbet according to instructions for your ice cream maker. (It may take 20 to 25 minutes longer to set than other ice creams.)

Meringue Sherbet with Cinnamon and Brandy

Llet Merengada

Makes about 1-1/2 quarts.

This is my version of the frothy milk meringue served in the summertime all over Spain in ice cream and coffee bars. Llet merengada came to Catalunya by way of Valencia, where it appeared for the first time in 1747 and was very popular throughout the nineteenth century.
Even today, on my frequent visits to Barcelona, my mother and I love to take my daughter Cristina to La Jijonenca, a place famous in Barcelona for its llet merengada. *The real version, of course, has no liquor in it, but I like to add a dash. This sorbet makes a lovely dessert on a hot summer evening accompanied by Crunchy Twice-Baked Almond Cookies (p. 135).*

1/2 cup sugar
Peel of 1 lemon
One 2-1/2-inch cinnamon stick
6 tablespoons orange liqueur
1 quart half-and-half
2 egg whites, at room temperature

1/4 cup finest-quality brandy, or to taste

Optional, as a garnish:
Ground cinnamon

In a medium saucepan, mix sugar, lemon peel, cinnamon stick, orange liqueur, and half-and-half. Cook over low heat, uncovered, for 10 minutes. Turn off heat, cover, and steep for 15 minutes. Transfer to a large bowl. Discard lemon peel and cinnamon stick.

Beat egg whites until stiff. Fold them into half-and-half mixture. Add brandy to taste. Chill. Make into sherbet according to the directions for your ice cream maker.

Sprinkle top with optional ground cinnamon and serve.

Rice Pudding Ice Cream

Gelat d'Arròs amb Llet

Makes about 5-1/2 cups.

Rice pudding is a rich and comforting dessert found all over Spain. I always enjoyed it at home, and this is my version made into a velvety ice cream studded with grains of rice.

4 cups half-and-half
2 cups milk
One 2- to 2-1/2-inch cinnamon stick
Peel of 1 lemon
1/2 cup short-grain rice (see p. 6)
2/3 cup sugar

In a heavy, medium saucepan, cook half-and-half and milk with cinnamon stick and lemon peel over medium-low heat for 5 minutes, or until just before it comes to a boil.

Meanwhile, blanch rice in boiling water for 1 minute; drain and run cold water over it. Stir rice and sugar into milk mixture and cook over low heat for 45 minutes, uncovered, stirring occasionally; don't remove the "skin" that forms on surface, simply stir it back into milk.

Remove cinnamon stick and lemon peel. Transfer to a blender and pulse a few times to just break up rice grains while keeping their texture. Chill. Make into ice cream according to directions of your ice cream maker.

Before serving, if you've kept ice cream in freezer, let it soften at room temperature so it will be easier to scoop it out—it is too hard right out of freezer.

Wine Recommendation: A glass of dessert wine such as Malvasia would be an ideal accompaniment to this refreshing, unusual ice cream.

Honey Ice Cream with Caramelized Nuts and Brandy

Gelat de Mel amb Fruits Secs

Makes 5 or 6 cups.

The caramelized nuts in this rich, velvety ice cream contribute an intriguing texture, while the honey rounds out the complex flavors of this special ice cream.

3/4 cup honey
1/2 cup blanched almonds, toasted (see p. 11) and coarsely chopped
1/2 cup hazelnuts, toasted (see p. 11) and coarsely chopped
1/2 cup walnut pieces, coarsely chopped by hand
4 cups half-and-half
8 egg yolks
1/4 cup finest-quality brandy

Note. To clean caramel from skillet, simply fill it up with water and bring to a boil; water will dissolve caramel. Oil skillet afterwards.

In a medium skillet, cook 1/4 cup honey over medium heat until it starts to foam. Add almonds, hazelnuts, and walnuts; cook, stirring with a wooden spoon, until nuts are coated with caramel and acquire a dark golden color. Transfer caramelized nuts to a large well-buttered plate, spreading them out. When they have cooled and hardened, grind half of them finely in a food processor. Set aside.

In a large, heavy pan, scald half-and-half. Meanwhile, beat egg yolks in a small bowl together with remaining 1/2 cup honey. Whisk egg mixture into half-and-half and cook over low heat, stirring constantly for 10 to 15 minutes, or until custard thickens and coats the back of a spoon. (If it should curdle, don't worry; it won't be noticeable after processing the ice cream.) Let cool to room temperature.

Whisk ground and chopped nuts, and brandy, into custard. Chill. Make into ice cream according to directions for your ice cream maker. (It may take 15 or 20 minutes longer to make than regular ice cream.)

Prune Ice Cream with Coffee and Brandy

Gelat de Prunes amb Cafè

Makes about 4 cups.

This is a rich, old-fashioned family recipe, with an ideal combination of flavors: coffee and brandy are naturals together, and the sweetness of the prunes adds an intriguing note.

6 ounces pitted prunes	2 cups half-and-half
8 tablespoons finest-quality brandy	3 cardamom pods
4 egg yolks	1 tablespoon instant coffee
1/2 cup sugar	1 cup heavy cream

In a small saucepan, combine prunes with 6 tablespoons brandy and water to cover. Cook over low heat for 15 minutes, or until prunes are tender and liquid is reduced to about 2 tablespoons. Purée prunes with their liquid in a blender or food processor. Set aside.

Beat egg yolks and sugar, and combine them in a medium saucepan with half-and-half. Break open the cardamom pods; crush seeds in a mortar with a pestle and add them to saucepan. Cook over low heat, stirring constantly, until custard thickens and coats the back of a spoon, about 15 minutes. Transfer to a large bowl and whisk in prune purée. Dissolve coffee in remaining 2 tablespoons brandy and stir it in, together with cream. Chill and make into ice cream according to the directions of your ice cream maker.

After-Dinner Treats

Dolços per a Picar

When I go out for dinner to fine restaurants, I always enjoy the moment when the plate of dainty petits fours arrives with the coffee. And I feel that at home, a little after-dinner treat is just as much appreciated, especially if it's homemade.

Variations on Yam and Almond Cookies

Panellets

Halloween is unknown in Spain; however, we do observe November 1 as All Saints' Day. It is a national holiday, and a particularly important date for those whose name is not in the official registry of saints, as they celebrate their saint's day on November 1. You see, birthdays pass almost unobserved in Spain—but saint's days are important celebrations.

Panellets ("little breads," in Catalan) are a traditional treat on All Saints' Day. The most typical are *panellets de pinyons*, made with the basic dough and rolled in pine nuts. But there are many variations, and we usually serve an assortment. I have chosen a few favorites here; I suggest making the basic *panellet* dough recipe, dividing it in parts, and then making several different flavors. You can also cut the basic recipe in half, for just a couple of flavors.

In Catalunya we would never make *panellets* at home; we bought them at a pastry shop. My favorites are from Vilaplana, one of the best pastry shops in Barcelona.

Basic Panellet Dough

Makes about 4 cups, or 3 pounds.

1 medium yam or sweet potato
  (1/2 pound)
2 cups sugar
3 cups (16 ounces) blanched
  almonds, finely ground

2 egg yolks
1 teaspoon vanilla extract
2 teaspoons minced lemon zest
  (see p. 10)

Boil yam until tender (about 30 minutes, depending on size). Peel and mash it; you should have about 1 cup. In a food processor, mix yam together with rest of ingredients until dough is soft. Let it rest for at least 30 minutes before using in any of the following recipes.

Pine Nut Panellets

Panellets de Pinyons

Makes 18 to 20 cookies.

1/4 recipe Panellet Dough (see
  above)

About 1 cup (5 ounces) pine nuts
1 egg yolk

Preheat oven to 350° F. After dough has rested, make small walnut-sized balls and coat them with pine nuts. Brush them lightly with egg yolk. Place on an oiled baking sheet, 1 inch apart. Bake in 350° F oven for 15 minutes.

Chocolate Panellets

Panellets de Xocolata

Makes 15 to 18 cookies.

1/4 cup unsweetened ground
  chocolate or cocoa (preferably
  Dutch process cocoa)

1/4 recipe Panellet Dough (above)
About 1/4 cup ground blanched
  almonds or hazelnuts (filberts)

Preheat oven to 350° F. Mix chocolate or cocoa with dough. Shape dough into walnut-size balls and roll them in ground almonds or hazelnuts. Place on an oiled baking sheet, 1 inch apart. Bake in 350° F oven for 10 to 15 minutes, or just until they start to color.

Chestnut Panellets

Panellets de Castanyes

Makes about 20 cookies.

6 ounces chestnuts, peeled
1 cup milk
1/4 recipe Panellet Dough (above)

Pinch of ground nutmeg
About 1/4 cup ground blanched
  almonds or hazelnuts (filberts)

Preheat oven to 350° F. Simmer chestnuts in milk for 35 minutes, covered. Grind chestnuts with milk in a food processor; add dough and nutmeg. Shape dough into walnut-sized balls and coat with ground almonds or hazelnuts. Bake as directed in Chocolate Panellets recipe (above).

Coffee Panellets
Panellets de Cafè

Makes 8 to 10 cookies.

1/8 recipe Panellet Dough (p. 133)
1 teaspoon instant coffee

About 1 tablespoon sugar
8 to 10 whole coffee beans

Preheat oven to 350° F. Mix dough with instant coffee, shape into walnut-sized balls, and roll them in sugar. Put 1 coffee bean on top of each cookie, pressing it in slightly. Bake as directed in Chocolate Panellets recipe.

Hazelnut Panellets
Panellets d'Avellanes

Makes 10 to 12 cookies.

1/8 recipe Panellet Dough (p. 133)
1/2 cup (2-1/4 ounces) toasted hazelnuts (filberts), toasted (see p. 11), and finely ground

About 1 tablespoon sugar
8 to 10 whole hazelnuts (filberts), toasted (see p. 11)

Preheat oven to 350° F. Mix dough with ground hazelnuts, shape in walnut-sized balls, and roll them in sugar. Place a whole hazelnut on top of each cookie, pressing it in slightly. Bake as directed in Chocolate Panellets recipe.

Clove Panellets
Panellets de Clau

Makes 8 to 10 cookies.

1/8 recipe Panellet Dough (p. 133)
1/4 teaspoon ground cloves

About 1 tablespoon sugar

Preheat oven to 350° F. Mix dough with ground cloves. Shape into walnut-sized balls and roll them in sugar. Bake as directed in Chocolate Panellets recipe.

Coconut Panellets
Panellets de Coco

Makes 10 to 12 cookies.

1/8 recipe Panellet Dough (p. 133)
1/2 cup shredded sweetened coconut

About 1 tablespoon sugar

Preheat oven to 350° F. Mix dough with coconut. Shape into walnut-sized balls and roll them in sugar. Bake as directed in Chocolate Panellets recipe.

Crunchy Twice-Baked Almond Cookies

Carquinyolis

Makes about 50 to 60 cookies.

Carquinyolis are another type of traditional cookie found in Catalan pastry shops. The different versions all have one thing in common: They are always hard—sometimes too much so for my taste. These are just delightfully crunchy.

3 cups flour
1 cup sugar
1 tablespoon baking powder
1/2 teaspoon salt
2 tablespoons minced lemon zest (see p. 10)
1/2 cup (1 stick) chilled unsalted butter, cut into small pieces

3 eggs
1 teaspoon vanilla extract
1 teaspoon almond extract
1-1/2 cups (1/2 pound) almonds, toasted (see p. 11) for only 5 to 10 minutes, just until they start to color

In a food processor, combine flour, sugar, baking powder, salt, and lemon zest. Cut butter into the dry ingredients with just a few pulses. Add eggs, vanilla, and almond extract. Pulse a few times; don't overmix, dough should not be too smooth. Transfer to a bowl and fold almonds into dough quickly with your hands, until evenly distributed.

Preheat oven to 350° F. Butter a cookie sheet. Shape dough into 3 logs lengthwise on the cookie sheet; they should be about 2 to 2-1/2 inches wide and 3/4 to 1 inch high. Dough will spread during baking, so leave 1 inch between each log.

Bake in 350° F oven for 25 to 30 minutes, or until dough starts to turn golden. Remove from oven and immediately, while still hot, cut logs into 3/4-inch-thick slices. Place slices, cut side down, on cookie sheet and return to oven. Bake for another 15 to 20 minutes, or until golden.

These delicious cookies will keep for quite a while, stored in a tightly closed tin—but I've never been able to make them last very long!

Almond Meringue Cookies

Ametllats

Makes 15 to 20 small cookies.

1 cup (5-1/2 ounces) blanched almonds, plus 1 blanched whole almond for each cookie
1/3 cup powdered sugar

1/2 teaspoon vanilla extract
2 tablespoons butter, melted
2 egg whites, at room temperature

Preheat oven to 400° F. Grind 1 cup almonds very finely in a food processor. Mix in sugar, vanilla, and melted butter. Transfer to a large bowl.

In a medium bowl, beat egg whites until very stiff (you should be able to turn bowl over without egg white falling out). Gently fold egg whites into nut mixture lightly, being careful not to overfold.

Line a baking sheet with parchment or brown paper. Using 2 small spoons, drop small round mounds of the batter onto baking sheet, spacing them 1 inch apart. Place 1 whole almond on top of each mound. Bake in the 400° F oven for 10 minutes, or until they start to brown.

These cookies are best eaten right after they are baked. (If baked ahead, they may absorb moisture from the air; to crisp them, bake in a preheated 350° F oven for 5 minutes.)

Fisherman-style Flamed Coffee and Brandy with Lemon and Orange Peel

Cremat

Serves six to eight;
yields about 6 cups.

This is a very old, classic recipe from the Catalan fishermen of the Costa Brava, the rugged coast north of Barcelona. Toward the end of the nineteenth century, many Catalans sailed to Cuba to seek their fortunes, and they prepared this comforting beverage to warm their bodies as well as their spirits as they sang habaneras, *haunting songs named after the city of Havana. It was in Havana that they created* cremat, *the soothing combination of Antilles rum and Cuban coffee, and back home they continued to enjoy this potent beverage—often substituting local brandy for the rum. Performances of* habaneras *are still held today during the summer in the Costa Brava, and the* cremat *flows abundantly. In Catalunya,* cremat *is traditionally prepared in a wide clay casserole. And it is more fun to make it in front of your guests; it can be heated over a chafing dish.*

1-1/2 cups finest-quality brandy or rum
1/4 cup sugar
3 strips *each* lemon and orange peel, cut with a vegetable peeler from top to bottom
One 2- or 3-inch cinnamon stick
5 cups freshly brewed, strong hot coffee
1 tablespoon coffee beans

In a shallow, wide flameproof casserole (preferably of clay) or a skillet, heat brandy or rum with sugar, cinnamon, and lemon and orange peels. When hot, ignite with a match and flambé (see p. 10) for about 1 minute, stirring with a ladle. Dowse flames with coffee. Add coffee beans and serve immediately, ladling into coffee cups.

THE VINEYARDS AND WINES OF

CATALUNYA

▼ ▼ ▼

ecause I come from a family of winemakers, it would have been impossible for me to write a book on Catalan cuisine without including a section on the great wines of my region. While this is not by any means a wine book, Catalan wines are today an important part of the wine world in America. More and more of them are available in this country, particularly on the East Coast where there are many Spanish restaurants (and now even a Catalan one in Manhattan, Eldorado Petit, which offers a fine list of Catalan—and Spanish—wines).

When I go back to Barcelona, I am amazed to see so many new labels when I explore the fine wine shops. I often visit El Celler de Gelida, one of Barcelona's top wine stores, and invariably I end up taking home more bottles to taste than originally planned. According to El Celler's owner, Antoni Falgueras, "the interest of Catalans in wine has increased dramatically in the last few years, and that interest is not restricted to Catalan wines, but extends to those from all over the world." Antoni currently carries in inventory 3,500 different labels—including, indeed, several California wines. "People are drinking less," he states, "but higher quality. At the same time, Catalan wines have improved, and more varietal and *pago* wines have entered the market."

Catalan wines today are a far cry from what they were just fifteen years ago. In the past, as in many other wine areas of Spain, quantity rather than quality was the rule. At the end of the nineteenth century, the most typical rural industry in Catalunya was the distillation of *aguardientes* (brandy and spirits) from the local wine. But in recent years, the vineyard acreage has decreased while the quality of the wines has improved dramatically. Creative Catalan winemakers have applied state-of-the-art technology in their cellars and are now experimenting in the vineyards by adapting nontraditional grape varieties (Cabernet Sauvignon, Chardonnay, Pinot Noir, Riesling, Gewürztraminer, and so on) to their own soil and climate.

As a result, Catalan wines have attained such a level of quality that they now rank with the finest in the world at international competitions. However, they have lost none of their local character. Each of the different *denominaciones de origen* (or "appellations of origin") in Catalunya has a distinct personality, yet all have something in common that sets them apart from the rest of Spanish wines. The whites are aromatic, fresh, and elegant; the reds are well aged, round, and full-bodied.

The emergence of these Catalan wines on the world market dates from the 1970s, but winemaking is an old art in Catalunya. As far back as the first half of the fourteenth century, writers praised the "subtle" and "tingling" sparkling wines of the area. But even the Romans found early on that this region was ideal for growing grapes, especially red varieties, with good color. The most prized Mediterranean wines in those days were the *generosos,* with deep color, high alcohol, and generally sweet. Throughout the Middle Ages, the Priorato district was known for the full-bodied, soundly structured wines made by monks in the monasteries. And the pale wines of Alella, brilliant and delicate, were very popular in Barcelona at the turn of the century. Catalan winemakers have always had a certain talent for adapting their wines to the tastes of the time, and today's taste favors wines with fruit and natural elegance over heaviness and excess oak.

In exploring the wines of Catalunya, I enlisted the help of my friend Mauricio Wiesenthal, author of several books on Spain, its art, peoples, and lifestyle. He is also an authority on wines and gastronomy, and a contributing editor to several Spanish food and wine magazines.

The Denominaciones de Origen

Diversity of climate and soil is an important factor in Catalunya's wine regions. The Mediterranean provides the area with mild temperatures, yet the high mountains of the Catalan coast contribute the cold winters and cool summer nights that are ideal for growing aromatic white grape varieties and producing fresh, fragrant white wines.

The most important Catalan *denominaciones de origen* are Alella, Ampurdán-Costa Brava, Costers del Segre, Penedès, Priorato, Tarragona, and Terra-Alta. Other small districts produce wines of great quality, especially *cavas*, or sparkling wines produced by the *méthode champenoise.* While 98 percent of the *cava* producers are located in Penedès, they are not technically part of the Penedès *Denominación de Origen.*

A Tour of Catalan Bodegas

As we discuss each of the wine districts in Catalunya, I have listed some of the best-known *bodegas.* Due to lack of space I cannot discuss all of them, so I have concentrated on those whose wines are exported to the United States and/or who have a long tradition of quality in Catalunya.

Alella

This appellation, north of Barcelona, is well known for its white wines of pale straw color, aromatic and fruity. The main wineries are Cooperativa de Alella, producer of the Marfil brand of dry and semi-dry white, rosé, and red wines; and Parxet, which markets the white Marqués de Alella label.

Parxet, S.A. (Alta Alella), Masia Can Matons—Santa Maria de Martorelles (Barcelona). Tel 93-593.71.73.

Since 1981, Ismael Manaut has been producing innovative white wines and *cavas* in the area of the Maresme. The old *masia*, or Catalan farmhouse, belies the modern cellar that produces Marqués de Alella Clásico, a straw-colored white wine with a fresh, fruity aroma, made from Xarel-lo (or Pansá), Macabeo, and Chenin Blanc grapes. His non-oak aged Marqués de Alella Chardonnay is exemplary, too. He also produces some excellent *cavas* under the name Parxet: Brut, Brut Nature, and Chardonnay.

Bodega Cooperativa Alella Vinícola, Rambla Guimerá, 70—Alella (Barcelona). Tel 93-555.08.42.

Founded in 1906, this energetic cooperative has managed to preserve their historic appellation despite the urban expansion of Barcelona. They make a variety of dry and semi-dry white wines with an unmistakable Mediterranean personality. The Marfil Blanco Semidulce, made from Garnacha Blanca and Pansá grapes and aged in old oak casks, is the most traditional wine of the area: a golden wine with the aroma of toasted almonds and walnuts.

Vinos Jaume Serra, S. L., Escuelas Pías, 1—Alella (Barcelona). Tel 93-555.03.50.

Founded in 1941, these *Bodegas* produce white and rosé wines from traditional varieties under the name Alellasol, as well as a *cava* called Jaume Serra. Recently, the firm has also set up a modern *bodega* in the Penedès.

Ampurdán–Costa Brava

This district's vineyards, located north of Girona, on the border with France, are probably the most ancient in Catalunya. The Greeks established their first settlements in Rosas and Ampúries, in Ampurdán (L'Empordà in Catalan). One of the oldest enology manuals in Europe was written in 1130 by the monk Ramón Pere de Novàs at the monastery of Sant Pere de Roda; its ruins can still be seen today on the rugged Mediterranean coastline. Most of Ampurdán's wines are fresh young rosés made primarily from Garnacha and Cariñena grapes.

Cavas del Ampurdán, Conde Zavella, s/n—Perelada (Girona). Tel 972-50.27.62.

Located in the thirteenth-century Castle of Perelada, this *bodega* dates back to the Middle Ages (although the present company was founded only in 1930). The Gothic cloister, impressive library, and private wine museum are worth a visit; every year on the second Sunday of September, a wine harvest festival is held in the romantic gardens. The firm produces white, rosé, and red wines, as well as *cavas* and Blanc Pescador, a slightly carbonated, very pleasant and refreshing white made from Parellada and Macabeo grapes.

Costers del Segre

Situated in the basin of the river of the same name northeast of Lérida, Costers del Segre has a long tradition in the production of quality wines going back to the twelfth century. The star of this recently created appellation is without question Raimat, a model estate founded by the Raventós family (of Codorníu) at the beginning of this century near the village of Raimat. Winters are hard and summers extremely dry in this region. To rescue these arid lands for vineyards, Manel Raventós had to create a sophisticated system of irrigation at great expense, but his investment has paid off in the quality of the wines.

Raimat-Coniusa—Raimat (Lérida). Tel 973-72.40.00.

Manel Raventós, one of the great figures of Catalan viticulture, whose family owns Codorníu in the Penedès, founded these *bodegas* in 1918. The winery buildings were designed by the architect Joan Rubió i Bellver, a pupil and collaborator of Gaudí, and include one of the first buildings constructed in reinforced concrete, the new technology at the beginning of the century. The facilities were enlarged in 1989, and a new *bodega* was built next to the old one, provided with the latest equipment. The extensive vineyards include Merlot, Pinot Noir, Cabernet Sauvignon, Chardonnay, and other European grapes, along with traditional Catalan varieties.

The wines are made with the latest technology, using temperature-controlled stainless-steel tanks; the reds are carefully aged in oak casks. Raimat's Chardonnay and Cabernet Sauvignon are their top wines; the reds are complex and velvety, the whites fresh and aromatic. They also produce a clean, well-balanced Cava Chardonnay and a range of other wines, including a recently released, well-aged Merlot and a Pinot Noir.

Priorato

This is another historic area, once under the jurisdiction of the Carthusian Scala Dei order of monks. The impressive ruins of the monastery still rise among the vineyards, just west of Tarragona. Garnacha was the classic grape variety of the aromatic, full-bodied, high in alcohol and generally slightly sweet Priorato red wines. Today, however, the vineyards are planted mainly with Cariñena, which yields a sturdy wine suitable for aging. Rich in color and alcohol, most of the district's wines are a blend of both grapes. When well made, the softness and aroma of Garnacha is nicely coupled with the powerful structure of Cariñena.

Cellers Scala Dei, Rambla Cartoixa s/n—Scala Dei (Tarragona). Tel 977-82.70.27.
Located in the heart of the lands surrounding the old monastery of Scala Dei and renowned for its wines in the nineteenth century, the present company was established in 1973 by a group of Barcelona businessmen interested in restoring the prestige of this historic wine region. Aged in large oak casks in the monastery's ancient cellars, the red wines are mainly made from Garnacha and Cariñena. Their best wine is Cartoixa Scala Dei, though the firm is experimenting with Chardonnay and Cabernet Sauvignon, too.

De Müller, S.A., Plaza, 3—Scala Dei (Tarragona). Tel 977-21.02.20.
This Tarragona firm has its aging cellars in Scala Dei and for many years has produced a classic red wine, Legítimo Priorato de Müller. At Christmas, they often release an exceptional older reserve.

Masía Barril—Bellmunt del Priorat (Tarragona). Tel 977-83.01.92.
In 1931, Rafael Barril acquired a *masia* (Catalan farmhouse) at El Priorato, once owned by the Charterhouse monks, where the family firm produces honest and typical wines of the appellation. The red is made from Garnacha with a small amount of Cariñena, and is aged in oak and chestnut casks. Rich and full-bodied, this wine has been compared to a robust southern Rhône.

Tarragona

The land of the old Tarraco, capital of the Roman empire in Spain, today has a serene and classic beauty. Olive, almond, and hazelnut trees stretch over the landscape among the vineyards. The area's wines were already famous in the days of Emperor Augustus. Its production is so bountiful that the wines are exported throughout the world; such abundance has sometimes undermined their historic reputation for quality. The main varieties planted are Macabeo, Xarel-lo, and Parellada for whites, and Tempranillo and Cariñena for reds.

De Müller, S. A., Real, 38—Tarragona. Tel 977-21.02.20.
The Müller family has deep roots in Catalunya, where they have been involved in politics, culture, and business, establishing their extensive *bodegas* at the port of Tarragona in 1851. In addition to mostly young, fresh white wines—the best is Viña Solimar—this large family firm, now directed by Joaquín de Müller, also produces outstanding wines for the Holy Mass, made according to canons dictated by the Vatican. Other specialties include aromatic sweet wines and a liqueur.

Penedès

This is the wine-producing district par excellence in Catalunya and home to my family's century-old *Bodegas* Torres. The Penedès not only yields the finest table wines, which constitute one of the great enological achievements in the second half of this century, but also is the home of the renowned Spanish *cavas,* or sparkling wines produced by the *méthode champenoise*. Grapes have been grown here since the fourth or fifth century B.C., when the Greeks and the Phoenicians colonized the area around Barcelona. The Penedès *Denominación de Origen* covers an area of 375,000 acres, of which about sixty-two thousand are planted with vineyards. The D.O.'s capital is Vilafranca de Penedès, thirty miles southwest of Barcelona.

The Penedès' climate and soil are very diverse. In less than twenty miles, the vineyards climb from sea level to an altitude well over 2,000 feet. The region is thus divided into three sub-zones: Low Penedès, with vineyards planted up to 400 feet; Middle or Central Penedès, planted up to 1,300 feet; and High Penedès, where vines grow at an elevation of up to 2,700 feet. Such variation allows the acclimation of very different grape varieties.

The traditional red grapes—Cariñena, Garnacha, Tempranillo, and Monastrell—are grown mostly in the Low Penedès, along the Mediterranean. The Middle Penedès is ideal for the classic whites from Xarel-lo and Macabeo, which are the basis for the area's sparkling wines. It is also most suitable for the noble European red varieties Cabernet Sauvignon, Cabernet Franc, Pinot Noir, and Merlot, and for the whites Chardonnay and Sauvignon Blanc. The High Penedès, with its rainier and cooler climate, is ideal for growing the fine, elegant local white Parellada and the French Sauvignon Blanc, as well as the aromatic Alsatian and German varieties Riesling, Gewürztraminer, and Muscat d'Alsace.

In the Penedès, dedicated winemakers grow their own grapes, select the rootstocks and grape varieties, oversee their pruning, and research the grapes most suitable for their special microclimate. From the large cooperatives to the small family wineries in the traditional *masias* (Catalan farmhouses), a wide range of wines is made: whites youthful and fragrant or complex and well aged; fresh fruity rosés; reds noble and complex or full-bodied and rustic; lively spritzy whites; elegant *cavas;* and sweet apéritif and dessert wines such as the traditional sweet Malvasía of Sitges.

The desire to create, change, and improve is a typical Catalan trait, and many vineyards are undergoing a transformation as the winemaker experiments with new grapes, new methods, and new blends. The *bodegas* of Penedès fall into two categories: those introducing more and more noble grapes from Europe and producing wines of a more international character, rather than traditionally Spanish ones; and those content with the typical grapes and the wines they have always made. In the middle are a number of wineries that are trying new varieties while continuing to rely on classic methods and varieties. Fortunately, *bodegas* of different styles can exist side by side, each producing some very successful wines.

The Sparkling Cavas

The small town of Sant Sadurní d'Anoia, seven miles from Vilafranca del Penedès and about an hour's drive from Barcelona, has been the headquarters for the sparkling wine industry in Spain since 1872. That is the year Josep Raventós and his son Manel, who had studied and worked in France, introduced the traditional methods used in the great Champagne houses of Reims and Epérnay to their *bodega,* Codorníu.

At first these sparkling wines from Penedès were known as *champán* or *xampany* (the Castilian and Catalan versions of the word *champagne*); later international legislation created the name *cava* specifically for sparkling wines from Spain produced by the *méthode champenoise.* The word *cava* (from the latin *cava,* which means "hole" or "gallery," refers to the underground *bodegas* where the wines are fermented and aged.

Sparkling wines have a long tradition in the Mediterranean. Virgil praised them in the *Aeneid,* and chronicles of medieval monasteries in Catalunya mention "swarming wines," which were most likely some sort of sparkling wine.

In Catalunya, *cavas* are generally made from a blend of traditional varieties: Parellada for elegance and finesse, Macabeo for aroma and fruit, and Xarel-lo for body and structure. The red grapes Garnacha and Monastrell are used in the rosés.

The reason Catalan sparkling wines can be sold for such a relatively low price on the American market, given their quality, is mainly due to the technology introduced by Codorníu in 1972, when Josep Maria Raventós was manager of the company. Committed to the *méthode champenoise* rather than to the less-expensive Charmat process, he set out to reduce the cost by mechanizing the traditional methods.

It used to take skilled specialists three to six weeks to finish the task of "riddling," or turning each bottle a little bit every day until the sediment produced by the second fermentation settles in the cork end and can be expelled. Because of the work of the Penedès pioneers, it can now be accomplished more efficiently either manually by a *girasol* ("sunflower") or mechanically by a *giropallet*, a huge crate with an octagonal base that holds 504 bottles and tilts them ever so slightly every eight hours. (This invention is now used in sparkling wine production in France and California.) However, only the large *cava* producers can afford this automated process; the smaller family-run firms continue to riddle by hand.

Bodegas Pinord, Doctor Pasteur, 6—Vilafranca del Penedès (Barcelona). Tel 93-892.32.50.
This is a traditional family firm that produces a wide range of wines, including dessert wines and sweet liqueurs. Their most characteristic wines are the lightly spritzy wines known as *vino de aguja*, or "needle" wines. Their La Nansa, made from Macabeo grapes, is a fresh, dry white with a fine and delicate aroma; Chateldon is a mature, velvety red, made mostly from a blend of Tempranillo and Monastrell aged in oak casks; and they also make a red from Cabernet Sauvignon.

Can Ràfols dels Caus, Can Ràfols—Avinyonet (Barcelona). Tel 93-897.00.13.
At this estate in the High Penedès, surrounded by vineyards and forests, Carlos Esteva produces outstanding wines from traditional and European varieties under the names Gran Caus for the white, Bitter Caus for the rosé made from 100% Merlot, and Gran Caus Negre for the oak-aged red, which is a blend of Cabernet Sauvignon, Cabernet Franc, and Merlot.

Castellblanch, Avinguda Casetas Mir, s/n—Sant Sadurní d'Anoia (Barcelona). Tel 93-891.00.00.
Established in 1908 and specializing in *cavas*, this firm is now part of the Freixenet group, and has a capacity for storing 10 million bottles in their extensive cellars. Brand names include Gran Castell, Brut Zero, Extra Castellblanch, and Gran Cremant.

Cavas Gramona, Industria, 36—Sant Sadurní d'Anoia (Barcelona). Tel 93-891.01.13.
Since 1881, the family Gramona Batlle has been devoted to the production of sparkling wines by the *méthode champenoise*, and makes several *bruts* as well as a rosé. They also produce a pleasant *vino de aguja*, Moustillant.

Cavas Hill, Buenavista, 2—Moja-Olérdola (Barcelona). Tel 93-890.05.88.
Hill is one of the traditional Penedès wine firms, dating back to 1660, when the English emigrant Mr. Hill acquired an estate called El Maset. One of his descendants, José Hill, built the first underground cellars in 1918, enlarged the family business, and devoted himself to the aging of great *reserva* wines. He also began producing sparkling wines. While they still produce a full range of still wines, they are best known for their *cavas*, sold under the names Brutísimo, Brut de Brut, Reserva Oro, and Sant Manel.

Cavas Masachs, Ponent, 20—Vilafranca del Penedès (Barcelona). Tel 93-890.05.93.
At the turn of the century, Josep Masachs started making *cavas* in this area, and Cavas Masachs remained a small family firm until the eighties, when Josep's grandsons Josep and Joan undertook a decisive renovation, enlarging both the cellars and the vineyards. Along with Macabeo, Xarel-lo, and Parellada, they have also planted Chardonnay vines. Their Louis de Vernier *cava* is made from the traditional varieties, while Carolina de Masachs *brut* also includes some Chardonnay.

Cavas Nadal, Can Nadal—El Pla del Penedès (Barcelona). Tel 93-898.80.11.
This family estate in the High Penedès, where traditional white varieties are grown, has been dedicated to viticulture since the sixteenth century. The Nadal family combines a technically advanced vinification cellar with old-fashioned methods such as riddling by hand. Of special note is their Brut Especial Gran Reserva, a perfect example

of a very dry *cava* with fine bubbles and the delicate floral aroma of Parellada.

Cavas Parés Baltà, Can Baltà, Afores s/n—Pacs del Penedès
(Barcelona). Tel 93-890.09.99
This small *bodega* produces traditional white wines from Macabeo, Xarel-lo, and Parellada, as well as sparkling wines made by the Charmat (Grand Vas) method.

Cavas Rexach Baqués, Santa Maria, 8—Guardiola de Font Rubí
(Barcelona). Tel 93-897.81.11.
The Baqués family has been producing sparkling wines in the Penedès since 1915. Although they are a small firm, their cellars are modern and the *cavas* are highly regarded.

Cavas Rovellats, Masia Rovellats, La Bleda—Sant Martí Sarroca
(Barcelona). Tel 93-898.01.31.
This century-old sparkling wine firm is surrounded by vineyards of Xarel-lo and Macabeo grapes; their Parellada and Chardonnay are planted in the High Penedès. The vinification cellars are thoroughly modern, while cool aging cellars are dug thirty feet underground and riddling is done by hand. The Gran Reserva Brut Natural is pale gold in color with a delicate perfume and well-balanced, fruity palate, while the Gran Cru has a fine mousse, and an elegant floral bouquet.

Cavas Torelló, Can Martí de Baix—Sant Sadurní d'Anoia
(Barcelona). Tel 93-257.16.58.
This family firm with *bodegas* in a beautiful sixteenth-century *masia*, or Catalan farmhouse, is surrounded with vineyards planted mainly with Macabeo and Xarel-lo. They made a still white wine, Blanc Tranquille, until recently, but now make only *cavas*.

Celler Ramón Balada, Anselm Clavé, 7—Sant Martí Sarroca
(Barcelona). Tel 93-890.35.30.
This firm is owned by the families Miret, Torrents, and Balada, who have been involved in viticulture in the High Penedès since the sixteenth century, but began to bottle their wines only in 1984. In addition to Xarel-lo, Macabeo, and Parellada vines, they also have some Cabernet Sauvignon, and are known for their fine-quality varietal wines. The Viña Toña Macabeo, a classic of this variety, is of special note, as is a recently released Vinya Sibil-la Cabernet Sauvignon.

Codorníu, Caserío, s/n—Sant Sadurní d'Anoia (Barcelona).
   Tel 93-891.01.25.
The main building of the Codorníu *bodega* is a nineteenth-century "national monument" of fascinating Modernist architecture, set in extensive gardens just outside Sant Sadurní. The firm dates from 1551 and has belonged to the Raventós family since 1659, when the Codorníu heiress, María Ana, married Miguel Raventós. Today its vast five-tier underground cellar is the longest in the world; it winds around for fifteen miles and holds more than 100 million bottles. The current managing director is Manel Raventós, representing the fourth generation since Josep Raventós started to make sparkling wines in 1872.

   If you are near Barcelona or Tarragona, a visit to Codorníu is a wine lover's must. Not only the wines but the cellars, the museum of old wine presses, the gardens, and the entire tour is memorable—including the five-hundred-year-old oak tree that welcomes you at the entrance. And Codorníu now has a winery in the Napa Valley.

   In the United States, Codorníu's handsomely packaged, vintage-dated *cavas* include Blanc de Blancs, Brut Clásico, and the top of the line, Anna de Codorníu Chardonnay. Even more exclusive is their new, excellent Jaume Codorníu *brut,* made from a blend of Chardonnay and Pinot Noir.

Conde de Caralt, Heredad Segura Viudas—Torrelavid (Barcelona).
   Tel 93-899.51.11.
Established in 1958, these *bodegas* belong to the Freixenet group and, like René Barbier, share the modern installations of Heredad Segura Viudas. They make several *cavas* as well as a white, rosé, and red wine under the Conde de Caralt label.

Freixenet, Plaça de l'Estació, 2—Sant Sadurní d'Anoia (Barcelona).
   Tel 93-891.07.00.
Freixenet's distinctive black bottle and creative marketing have made it the number-one-selling sparkling wine imported into the United States and one of the world's leading firms in the production of cavas. Besides the Cordón Negro brand in the black bottle, the firm's line includes the less expensive Carta Nevada, the premium brand Brut Nature, and the top of the line Reserva Real.

   The estate of La Freixeneda ("ash grove" in Catalan) has belonged to the Ferrer family since the thirteenth century. In 1889, Pere Ferrer, nicknamed "Freixenet," started to make sparkling wine. His son

Josep Ferrer is the current president. After Freixenet's purchase in the mid-eighties of the firms Castellblanch, Segura Viudas, Conde de Caralt, and René Barbier, it has become the sparkling wine leader in Spain. The Freixenet group also includes the Gloria Ferrer winery in the Sonoma region of California, the historic cellar of Henri Abelé in the heart of the Champagne region, and the Mexican Sala Vivé.

In the mid-seventies, a large investment was made to transform Segura Viudas into one of the most modern sparkling wine *bodegas.* The entire operation is mechanized, and their cellars house about 10 million bottles. Besides the Segura Viudas label, it produces the Paul Cheneau brand exclusively for the American market.

Heredad Segura Viudas—Torrelavid (Barcelona). Tel 93-899.51.11. This estate, which dates back to the eleventh century, and its medieval *masia,* or Catalan farmhouse, are today part of the Freixenet group. Besides Segura Viudas, two other lines, Conde de Caralt and René Barbier—a historic label established in 1880—are made at the winery. The facilities are modern and efficient, with a beautiful bottling plant, an extensive underground, multileveled aging cellar, and a wine library of the estate's best *reservas.*

The sparkling wines are sold under the brand name Segura Viudas; Conde de Caralt are white wines, and René Barbier are whites and reds, including some well-aged *reservas.* All of them are made from the traditional Penedès grapes, except for Barbier's Cabernet Sauvignon.

Jean Leon, Château Leon—El Plà del Penedès (Barcelona).
Tel 93-899.50.33
Born in Spain, Jean Leon went to America in the fifties and eventually opened La Scala restaurant in Beverly Hills, where his customers have included Hollywood's elite. In 1962 he acquired a 375-acre vineyard in Plà del Penedès, three miles from Vilafranca, with a small farmhouse that he turned into a winery. Convinced that the Penedès could produce great wines from noble European varieties, he planted his vineyards with cuttings of Cabernet Sauvignon, Cabernet Franc, Chardonnay, and Pinot Noir from France. His buttery Chardonnay is fermented and aged in small oak barrels, while his spicy Cabernet Sauvignon, rich in tannins, is aged for two years in wood. His production is around 150,000 bottles of Cabernet and 40,000 of Chardonnay per year, mostly sold locally and in the United States.

J. Sardá, Masia Olivella—Castellví de la Marca (Barcelona).
  Tel 93-772.09.25.
Founded in 1900, this firm recently planted their own vineyards on
the estate of Can Olivella, where they are experimenting with noble
European varieties such as Cabernet Sauvignon and Chardonnay.
Their white wines are made with the traditional grape blend of the
Penedès: Xarel-lo, Macabeo, and Parellada for whites; and Tem-
pranillo, Garnacha, and Monastrell for reds. They also produce *cavas,*
including an excellent Extra Brut.

Jaume Serra—Vilanova i la Geltrú (Barcelona). Tel 93-245.35.06.
This firm, which has been producing wines in the Alella region for
almost half a century, recently established a *bodega* in the Penedès,
where they have planted the noble red varieties Cabernet Sauvignon
and Merlot as well as Tempranillo.

Juvé & Camps, Ctra. Gelida, s/n—Sant Sadurní d'Anoia
  (Barcelona). Tel 93-891.10.00.
Another family firm, now in its third generation, founded in 1916 by
Joan Juvé i Camps. They specialize in *cavas,* but also a produce an
interesting dry white wine called Ermita d'Espiells, made from a blend
of Macabeo, Xarel-lo, and Parellada. Their elegant Reserva de la Fa-
milia *brut* is one of the most internationally appreciated *cavas,* and
the Grau Juvé y Camps is their top-of-the-line. They've also planted
some Chardonnay on their Espiells estate, in the middle Penedès.

Marqués de Monistrol, Pza. Iglesia, s/n—Monistrol d'Anoia
  (Barcelona). Tel 93-891.01.19.
In 1882, the great enologist and promoter of Spanish agriculture José
María Escrivà de Romaní, Marquis of Monistrol, established this
winery and excavated the first underground galleries for aging his
sparkling wines. The picturesque village of Monistrol d'Anoia, near
San Sadurní, grew up around the winery, now owned by the Italian
firm Martini.
  Monistrol's whites, rosés, reds, and *cavas* are vinified using the
most modern technology and aged in impressive underground cellars.
Among their top brands are the fresh, fruity Blanc de Blancs with a
touch of spritz; a white Blanc en Noirs made from red grapes, first
released in 1989; a delicate dry Blanco Seco made with the traditional
Penedès varieties; and the red Gran Reserva, aged two years in casks,
two years in the bottle. They also produce an excellent *brut* called
Gran Tradición.

Mascaró, Casal, 9—Vilafranca del Penedès (Barcelona).
   Tel 93-890.16.28.
Established in 1870, this prestigious family firm counts four genera-
tions in the production of brandies and liqueurs. They also produce
famed *cavas* under the brand name Mascaró, and a very good
Cabernet Sauvignon called Anima.

Masía Bach, Ctra. Capellades, s/n—Sant Esteve de Sesrovires
   (Barcelona). Tel 93-771.40.52.
After making their fortune in the textile industry in the twenties, the
enterprising brothers Pere and Ramón Bach decided to become winemakers and acquired a beautiful 850-acre estate near Sant Sadurní.
They planted it with vineyards and olive trees, built a handsome Catalan mansion, and established Masía Bach in 1929. In the aftermath of
the Spanish Civil War, the firm went into decline and was acquired by
Codorníu in 1975.
   Under the auspices of winemaker Angel Escudé, they set out to
revive the old *bodega,* with great success. The modernist mansion,
with its charming salons decorated with stained glass and tiles, has
been restored to its old luster and is truly worth a visit. A special
point of interest is their half-mile long, eighty-foot-deep cellar built in
1924, destined for oak aging of their red wines.
   The firm's flagship is the white Extrísimo Bach, a luscious, mellow,
well-aged sweet wine of silky texture. Extrísimo Seco is a fine dry
white, characteristic of Penedès, with the fresh aroma of Parellada;
while the Bach Tinto Viña Extrísima is a well-balanced red wine
made from Tempranillo blended with Garnacha and Cabernet Sauvignon.

Masía Valldosera, Finca Les Garrigues—Olérdola (Barcelona).
   Tel 93-890.12.16.
In just a few years, this family *bodega* has created an image of interna-
tional prestige and quality with their varietal wines, which include
Xarel-lo, Macabeo, and a Chardonnay.

Masía Vallformosa, La Sala, 45—Vilobí del Penedès (Barcelona).
   Tel 93-897.82.86.
Involved in the wine business since 1936, the Domènech family began
bottling their wines only in 1972, and in 1981 started to produce their
own *cavas* from grapes grown on their estates in the Penedès. Of
special interest: the Brut Reserva with delicate bubbles and an aroma

of hazelnuts and honeysuckle, and a Vallformosa Reserva red made from Tempranillo and Cabernet Sauvignon.

Mestres Sagués Vins de Cava, Ajuntament, 8—Sant Sadurní d'Anoia (Barcelona). Tel 93-891.00.43.
Like a few firms in Champagne continue to do, this small family firm ferments the base wines for their sparkling wines in wood and ages them from two to five years.

Mata & Portabella, Montaner Oller, 2—Sant Sadurní d'Anoia (Barcelona). Tel 93-891.25.52.
With a viticultural tradition that dates back to the nineteenth century, this firm ages their youngest *cava* for fourteen months, while the Nature and Grand Cru are aged three and four years respectively.

Mont Marçal, Finca Mont Marçal—Castellví de la Marca (Barcelona). Tel 93-891.82.81.
Established in 1975 by Manuel Sancho, Mont Marçal has acquired a well-deserved reputation among wine lovers in the few years since it was founded. Its 150 acres of vineyards are planted with the traditional Penedès varieties—Parellada, Xarel-lo, and Macabeo—as well as with some noble European grapes such as Chardonnay and Cabernet Sauvignon; Sylvaner is also in the experimental stages. The wines are made with the most modern technology, in cold-fermented stainless-steel tanks, and the reds are aged in oak casks. Of particular interest are their fresh and aromatic white Vi Novell (Catalan for "new wine"), another white made with some Chardonnay, and a *reserva* red with great character and breed.

Parató Vinícola, Can Raspall de Renardes—El Pla del Penedès (Barcelona). Tel 93-898.81.82.
José Elías, who founded this firm in 1977, is a passionate winemaker who only recently began producing *cava*. The microclimate of his estate in the High Penedès is perfect for producing the aromatic Parellada for his Blanco Parató Nature; he also grows other traditional varieties, as well as some Pinot Noir and Chardonnay.

René Barbier, Heredad Segura Viudas—Torrelavid (Barcelona). Tel 93-899.51.11.
Léon Barbier, a French wine grower who settled in Catalunya, founded this firm in 1880, and his son René gave it his name in 1934.

The firm is now part of the Freixenet group, with Conde de Caralt and Segura Viudas, and the wines are vinified at the Segura Viudas facilities.

The white and rosé wines are bottled young; only the red wines are aged in oak casks. Wines include Kraliner, a clean, fruity white wine made with local varieties, and a lively traditional rosé with an attractive strawberry color. A young, fresh wine made from Cabernet Sauvignon has recently been released.

Torres, Comercio, 22—Vilafranca del Penedès (Barcelona). Tel 93-890.01.00.

It is appropriate to end this tour of Catalan wineries with a visit to my family's *bodega,* sharing our history and what I feel we have contributed to Spanish viticulture. I am very proud of the fact that Torres is the largest independently owned producer of premium wines in Spain, and that they are sold in eighty-five countries all over the world. But it has taken well over three hundred years to get to where we are today.

My family has owned vineyards and made wine since the seventeenth century, but our entry into the world market actually had its beginnings in 1858, when Jaime Torres set off for America to make his fortune. Eventually settling in Havana, Cuba, he worked and saved diligently for seven years and in 1865 invested his savings in a fledgling oil company. Shortly thereafter, a worldwide oil boom made him a wealthy man.

Jaime reinvested in oceangoing sailing ships and organized the first shipping line between Barcelona and Havana. Then he returned to Barcelona and began construction of a large wine cellar, inaugurated in 1870 and still in use today. Upon his death in 1906, his brother Miguel took over the winery operation. Miguel's eventual successor was his son Juan, my grandfather.

My father, Don Miguel—who died in May 1991—was only twenty-three when his father died in March 1932; but assisted by his mother, Josefa, he took charge of the winery management. Those were difficult days in Spain, and in all of Europe. The Spanish Civil War broke out in July 1936 and lasted three years. And in 1939, during an air raid in Vilafranca del Penedès, several bombs hit our winery. A huge 160,000-gallon vat full of wine was destroyed during the explosions. The streets became actual rivers of wine; the damage was overwhelming. The efforts of three generations lay in ruins.

However, from the ashes and debris arose the will to rebuild. There was no capital left, so Miguel applied for credit. In spite of the difficulties of that time, reconstruction began very soon and was finished in early 1940. While former generations had always exported wine and brandy in bulk, it was Miguel who decided to embark on the estate-bottling venture and to create prestige for the brand and for each Torres label.

My father always remembered with nostalgia and pride his first sales in Barcelona. He would visit the finest restaurants, pull some samples of wine or brandy out of his briefcase and persuade the prospective buyer to taste them, as he knowledgeably explained how they were produced. His enthusiasm never failed to make a sale! By the late fifties, Torres brandy had acquired a small but influential share of the market. Compared with the popular brandies from the south of Spain, Miguel's was different: it had a softer bouquet and a French style.

The Torres family is marked by individualism and a pioneering spirit. If my father was an innovator in wine marketing, my brother Miguel Jr. has played the same role in wine production. It was in the mid-sixties that, after studying winemaking in France, he set my family's business on a path from which it has never looked back. Just as there has been a revolution in wine growing in the New World vineyards of California, Australia, New Zealand, and now Chile, so too has there been a revolution in the Old World vineyards of Spain, France, Italy, and Germany. With the advent of new technology, new clones of grapes, and just as important, a global outlook and market, every facet of wine growing, from site selection to the appreciation of wine, has undergone intense scrutiny. Miguel Jr. been a pioneer in Spain for the past thirty years, and today he is recognized as a member of the very small group of leading winemakers in the world.

He began where all good winemakers must, in the vineyards. Like all sons of a strong-willed father, Miguel Jr. had to work very hard to convince our father of the validity of his ideas. Fortunately, he was successful from the beginning and he has never stopped acquiring and planting prime vineyard land, so that today we have more than twenty-five hundred acres of vineyards. These have been essential not only to the quality of Torres wines, but also as a showcase and classroom for neighboring grape growers.

Like winemakers in California, Italy, and elsewhere, Miguel Jr. began very early on to experiment with adapting the noble European grape varieties to our soils and microclimates. First he planted Cabernet Sauvignon and Pinot Noir, then followed Chardonnay, Sauvignon Blanc, Riesling, Gewürztraminer, Muscat d'Alexandria,

Cabernet Franc, and lately Merlot and Syrah. By trial and error, Miguel has found sites well adapted to expressing the individuality of each variety—a tribute to the quality and diversity of our native Penedès region.

These noble grapes have changed the whole picture of Penedès wines. Today many fine winemakers in Spain—not only in Catalunya, but in other Spanish wine regions as well—are following the path my brother has taken since the 1960s.

Now he has gone full circle and is experimenting with some of the indigenous Catalan varieties such as Garnacha and Monastrell. We have great hopes that these grapes will contribute to the excitement and originality of the Torres wines in the nineties.

Miguel's interest in Catalan wines extends far back into history. He has just published, in conjunction with a number of noted experts, *Mil Años de Viticultura en Catalunya* ("One Thousand Years of Viticulture in Catalunya"), a volume dedicated to tracing the traditions of wine growing from its roots in the ancient Phoenecian, Greek, and Roman civilizations to the present day. The book includes a list of 124 Catalan varieties, with detailed notes on twenty-four of the most interesting. Perhaps even more important, Miguel has established many of these varieties in an experimental vineyard to rediscover and preserve the old Catalan grapes and their traditions.

The revolution has gone on in the cellar, too. Every piece of modern winemaking technology is studied, experimented with, and adapted to our needs. In 1973, our winery pioneered in Spain the use of temperature-controlled fermentation for white wines; keeping the temperature low to ensure a slower fermentation produces more aromatic and fruity wines. At the same time, we also began using stainless-steel tanks to ferment our reds. Many wineries all over Spain are now using these methods to make their wines.

But high technology is not the universal key to great winemaking. Here again we have come full circle, experimenting with traditional techniques such as whole-cluster pressing and barrel fermentation for whites, and whole-cluster maceration and "punching down" for reds. Though these old winemaking traditions are today very costly, they accomplish many complex tasks in a single step and are thus very sophisticated.

All of these efforts find their highest expression in our single-vineyard selection (*pago*) wines: Mas la Plana (Gran Coronas "Black Label") Cabernet Sauvignon, Milmanda Chardonnay, Mas Borrás Pinot Noir, and Fransola Sauvignon Blanc/Parellada.

For the past ten years Miguel has also been developing a wine estate we purchased in Chile in 1979. And in 1985 I began planting a vineyard—named "Don Miguel" after my father—in Sonoma Green Valley, north of my home in the San Francisco Bay area. Naturally, everything we have learned in Spain is being applied to these two projects as well. Our first Sonoma Chardonnay, the '89 vintage, was released in 1991 under the label Marimar Torres Estate, Don Miguel vineyard; and our new winery on the estate is under way.

Perhaps the main contribution my family has made to Spanish winemaking has been to change the concept of wine appreciation in Spain. Today most Spaniards realize that wine does not necessarily have to be old—or to taste old—in order to be good; that the varietal character and nobility of the grape are extremely important; that Spanish wines do not have to be an imitation of French wines—they can stand on their own and reflect the winemaker's individual style. A perfect example of this is our Mas la Plana (Gran Coronas "Black Label") Cabernet Sauvignon. Though it is made from a classic Bordeaux variety, many tasters have remarked that it actually has a Burgundian style. Of course we associate it with neither Bordeaux nor Burgundy—it is a Penedès wine and, what is most important, Torres.

GRAPE GLOSSARY

The White Varieties

Chardonnay
One of the noble European varieties, Chardonnay is grown in Penedès, Costers del Segre, and in a small section of the Alella wine district. It adds elegance to some of the best Catalan whites, and is also used in some *cava* blends.

Gewürztraminer
This noble Alsatian variety also does very well in the higher elevations of Penedès, especially on sites with a sunny exposure. The small rosy grapes have a thick, highly perfumed skin; and the spicy character is particularly interesting when blended with wines from other aromatic varieties, such as Muscat.

Macabeo
One of the traditional varieties, known in Rioja as Viura. The large golden grapes yield wines moderately rich in alcohol with a fine aroma. Macabeo is used for the traditional "coupage" of *cavas*.

Malvasía
Native of Greece, this variety is limited to the area around Sitges, south of Barcelona, and to a few vineyards in Central Penedès, where it is used to make a luscious, slightly fortified sweet wine.

Muscat
Grown in the Mediterranean since ancient times, Muscat produced famous wines in Catalunya during the Middle Ages, and in France during the time of Charlemagne. Today, the delicate *moscatel de grano pequeño* (or "small grape muscat") is grown in the Low Penedès, near the sea, where it produces elegant wines with a fragrance of rose, geranium, and honey. Another variety, Muscat of Alexandria, is more widely planted.

Parellada
The most delicate and aromatic of the traditional Catalan varieties, Parellada contributes a lovely floral aroma to the best *cavas*, and is also prized for its freshness and acidity when used in the still white wines from the Penedès area.

Riesling
Another of the noble varieties, this native of the Rhine, Mosel, and Alsace is planted in several vineyards of the high Penedès, where the small compact grapes produce a wine prized for its refreshing acidity and scent of peach and honey.

Sauvignon Blanc
A nontraditional variety adapted from the Loire Valley in France, its small oval berries bear a slight taste of musk and in Penedès produce dry, aromatic white wines, which are often aged briefly in oak.

Xarel-lo
This classic white variety with compact golden grapes is often used in the blend for *cavas*, where it contributes a robust structure and alcoholic strength.

The Red Varieties

Cabernet Franc
A noble French variety, grown in small quantities in Penedès, it produces pleasant fruity wines with a less complex bouquet than Cabernet Sauvignon. The two are often blended together.

Cabernet Sauvignon
This well-known variety produces the best aged reds of Penedès. The wines are dark in color, with rich floral and fruity aromas and a characteristic note of green pepper. Because of their great tannic structure, they need aging, preferably in wood, to open and develop.

Cariñena
A native of Aragón and Catalunya, this variety has been known in France since the 12th century under the name *carignan* and in Mediterranean climates produces wines rich in pigment and alcohol. Because wines from this grape require aging, Cariñena is often blended with Garnacha in order to hasten the wine's evolution.

Garnacha
Another Mediterranean variety with an old lineage, Garnacha is known in France as *grenache*, and produces wines of high alcoholic strength which evolve quickly. For this reason, in Catalunya it is often vinified with varieties which have a better structure and stronger tannins. It is included in almost all Catalan rosés, and is also part of the blend of traditional red wines.

Merlot
Appreciated for its velvety tannins and soft, youthful aromas, this French variety is often blended with Cabernet Sauvignon. In Penedès, it is vinified as a fresh, young wine, in which notes of violet and ripe berries predominate.

Monastrell
This traditional Mediterranean variety, originally from the town of Murviedro, in Valencia, goes by the name of *mourvèdre* in France and *mataró* in California. In Catalunya, the rich, deeply-colored wines require a certain amount of aging. They are used in the blend of some red wines, but are the most used in the production of rosé sparkling wines.

Pinot Noir
The variety used to make the best red wines of Burgundy has been grown very successfully in Penedès where it produces ruby-colored wines with a floral aroma and velvety palate.

Tempranillo
The finest indigenous red variety grown in Spain, it is known under different names in different regions: Cencibel in La Mancha, Tinto Fino in Ribera del Duero, and Tempranillo in Rioja and Catalunya, where it is also known as Ull de Llebre (or "eye of the hare"). In Penedès, its wines exhibit deep color and extract, elegance, and a structure suitable for aging.

Barrica
The Castilian and Catalan term for small oak barrels used for aging wine.

Bodega
Castilian or Catalan for wine storage building or cellar; it can also refer to a winery.

Cava
The word *cava* comes from the latin word for hole or gallery; it refers to the underground cellar where wines are aged. Also the term for Catalan sparkling wine made by the *méthode champenoise*, used traditionally in the Champagne region of France, and first produced in Spain by José Raventós at Codorníu in 1872. Under the EEC law of 1986, *cava* is a VMQPRD wine (*Vin mousseux de qualité produit dans une region determinée*, or "quality sparkling wine produced in a specific region").

Cosecha
Castilian for the vintage, or harvest—and the wines made—in one particular year.

Crû
A French term which literally means "growth" and in the case of wine, indicates a wine that "grew" in a particular vineyard. Like its Catalan equivalent "pago," here the grape growing and winemaking are combined in a single concept: wine growing associated with its place of origin.

Denominación de Origen
Specific wine-growing region controlled by legislation that regulates its viticulture and winemaking practices—equivalent to the French Appellation Contrôlée or the Italian Denominazione d'Origine Controlata.

Masia or mas
Catalan for farmhouse (spelled "masía" in Castilian).

Méthode champenoise
The French term used to designate the classic methods for making sparkling wine employed in the Champagne region of France, in which still wines undergo a second fermentation in the bottle by adding a dose of sugar and yeast.

Noble European Varieties
They are Cabernet Sauvignon, Pinot Noir, Merlot, Riesling, Chardonnay, Sauvignon Blanc, Garnacha, and Tempranillo.

Pagès
Catalan for peasant. The word means "inhabitant of the *pago*."

Pago
The Catalan equivalent of *crû* (see above). The word *pago* is derived from the Latin *pagus*, which means "rustic place" or "place in the field."

Reserva
The Castilian term for wines that have been given special aging; it is meant to be an indication of quality. For red wines, it means a minimum of three years aging (which includes at least one year in wood casks or barrels). For white and rosé wines, it means a minimum of one year's aging in wood and bottle.

Varietal
A U.S. designation for a wine that takes its name from the grape variety from which it is entirely or primarily made (at least 75% by U.S. law). For example, a wine labeled Chardonnay or Cabernet Sauvignon.

Verema
Catalan for grape harvest. (In Castilian, it is called *vendimia*.)

Vi blanc
Catalan for white wine.

Vi negre
Catalan for red wine.

Vi novell
Catalan for "new" wine.

Vi rosat
Catalan for rosé wine.

APPENDIX

▼ ▼ ▼

EQUIVALENTS

1 small onion	= 1/3 pound
1 large onion	= 1/2 pound
1 medium carrot	= 1/4 pound
1 large carrot	= 6 ounces
1 large tomato	= 1/2 pound
1 large pepper	= 6 to 8 ounces
1 small pepper	= 4 to 6 ounces
1-1/4 cups chopped onion	= 1 large
1 cup chopped onion	= 1 medium
1 cup chopped carrot	= 2 medium
1 cup chopped tomato (unpeeled)	= 1 large
1 cup chopped tomato (peeled and seeded)	= 2 large
1 cup chopped pepper	= 1 large
1 cup chopped leek	= 1 small (white part and one third of green part)
1 tablespoon minced garlic	= 3 large cloves
1 head garlic	= 20 garlic cloves
1 tablespoon minced shallots	= 1 medium
1/4 cup minced shallots	= 2 large
1 cup grated Gruyère cheese	= 1/4 pound
1 cup grated Parmesan cheese	= 3 ounces
1/4 cup lemon juice	= 1 large lemon
1/2 cup orange juice	= 1 to 1-1/2 large oranges

1 tablespoon orange zest	= 1 large orange
1 tablespoon lemon zest	= 2 medium lemons
2 teaspoons minced lemon zest	= 1 large lemon
1 large (1/2-inch) slice white bread	= 1 ounce
1 cup bread crumbs (without crusts)	= 3 ounces bread (before trimming crusts)
1 cup sugar	= 1/2 pound
1 cup unsifted powdered sugar	= 4-1/4 ounces
1 cup unsifted flour	= 4 ounces (1/4 pound)
1 cup mashed potatoes	= 3/4 pound
1 cup blanched almonds	= 5-1/2 ounces
1 cup whole almonds	= 5 ounces
1 cup ground almonds	= 3-1/2 ounces
1 cup hazelnuts	= 4-1/2 ounces
1 cup walnuts	= 3-1/2 ounces
1 cup pine nuts	= 6 ounces
1/2 cup pitted olives	= 1/4 pound
1 cup unpitted olives	= 1/3 pound
One 2-ounce can flat anchovy fillets	= 8 anchovy fillets
1 stick butter	= 1/2 cup (8 tablespoons), or 4 ounces

RESTAURANT ADDRESSES

Agut d'Avignon
Trinitat, 3 y Avignó, 8
Barcelona
Tel 93-302.60.34
Closed Holy Week.

Ampurdán
Antigua Carretera Francia, s/n
Figueres (38 km from Girona)
Tel 972-50.05.62.
Never closed.

Azulete
Vía Augusta, 281
Barcelona
Tel 93-203.59.43
Closed Sundays, holidays, Holy
Week, and Saturday lunch, plus
Christmas and the first two
weeks of August.

Cal Joan
Plaça Estació, 8
Vilafranca del Penedès
Tel 93-890.31.71
Lunch M–F; Dinner Saturday.
Closed Sunday, holidays, Holy
Week, September, and
Christmas.

Can Boix
Carretera Lleida-Puigcerdà
Martinet (in the Pyrenees)

Tel 973-51.50.50
Closed Tuesday from October
15 to June 30.

Can Borrell
Represo, 3
Meranges (in the Pyrenees)
Tel 972-80.00.33
Closed Sunday night and Mon-
day (except in summer).

Carles Camós Big-Rock
Fanals, 5
Platja d'Aro (35 km east of
Girona, on the Costa Brava)
Tel 972-81.80.12

Casa Isidre
Flors, 12
Barcelona
Tel 93-241.11.39
Closed Sunday, holidays, Satur-
day night in summer, July 5 to
August 15, and one week at
Christmas and Holy Week.

El Celler del Penedès
(no street address)
Sant Miquel d'Olérdola (3 km
from Vilafranca del Penedès)
Tel 93-890.20.01
Never Closed.

El Racó d'en Binu
Puig i Cadafalch, 14
Argentona (30 km north of
Barcelona)
Tel 93-797.01.00
Closed Sunday night and
Monday.

Eldorado Petit
Rambla Vidal, 11
Sant Felíu de Guixols (on the
Costa Brava)
Tel 972-32.18.18
Closed Wednesday from Octo-
ber to April, and all of
November.

> Dolors Montserdá, 57
> Barcelona
> Tel 93-204.55.06
> Closed Sunday.

> 45–47 West 55th Street
> New York, NY
> Tel 212-586.34.34.

Els Perols de L'Empordà
Villarroel, 88
Barcelona
Tel 93-323.10.33
Closed Sunday night, Monday,
Holy Week, and August
15 to 31.

Eugenia
Consolat de Mar, 80
Cambrils (on the coast, 20 km
south of Tarragona)
Tel 977-35.01.68
Closed Tuesday night and
Wednesday in winter; Wednes-
day and Thursday lunch in
summer; and November and
December.

Galbis
Avenida Antonio Alméla, 15
L'Alcudia de Carlet (29 km
south of Valencia)
Tel 96-254.10.93
Closed Sunday, holidays, and
August.

Jaume de Provença
Provença, 88
Barcelona
Tel 93-230.00.29
Closed Sunday night, Monday,
Holy Week, and August.

L'Avi Pau
Avenida Diagonal, 20
Cunit (on the coast south of
Barcelona about 40 km north
of Tarragona)
Tel 977-67.48.61
Closed Tuesday and mid-
November to mid-December.

L'Olivé
Muntaner, 171
Barcelona
Tel 93-230.90.27
Closed Sunday and two weeks
in August.

Neichel
Avenida Pedralbes, 16 bis
Barcelona
Tel 93-203.84.08
Closed Sunday, holidays, Holy
Week, Christmas, and August.

Peixerot
Paseo Marítimo, 56
Vilanova i la Geltrú (on the
coast, 45 km south of
Barcelona)
Tel 93-815.06.25
Closed Sunday night (except in
summer) and Christmas day.

Roig Rubí
Sèneca, 20
Barcelona
Tel 93-218.92.22
Closed Sunday, holidays,
Christmas, Holy Week, and
second week of August.

Sa Punta
Urbanización Sa Punta
Platja de Pals (on the Costa
Brava 45 km from Girona)
Tel 972-63.64.10
Closed Monday from October
to Holy Week, excluding
holidays.

MAIL ORDER SOURCES
FOR SPECIAL INGREDIENTS AND EQUIPMENT

▼   ▼   ▼

Corti Brothers
5810 Folsom Boulevard
Sacramento, CA 95819
Tel (916) 736-3800
Catalog.
Catalan olive oil, Costa Brava anchovies, salt cod, and saffron.

Dean & DeLuca
560 Broadway
New York, NY 10012
Tel (212) 431-1691 ext. 223 or 270;
1-800-221-7714 outside New York state;
Fax (212) 334-6183
Spanish saffron threads, Catalan olive oil, and short-grain rice from Valencia.

G.B. Ratto International Grocers
821 Washington Street
Oakland, CA 94607
Tel 1-800-228-3515 in California;
1-800-325-3483 outside California.
Catalog.
Spanish saffron, Valencian paella rice, Catalan olive oil, salt cod fillets, and paella pans.

Peet's Coffee, Tea and Spices
P.O. Box 8247
Emeryville, CA 94662
Tel 1-800-999-2132;
Fax (510) 653-0672.
Saffron threads (Mancha Superior grade).

Vanilla Saffron Imports
949 Valencia Street
San Francisco, CA 94110
Tel (415) 648-8990;
Fax (415) 648-2240.
Saffron threads (Mancha Superior), Spanish Truffles, and pine nuts.

Williams-Sonoma
P. O. Box 7456
San Francisco, CA 94120-7456
Tel 1-800-541-2233
Catalog.
Spanish saffron threads (Mancha Select), Catalan olive oil (Verge de Borges brand), and speckled enamel paella pans by mail order. Check the more than ninety Williams-Sonoma cookware shops throughout the country for imported clay casseroles and Valencian short-grain rice.

INDEX